Our Hallowed Ground

The University of Minnesota Press gratefully acknowledges assistance
provided for the publication of this book
by the John K. and Elsie Lampert Fesler Fund.

Our Hallowed Ground

WORLD WAR II VETERANS OF
FORT SNELLING NATIONAL CEMETERY

Stephen Chicoine

University of Minnesota Press
Minneapolis • London

Map of Fort Snelling National Cemetery by Parrot Graphics

Published by the University of Minnesota Press
111 Third Avenue South, Suite 290
Minneapolis, MN 55401-2520
http://www.upress.umn.edu

Library of Congress Cataloging-in-Publication Data

Chicoine, Stephen.
Our hallowed ground : World War II veterans of Fort Snelling National Cemetery /
Stephen Chicoine.
p.   cm.
Includes bibliographical references.
ISBN 0-8166-4674-0 (pb : alk. paper)
1. World War II, 1939–1945—Biography.   2. World War II, 1939–1945—United States.
3. World War II, 1939–1945—Veterans—United States—Biography.   4. Fort Snelling
National Cemetery (Fort Snelling, Minn.)   I. Title.
D769.2.C55   2005
940.54'65776581—dc22
2005012830

12   11   10   09   08   07   06   05   10   9   8   7   6   5   4   3   2   1

This book is dedicated to those brave Americans
who gave their lives in the defense of freedom and democracy
but who have been forgotten.

That from these honored dead we take increased devotion to that cause for which they here gave the last full measure of devotion, that we here highly resolve that these dead shall not have died in vain, that this nation under God shall have a new birth of freedom, and that government of the people, by the people, and for the people shall not perish from the earth.

—Abraham Lincoln, at the commemoration of the national cemetery at Gettysburg

Contents

Preface

Row after row of white markers stretch across the green expanse of Fort Snelling National Cemetery. The marker for each individual who served our nation tells us little about the person whose remains lie there. Some markers do not even include the designation of the individual's unit. Stories of their service to a grateful nation deserve to be told, the somber details along with the heroic deeds. One can best appreciate the importance of the cemetery by learning of the personal experiences of these American heroes.

Fort Snelling National Cemetery, perhaps the most important shrine to democracy in the Upper Midwest, was established in 1939 and contains the remains of almost 170,000 U.S. servicemen and servicewomen and their immediate families. They represent the strength of the nation, citizens who rose to its defense in time of need. We Americans recognize that we must sometimes resort to military force to defend democracy here and abroad, and at no time was this more necessary than in World War II. Many veterans of the Second World War lie buried in Fort Snelling National Cemetery. Humility was a common trait among America's citizen-soldiers who defeated the seemingly invincible military forces of Nazi Germany and Imperial Japan. Yet such men and women deserve to be remembered and their courage and gallant deeds recognized. This book is not intended to glorify war, but to pay honor to the valor of those who sacrificed for the nation.

The outlook was grim in the aftermath of the Japanese attack on Pearl Harbor, and the strength of resolve of the United States was the country's only hope. Perhaps some citizens left home for war with a sense of youthful adventure, but all soon learned the harsh reality of war. The lives of some were cut short. Others survived the conflict, having lost their innocence on the field of battle. Some died in the attack on Pearl Harbor, while others lost their lives in the final few days as the long and bloody war came to a close. Some took part in epic events, while others fought in obscure actions in remote locales. All were brave, but only a chosen few were cited for their bravery. Their final honor is to lie at rest in a national cemetery for defending democracy for future generations. These stories are but a few of the many thousands left untold, and we can only hope that they inspire a far greater appreciation for the sacrifice of what we have rightly come to call "the greatest generation."

Sixteen million Americans served during the war and more than four hundred thousand died. The government reinterred the remains of many Americans killed in action during World War II in national cemeteries across the country. This took place at Fort Snelling National Cemetery during 1947 and 1948. Some World War II veterans returned to war and gave their lives in the Korean War from 1950 to 1953. Veterans who suffered wounds and trauma in World War II and never fully recovered died in the 1950s. Young men and women who entered the military service at the age of eighteen in 1940 are now in their eighties. Even the youngest veterans, who entered the war in 1944 or 1945, are in their late seventies. These American heroes are dying off at a rate of well over one thousand per day... every day.

The World War II veterans buried in Fort Snelling National Cemetery represent a broad cross section of this generation. The veterans whose stories are included in this book are in no way intended to be representative of all the men and women whose remains lie there. Their inclusion is the result of hours and hours of walking in the cemetery and researching their names as I looked for stories. I recognized some as veterans of certain battles or campaigns from the dates of their deaths. Others intrigued me because of their particular unit designations. I spoke to groups of veterans and gave my card to them as I searched for leads. Over time, the stories came from a multitude of sources. Years of scanning obituaries led to many worthwhile tales and several dead ends. While I made every effort to gather a representative sample of service, theater, officer and enlisted, gender, race, and hometown, that in the end was not entirely possible. However, it is my hope that the stories and their accompanying photographs convey a sense of the extraordinary contributions of ordinary American citizens and of their heroic service to the nation and its ideals.

Acknowledgments

My interest in the human experience of the Second World War began when I was a boy, devouring every book on the subject in the Carnegie Library in Decatur, Illinois. That foundation of knowledge grew over the years through reading more in-depth accounts and also by listening to the recollections of friends and relatives, including Chuck and Adeline Hendrix, Harry and Mary Cummins Jr., and Duane and Bea Chicoine. The initial inspiration for this book was a visit to Washington, D.C., during which I spent the better part of a day working through the crowds in Arlington National Cemetery. At the end of that visit I felt that Fort Snelling National Cemetery deserved as much respect and attention. Brent Ashabranner—a U.S. Navy veteran of the Pacific theater, my longtime writing mentor, and the author of *A Grateful Nation: The Story of Arlington National Cemetery*—encouraged my belief in the potential for a good story concerning the military exploits of those buried in Fort Snelling National Cemetery. Furthermore, the topic was on my mind, professionally speaking: I recently had completed a book on Texas history, which used as its basis stories of Civil War soldiers buried in an old rural cemetery.

This book is the result of countless hours of research. The Minnesota Historical Society and its excellent staff played an important role in much of the initial research. Certain holdings in the MHS manuscript collection came from veterans who were later buried in Fort Snelling National Cemetery. The society's vast collection of microfilmed state military records was indispensable. The microfilmed Minnesota newspaper collection also proved to be useful for articles from 1941 to 1945, as well as for obituaries from 1946 to the present. The University of Minnesota's Wilson Library, the

Minneapolis Public Library, and the Hennepin County Library System were important resources throughout the course of my research. The InterLibrary Loan Department of the Hennepin County System in particular had much otherwise unattainable information. The *Star Tribune* and the *St. Paul Pioneer Press* contained not only important feature articles of the times, but also more recent obituaries of the past several years, which introduced me to potentially powerful stories and allowed me to make contact with family members of veterans.

Curator Doug Bekke and archivist Leland Smith of the Minnesota Military Museum at Camp Ripley, near Little Falls, were helpful in sharing insights and information as well as photographs of certain veterans, as were JoEllen Haugo, librarian in the Special Collections department of the Minneapolis Public Library; Noel Allard, founder and executive director of the Minnesota Aviation Hall of Fame; and Don Patton (retired colonel, U.S. Army) of the Harold C. Deutsch World War II History Round Table.

Numerous individuals at various U.S. military agencies made special efforts to assist this research. They include Dan Crawford, head of the reference section of the History and Museums Division of the Marine Corps Historical Center; Lena Kaljot, photograph historian with the Marine Corps Historical Center; Kenneth Smith-Christmas, curator of material history at the U.S. Marine Corps Air-Ground Museum at Quantico, Virginia; Mark L. Evans, historian at the Naval Aviation History Branch of the Naval Historical Center; Kathleen M. Lloyd, head of the Operational Archives Branch of the Naval Historical Center; and Lieutenant Colonel Robert L. White Jr., chief of the Military Awards Branch of the Department of the Army in Alexandria, Virginia.

County historical groups, including the Blue Earth County Historical Society in Mankato, Minnesota, provided valuable information. Information otherwise unavailable came from various veterans associations and their historians, including the 390th (Bomb Group) Memorial Museum Foundation in Tucson, Arizona; the 401st Bomb Group Association; Richard F. Gelvin of Mesa, Arizona, with the 445th Bomb Group; Bill Davenport of Santa Ana, California, group historian of the 446th Bomb Group; Bill Hoffland of the Ninety-ninth Infantry Battalion (Separate) Association; and others.

Many Web sites were useful, including www.99thinfbnsep.org; www.uss-hornet.org; www.vf2.org; www.blueangels.org; www.1stfighter.org; www.acepilots.com; the Web site of the U.S. Navy Office of Information, http://www.chinfo.navy.mil/navpalib/ships/; and many others. The cemetery Web site at http://www.cem.va.gov/nchp/ftsnelling.htm is both detailed and informative.

The most important sources of information were the immediate family members and close friends of many of the World War II veterans profiled in this book. There are too many to thank individually in this brief section. Suffice it to say that the book would have been much less personal without their contributions of time, memories, and photographs.

My thanks to associate editor Pieter Martin of the University of Minnesota Press for all of his efforts gathering additional images to make this book so powerful and to Michele Hodgson for her copyediting. Special thanks to Todd Orjala, senior acquisitions editor, for his vision to recognize the importance of this work and for his constant encouragement along the way.

Finally, I must give special thanks to my wife and daughters, who not only allowed me the freedom to pursue my passion but who also accompanied me at times during the course of my research. This considerable effort would not have been possible without their understanding and encouragement.

Photograph by Richard Hamilton Smith

Overview of Fort Snelling National Cemetery

The U.S. Army took control of the Upper Midwest (then known as the northwest frontier of the young nation) after the War of 1812 and established a chain of forts at strategic locations across the region. One site of particular importance was the confluence of the Mississippi River and the Minnesota River in what was then the Minnesota Territory. Soldiers of the Fifth U.S. Infantry under the command of Colonel Josiah Snelling constructed the first permanent fort on the site in 1820. Brigadier General Winfield Scott came to inspect the fort in 1824. Scott was a hero of the War of 1812 who would distinguish himself in the Mexican War and ultimately serve as commander in chief during the Civil War. He recommended the post be named Fort Snelling, which the War Department approved in 1825. Fort Snelling subsequently served as the assembly point and training ground for Minnesotans and others from the Upper Midwest who were going off to serve the nation in the Civil War, the Spanish-American War, World War I, and World War II. Nearly three hundred thousand young men entered the U.S. Army and made their way to the battlefields of World War II through Fort Snelling.

In its earliest years, Fort Snelling maintained a small cemetery for soldiers who died while stationed there. Twenty-one or more Civil War soldiers appear to have died at the post of disease or wounds before they could muster out. Veterans of the Indian wars passed away in their later years at Fort Snelling and were laid to rest in the post cemetery. The Twenty-fifth U.S. Infantry Regiment, an African American unit, was posted at Fort Snelling in the 1880s after fighting the Comanches for ten years on the Texas frontier. Two Native Americans of the Blackfoot Nation served at Fort Snelling in Company I (the Indian company, as it was known) of the Third U.S. Infantry in the 1890s and died of tuberculosis. They too were buried in the post cemetery.

President Abraham Lincoln authorized the establishment of the national cemetery system in 1862, only days after the bloody Battle of Gettysburg. Congress enacted legislation after World War I to expand eligibility requirements for interment in national cemeteries. While many of the 115,000 American dead from that war were buried in France, some bodies were returned home, along with more than two hundred thousand wounded. Having mobilized 3.8 million soldiers during World War I, the federal government recognized that the vast number of veterans would necessitate expansion of the national cemetery system.

Certain organizations in Minneapolis–St. Paul petitioned Congress to establish a national cemetery in the area during the postwar years. Legislation passed in 1936–37 authorized the secretary of war to set aside land at Fort Snelling for that purpose. In fact, the federal government recognized the need to establish national cemeteries in twelve or more metropolitan areas across the nation. The first burial at Fort Snelling National Cemetery—that of a World War I veteran—took place on July 5, 1939. George H. Mallon, a Minneapolis resident who installed automatic sprinkler systems before the First World War, had attended officers training camp at Fort Snelling. He went overseas as captain of Company E, 132nd Infantry Regiment, Thirty-third Infantry Division. General John J. Pershing decorated Mallon with the Medal of Honor for conspicuous gallantry on September 26, 1918, the opening day of the Meuse-Argonne offensive. This major push by Pershing's American Expeditionary Force was the last battle of World War I. Mallon's medal citation reads:

> Becoming separated from the balance of his company because of a fog, Captain Mallon with nine soldiers pushed forward and attacked nine active and hostile machineguns, capturing all of them without the loss of a man. Continuing on through the woods, he led his men in attacking a battery of four 155mm howitzers, which were in action, rushing the position and capturing the battery and its crew. In this encounter, Captain Mallon personally attacked one of the enemy with his fists. Later, when the party came upon two more machineguns, this officer sent men to the flanks while he rushed forward directly in the face of fire and silenced the guns, being the first one of the party to reach the nest. The exceptional gallantry and determination displayed by Captain Mallon resulted in the capture of one hundred prisoners, eleven machineguns, four 155mm howitzers, and one antiaircraft gun.

Less than two weeks later, a fragment from a high explosive ripped through Mallon's right thigh. He spent three months in a military hospital before he returned home to

Minneapolis, a hero, in 1919. He became prominent in political and labor circles, serving as Hennepin County commissioner for eight years. George Mallon died in 1934 at the age of fifty-seven after a long illness. The government reinterred his remains in Minnesota's new national cemetery on July 5, 1939. The official dedication of Fort Snelling National Cemetery had occurred just one day earlier.

The remains of veterans buried at Fort Snelling's old post cemetery were reinterred in the new national cemetery, which encompasses 436 acres adjacent to Minneapolis–St. Paul International Airport. Most of the Civil War soldiers were buried in section A-2, near the flagpole, as were the two Blackfoot soldiers. The unidentified remains of 680 soldiers from the post cemetery were reinterred in section A, block 23, just inside the cemetery from the Gate 2 entrance. Each of these white marble markers bears a single word, "Unknown."

The deceased of the Twenty-fifth Regiment of African Americans were reinterred in section A-5, the next block from A-2. African American soldiers who died in the 1940s and early 1950s were laid to rest in sections A-3 and A-6, along the fence on Thirty-fourth Avenue. While most served in labor battalions in the Spanish-American War and World War I, African American combat veterans are also buried at Fort Snelling. The segregated arrangement in the national cemetery at that time paralleled the segregation practices in the U.S. military and across the nation as a whole.

A Spanish-American War veteran who passed away just four months after the dedication of the cemetery was buried in section A-2. Other Spanish-American War veterans who died during the 1940s were buried in sections A-5, A-21, and A-22, among others.

World War II led to another massive nationwide mobilization and, ultimately, to vast numbers of deaths. The remains of many Americans killed in action in World War II were not returned to the States until 1948. They were laid to rest in block 1 of section B (B-1) and blocks 1 and 3 of section C (C-1 and C-3). The road leading into the cemetery from the main flagpole was named Mallon Road, for the first veteran buried at the new site. The graves on either side of Mallon Road (the DS section) are those of men decorated with the Medal of Honor, the Distinguished Service Cross, and the Navy Cross.

Today, Fort Snelling National Cemetery is the final resting place of the remains of almost 170,000 servicemen and servicewomen and their immediate families. All veterans and members of the armed forces (army, navy, air force, Marine Corps, Coast Guard) are eligible for burial in a national cemetery so long as they have an honorable discharge. Merchant marines with oceangoing service during World War II are also eligible, as are reservists and National Guard who meet certain criteria. Others, including commissioned officers of the National Oceanic and Atmospheric Administration and commissioned officers of the Public Health Service, may be eligible. Spouses and minor children of those eligible may also be buried in a national cemetery.

Memorial Rifle Squad of Fort Snelling National Cemetery

George Weiss served in the U.S. Marines near the end of World War II. Weiss later became active in Veterans Affairs, particularly with the Veterans of Foreign Wars. He is a past post commander and district commander with the Minnesota VFW and remains a busy man. Twenty-five years ago, he and five other veterans formed the Memorial Rifle Squad at Fort Snelling National Cemetery. They borrowed rifles from an American Legion Post and provided their first military ceremonial burial services for three interments on June 19, 1979.

The original group became the Tuesday Squad. They gathered enough men by September 1979 to form a second unit, which became the Friday Squad. Eventually a rifle squad was formed for each weekday. Each squad has a bugler assigned to play taps after the rifle salute is fired over the grave. The men in each squad come to know each other well, seeing each other as they do once a week year-round. Jokes fired off from one branch of the service at another are quickly returned. There is good food and good company. "The camaraderie we get here is almost what we got in the service," Weiss remarked. Their demeanor turns serious, however, as ten o'clock approaches. The deep sense of purpose within the squad becomes immediately apparent.

The Memorial Rifle Squad has not missed a scheduled funeral in twenty-five years of service. Weather is not a factor; the squads have done their duty in summer temperatures of 100 degrees and throughout the harsh Minnesota winter in subzero temperatures accompanied by snow and ice. The squad of the day may participate in as many as seventeen funerals between the hours of 10:00 a.m. and 2:00 p.m. on any given day. It is not unusual for the squads to provide honors for fifteen funerals on a single day more than once in a given week. The Fort Snelling Memorial Rifle Squad has provided military ceremonial honors at more than forty thousand burials since its inception.

This all-volunteer rifle unit was the first among all cemeteries in the National Cemetery Administration of the Department of Veterans Affairs. The rifle squad rarely ventures from Fort Snelling National Cemetery, other than to participate in a special event at the nearby Minnesota Veterans Home. All squad members are veterans; previous military service is a requirement of eligibility. The 120 members represent all branches of the service. The original core of the group consists of World War II veterans. The average age of the members is 74.6 years.

The federal government provides the squad's meeting room on the cemetery grounds as well as the rifles and ammunition. Financial support for the squad's additional expenses comes from local veterans groups, not the Veterans Administration. Some support also comes from the families for whom the squad performs the service.

George Weiss and his fellow squad members carry the same determination and dedication to service that defined them as young men fifty years ago. Weiss is unwavering when he says, "We are doing what we think is necessary. We take care of our own." Their own is anyone who has ever worn the uniform of the U.S. armed forces. The Memorial Rifle Squad exemplifies service.

Our Hallowed Ground

Chapter 1

Pearl Harbor through Guadalcanal

On December 7, 1941—"a date which will live in infamy"—a wave of Japanese torpedo bombers and dive-bombers appeared over the horizon at the U.S. naval base at Pearl Harbor in Hawaii. It was just before eight o'clock on a sunny Sunday morning. Confusion and disbelief were followed by chaos as explosions rocked the harbor. Dark plumes of smoke rose into the skies from burning warships. Leaking oil spread across the water and caught fire, adding to the apocalyptic scene. The surprise attack by Imperial Japan plunged the United States into the Second World War. Although heroism abounded on that December day, the full extent of the deeds will never be known.

Karl Lasch and Ambrose Domagall

The first tangible indication of an immediate Japanese threat to the U.S. Pacific Fleet at Pearl Harbor was the sighting of a midget submarine at four o'clock on the morning of December 7, 1941—four hours before Japanese bombers flew over the harbor. Japanese Admiral Isoroku Yamamoto's plan to attack Pearl Harbor included five midget submarines, each eighty feet long and armed with two torpedoes. They were to destroy any American ships attempting to leave Pearl Harbor and escape into the open sea. The sinking of ships in the harbor entrance would further bottleneck the American fleet and damage the operational capability of the base in the foreseeable future.

The patrol ship sent to investigate the sighted midget submarine was the USS *Ward,* an obsolete flush-deck destroyer launched in 1918 that had been placed in reserve in 1922. The navy reactivated the *Ward* on January 15, 1941, and sailors from the Minnesota

The number-one gun crew on the destroyer USS *Ward* fired the first shot by the U.S. military in World War II on December 7, 1941. Coxswain Karl Lasch, the sight setter, and Seaman Second Class Ambrose Domagall, a loader, both of St. Paul, Minnesota, are buried in Fort Snelling National Cemetery. Photograph courtesy of the Naval Historical Foundation.

Navy Militia were called to active duty and ordered to crew the destroyer. The Minnesota Navy Militia, based in the seaport of Duluth, Minnesota, had been in existence since 1903 for the express purpose of training men for the U.S. Navy. The militia used the USS *Paducah,* a two-hundred-foot-long gunboat launched in 1905, for training.

The *Ward* was patrolling the approach to Pearl Harbor throughout the night of December 6 and into the early morning of December 7 when the minesweeper *Condor* sent a blinker message to the *Ward* at 4:00 a.m. The *Ward* steamed to the approximate location but found nothing. It was 6:00 a.m. before the *Ward* ceased the search. Not long afterward, Seaman Second Class Ambrose Domagall of St. Paul on lookout duty on the *Ward* spotted something in the water near the supply ship *Antares.* The *Antares* confirmed the sighting moments later at 6:30. The officer on deck sounded the alarm for general quarters and the crew rushed to battle stations. Meanwhile, a PBY plane spotted the Japanese submarine from overhead and dropped smoke floats near it. The *Ward*'s number-one gun fired the first shots by the U.S. military in World War II at 6:45 a.m. Coxswain Karl Lasch of St. Paul was the sight setter on the gun and Seaman Domagall was the loader. A change of course ordered moments earlier by the captain caused the *Ward* to roll and the round of shots sailed over the sub. The *Ward* steamed past the sub and the number-three gun crew on the aft deck hit it with a round at point-blank range. Several depth charges finished off the wounded sub and sent it to the bottom of the harbor. The *Ward* reported the incident at 6:52 a.m. to Naval District Headquarters, but no one there apparently thought the brief engagement worthy of attention. The *Ward* and her crew became a footnote of history rather than heroes for saving battleships of the U.S. Pacific Fleet that might otherwise have been lost.

Karl Lasch died in 1981. He is buried in section R of Fort Snelling National Cemetery in grave site 3252. Ambrose Domagall, who died in 2001, is also buried in section R, in grave site 800.

Gordon Tengwall

The Japanese air raid on Pearl Harbor began at approximately 7:43 a.m. Three dive-bomber torpedoes struck the port side of the USS *Oklahoma* at 7:50. The ship immediately began to list. Oil and water on the deck made it difficult for crews to get to their battle stations. A fourth torpedo hit the *Oklahoma* at 7:55. The *Utah* also took a torpedo from this first wave, began to list, and soon capsized. Three torpedoes hit the USS *West Virginia* and she began to list. The USS *Arizona* erupted into an inferno, sending forth plumes of black smoke after a bomb hit the ship's magazine. The *Oklahoma* was hit by up to nine torpedoes. Her port side opened almost completely along a 250-foot length of her hull. She listed and quickly rolled. The U.S. Pacific Fleet was devastated.

The human toll was far more tragic. Thousands of men felt the shock of exploding torpedoes rocking their battleships, sensed a moment of fear, then composed themselves and began to move. They alerted their sleeping friends and headed to battle stations. For some, the ship listed and rolled so quickly that they had no chance of getting to their stations. They heard the ominous creaking as the ship began to roll and realized with terror that they must jump into the burning, oil-slicked waters of the harbor. Many died in explosions or were trapped within capsized ships. Strafing Japanese planes took lives on the decks and in the water. Many sailors drowned.

Gunner's First Mate Gordon Tengwall survived the sinking of the USS *Oklahoma* at Pearl Harbor on December 7, 1941. He served through the war on the heavy cruiser USS *Louisville* in the Pacific theater. Photograph courtesy of the Tengwall family.

Gordon Tengwall of Pennock, Minnesota, joined the U.S. Navy to get off the farm and see the world. His first year of service had been uneventful, but on December 7 he was a gunner's first mate aboard the *Oklahoma*. Seaman Tengwall was helping in the ship's mess that morning. He was on deck, having just returned from the garbage scow off the *Oklahoma*'s port side, when he heard explosions. He turned to see the parked American planes burning on nearby Ford Island and a Japanese plane diving at the *Oklahoma*. Tengwall dropped his buckets and raced below to warn fellow crew members, many of whom were still asleep in their berths. "I was running down the ladder and I was met by a torpedo," he recalled. "There was an explosion, and then I could see the light out the side of the hull and water was gushing in it. I turned around to go back and the second torpedo hit. It raised me a foot off my feet."

Movement along the passageways was difficult as the ship was listing hard to port. Pandemonium reigned. Seaman Tengwall tried to persuade a friend below to let go of a stair railing, but the man refused, despite water everywhere. Tengwall finally crawled out a port window as the ship's list became a roll toward capsizing. He and others who made it out scrambled along the hull as the massive warship turned over, slipping and cutting themselves on barnacles. The crew on top became easy targets as Japanese planes sprayed the hull with machine-gun fire. Tengwall looked for a way off, but feared being sucked into the vortexes created by all the water pouring into the capsized ship. After two attempts, he finally plunged in, trying to miss the oil burning on the surface of the water. But he swallowed oil every time he came up struggling for air, and he would be sick for days afterward. As a rescue launch passed by, it seemed he would be left behind, but a sailor reached down and dragged the half-drowned Minnesotan into the boat.

Once they were ashore, there was little the surviving sailors could do. Tengwall later recalled there being "no battle stations, no guns. The planes were still coming— you could actually see the faces of the pilots—but there was nothing we could do." He slept that night on the floor of an ammo dump. The *Oklahoma*'s starboard hull showed just above the water's surface in the aftermath. Many of the crew were trapped inside and rescue crews worked feverishly for two days to save them. They brought out thirty-two men, but another four hundred perished.

Seaman Gordon Tengwall went to war soon after his recovery. The navy assigned him to the heavy cruiser USS *Louisville*, which escorted aircraft carriers raiding in the Central and South Pacific in early 1942. In 1943 the cruiser's assignments covered the Pacific, including the battle of Rennell Island off Guadalcanal in January and the pre-assault bombardment of Attu and Kiska in the Aleutian Islands in April. The *Louisville* took part in a series of naval bombardments in the Marshall Islands in early 1944. She was the leading unit in the bombardments and fired continuously for the first eleven days of the battle of Saipan. As a gunner's mate, Tengwall saw considerable action.

The *Louisville* joined the vast armada supporting the American invasion of Leyte in the Philippines in October 1944. The Japanese responded with a formidable force of two battle fleets. The resulting clash on October 24–25 became known as the Battle of Leyte Gulf, where Tengwall and his crewmates took part in the third of four major air and naval battles. The battle of Surigao was the last battle-line naval action in history. Tengwall must have been excited to discover among the line of American battleships the *West Virginia,* the *California,* the *Tennessee,* and the *Pennsylvania*—all vessels whose fighting days had seemed finished in the aftermath of Pearl Harbor. The ships and heavy cruisers engaged the Japanese fleet as it came single file out of the straits. The result was a resounding victory, not only in sinking five Japanese warships, but also in ensuring that the fleet would not be able to wreak havoc on the hundreds of American supply ships just off the landing beaches on Leyte.

The *Louisville* continued on duty, defending the Leyte beachhead into early 1945. Kamikazes (suicide bombers) were a daily event in the waters just off Leyte. Observers said there seemed always to be a couple or more ships burning. Two kamikazes hit the *Louisville* on January 5–6, but the ship was repaired in time to take part in the Okinawa action, only to be struck again by a kamikaze on June 5. The *Louisville* earned thirteen battle stars for her service in the war. Gordon Tengwall had every right to feel he had done his part. He later shared with his son, Doug, that the kamikazes were among his greatest fears of the war.

Doug Tengwall recalls that his dad "never spoke about the war when we were young." He does remember him being clear that he felt no animosity toward the Japanese after the war in the Pacific. His father did not say much about his war experiences until 1991, when Congress authorized a Bronze Medal for Pearl Harbor survivors and the Tengwall family gathered for the formal presentation.

Gordon Tengwall died May 18, 2001. He is buried in section 13, grave site 1779, at Fort Snelling National Cemetery. It was his fervent hope that nothing like Pearl Harbor would ever happen again to the United States.

Franklin Van Valkenburgh and Ira Weil Jeffrey

A 1,760-pound bomb released from a high-altitude bomber struck the number-two turret of the *Arizona* at 8:10 a.m. on December 7 in Pearl Harbor, penetrating deep into the battleship before exploding near the forward magazine. The *Arizona* blew up with immense force, instantly killing 1,177 of the seamen on board. The ship's burning superstructure, barely visible through the billowing smoke, became a vivid reminder for shocked Americans of the tragic loss of lives. Among the casualties were ship commanders Rear Admiral I. C. Kidd and Captain Franklin Van Valkenburgh. Van Valkenburgh grew up in Minneapolis before going off to pursue a naval career. Both he and Kidd were posthumously awarded the Medal of Honor. There were no remains to be buried.

Ensign Ira Weil Jeffrey, a Minneapolis resident and a 1939 graduate of the University of Minnesota, was on the USS *California* on December 7. He had written his mother from San Diego in October: "Where'll *[sic]* we'll be going, who knows. But it will probably be Pearl, where we'll just continue doing as we have. How dull!" Jeffrey was commended posthumously for heroism at Pearl Harbor for organizing a human-chain relay of supply ammunition to the *California*'s antiaircraft guns after the mechanical loading systems failed. Minneapolis newspapers recognized Jeffrey as the first man from the city to die in the war. His remains were never recovered.

Earl T. Nermoe

The *West Virginia* was moored so close to the *Arizona* that fiery debris from explosions on the *Arizona* showered down on the *West Virginia*'s quarterdeck. Meanwhile, seven torpedoes ripped into the *West Virginia*'s port side and two bombs burst through her superstructure. The ship began to list sharply to port as water rushed in. Captain Mervyn Bennion, mortally wounded by the bombs, refused to leave his station. He died that day and subsequently was awarded the Medal of Honor. Mess Attendant Doris Miller, an African American, also earned the Medal of Honor for taking an idle antiaircraft gun and returning fire for some time on the attacking planes. Quick decisions resulted in counter-flooding the *West Virginia* as she began to list, allowing the ship to settle on the bottom of the harbor on an even keel. The result was a significantly lower number of lives lost.

Among the 105 sailors on the *West Virginia* who lost their lives on December 7 was Seaman First Class Earl T. Nermoe, a twenty-two-year-old from Upham, North Dakota (population 155). The American Legion Post in Upham is named in his honor. Nermoe's remains were returned to the Upper Midwest after the war and buried in Fort Snelling National Cemetery, section B-1, grave 352-N. The U.S. Navy salvaged the wreck of the

The flaming wreckage of the USS *West Virginia* at Pearl Harbor. Seaman First Class Earl Nermoe was one of more than one hundred seamen who lost their lives aboard the ship on December 7, 1941. Quick thinking and counter-flooding measures kept the *West Virginia* from capsizing and saved countless other lives. Photograph courtesy of the Library of Congress, Prints and Photographs Division, FSA-OWI Collection, LC-USW33-018433-C DLC.

West Virginia, but months of restoration were necessary before she returned to action. She did so before the end of the war, a symbol of the indomitable spirit of the United States. Earl Nermoe would have been proud.

Allen Goudy

While Japanese torpedo bombers and dive-bombers wreaked death and destruction in Pearl Harbor, enemy fighter pilots were strafing Hickam and Wheeler Fields on the island of Oahu. Only a few American fighter planes at the airfields got off the ground before the others were destroyed. U.S. Army Air Force personnel at Wheeler Field attempted to organize amid the chaos and return the fire. Some used antiaircraft guns, but many others defiantly returned fire with rifles and even pistols. Nearly seven hundred Army Air Force personnel were killed or wounded in the attack. Twenty-four-year-old Allen Goudy of Wayzata, Minnesota, was serving at Wheeler Field with the Seventy-second AAF Pursuit Squadron. Goudy entered the service in March 1941, went overseas the following month, and died in action on December 7. His remains were returned to the Upper Midwest after the war. He is buried in section C, grave 7359, at Fort Snelling National Cemetery.

Byrl Carson

Byrl Carson of Fairmont, Minnesota, was on the USS *Utah* at Pearl Harbor. Carson graduated from high school in 1939 and persuaded his parents to allow him to enlist at age seventeen in the U.S. Navy. He had read much about the navy, seen the movie newsreels, and wanted to do his part for his nation with what he referred to as "the finest, fightenest organization in this world today." War seemed imminent, and his two older brothers already were in the service. One was a Marine and the other was training to be an army bomber pilot.

A torpedo exploded on the *Utah*'s port side at eight o'clock, just as her colors were being hoisted. Another torpedo hit the ship moments later, and by 8:05 the *Utah* listed a perilous forty degrees. Carson and his crewmates rushed topside. Japanese planes with the distinctive red sun painted on their wings swooped through Battleship Row. The crew scrambled to starboard, the high side, while the planes strafed the deck. The men began to jump off the burning ship, most of them unable to grab the life jackets that were stored away. Carson and others slid down the ropes that tethered the ship to its mooring. The *Utah* capsized at 8:12, just twelve minutes after the first torpedo hit. Carson was halfway down the rope when the ship began to roll. He jumped into the water, which was, he recalled, "all afire from the oil." The sailors did their best to make their way to shore, mostly swimming underwater below the inferno at the surface. "We lost an awful lot of people when we were swimming ashore," Carson recalled. "We were being strafed by Zeroes." The battleship *Arizona* exploded into an inferno just before the *Utah* capsized.

On shore Carson joined a group of sailors rushing to save the *California,* moored southwest of Battleship Row in a shallow bay on Ford Island. Flagship of the Pacific Fleet, the *California* suffered torpedo hits fore and aft in the early minutes of the

Two ships sank from under Seaman Byrl Carson at Pearl Harbor that fateful day, first the USS *Utah* and later the USS *California*. Photograph courtesy of the Carson family.

attack. At 8:40, eight groups of Japanese high-altitude bombers appeared over the harbor. The *California* was rocked by four near misses. At 9:00 a fifth bomb struck the ship, penetrated to the second deck, and exploded. The battleship listed to port and fire broke out on the deck at 9:30, but the crew did not give up the fight. The *California* was getting steam up to get under way and head to the open sea. By the time the Japanese aerial onslaught ceased at about 9:45, a vast sheet of burning oil drifting down from Battleship Row enveloped the *California* and ignited more fires onboard.

The captain ordered the ship abandoned at 10:02. For the second time that day, Byrl Carson jumped into the burning water and swam underwater to shore.

The Japanese sank or severely damaged eighteen U.S. warships, eight of them battleships, that morning at Pearl Harbor and took the lives of more than 2,004 Americans. Forty-eight hours later, the navy assigned Carson and many others to bury the dead. The task went on for days. The ordeal was such that Carson told his family, "None of us on burial duty could eat." Meanwhile, the navy initially listed Carson as missing in action. On the same day she learned he was missing, Carson's mother received another telegram from the War Department, telling her that the Japanese had captured Byrl's brother Morris, a Marine serving at the U.S. Embassy in Peking. Byrl Carson's military records indicate he was transferred to the light cruiser USS *Honolulu* just days after the Japanese attack. The navy sent Carson to San Diego in April 1942 for instruction in operating special landing boats. This knowledge would prove useful in a matter of months.

Pearl Harbor, while a costly setback to the United States, galvanized the nation into action. Survivors of the day, Byrl Carson among them, were ready to continue the fight with the Japanese on more equal terms. Meanwhile, thousands and thousands of American civilians rushed to enlist and join them. America was at war.

The United States rose from defeat at Pearl Harbor to strike back at Imperial Japan within six months. Two resounding victories at the Battle of Coral Sea on May 9, 1942, and the Battle of Midway on June 6, 1942, stopped the Japanese momentum. The United States commenced its first major offensive in the Pacific in August 1942 at a time when Japan still maintained naval superiority in the Pacific. The objective was possession of the island of Guadalcanal in the Solomon Islands.

The First Marine Division went ashore at Guadalcanal on August 7, 1942. Seaman Byrl Carson was aboard the navy cargo ship *Betelgeuse*, which was just offshore and unloading supplies. The navy command lacked experience in matters of logistics on this scale. The pioneer battalion assigned to unload the supplies and move the material off the beach was inadequate. Many of the landing boats lacked movable bow ramps and the laborers had to lift the supplies up and over the gunwales. Supplies, including piles of ammunition, stacked up on the beach while landing craft waited just outside the surf. The navy command sent Carson and other sailors ashore to assist in unloading and moving the supplies. The men worked in the extreme heat to the point of exhaustion, yet somehow kept on. Japanese bombers attacked the fleet twice that afternoon. One hundred landing craft were beached by nightfall, waiting to be unloaded. Unloading continued through the night.

The USS *California* before sinking at Pearl Harbor. Photograph courtesy of the National Archives (80-G-32463).

The Japanese navy responded quickly to the American landing in the Solomon Islands, sending a strong naval force toward Guadalcanal on August 8. The U.S. carrier force withdrew, leaving the amphibious force without air cover. Navy and Coast Guard personnel continued to frantically move supplies ashore for as long as possible. The Battle of Savo Island took place in the early morning of August 9. The Japanese sank four cruisers in minutes, severely crippled a fifth, and damaged a sixth. All other American ships cleared from the area that day. The disastrous defeat stranded slightly fewer than eleven thousand Americans on Guadalcanal without naval support or sufficient supplies. Carson began a three-month stint on Guadalcanal, where he and fellow servicemen did not go on full rations until mid-September. He later recalled, "Nothing to eat except Japanese rice and hardtack we found in a cave they abandoned. And coconuts. Eat them and get diarrhea. Lots of men died of that." Carson's military records state that he was "commended . . . for meritorious work without rest while under fire during GUADALCANAL OPERATIONS Aug. 7–8–9, 1942." The navy officially transferred him to Naval Local Defense Headquarters for temporary duty on Guadalcanal on September 1. Lieutenant Commander Dwight Hodge Dexter of the U.S. Coast Guard, which was part of the navy at the time, was in command (Dexter retired as a rear admiral). Eighteen of the twenty-two troopships involved in the Guadalcanal landing carried Coast Guard personnel to operate landing craft.

Wrote Carson: "Up to August 21 we never had a plane with which we could counter-attack. . . . It was on the 21 that we had our biggest joy for a long time. There were a few Grummans [Marine Wildcat fighters] that were coming to fight back at the Japs. It was an entirely different story too after they arrived. Instead of having to hide all the time we would get out and watch the dogfights. . . . Every time we would see a Jap plane go down in flames we would holler like hell."

Of his Guadalcanal experience after the war, Carson remarked: "None of us figured we'd make it. Stopped thinking about it, just faced the reality of not living. Everybody did everything, no matter what the assignment was." He began ferrying Marine raiding parties along the coast of Guadalcanal and up its rivers, dropping them off and later extracting them, at times under fire. They were most likely aboard Higgins boats—rugged, shallow-draft, and highly maneuverable craft used in the landing and subsequent supply of the Marines on Guadalcanal. Carson would have learned to operate and maintain Higgins boats in San Diego. He wrote of one day being caught in a cross fire from the beach while dropping off a group of Marines. Casualties were high. A Japanese sniper killed Carson's engineer, who was standing right next to him. Carson later fought on the line with the Marines for a time when the Japanese threatened to overrun Guadalcanal's Henderson Field.

Guadalcanal was constantly under threat of bombardment from the air or shelling from the sea. Carson counted 155 air raids and eighty-seven shellings during his stay. An aerial bombing ends in minutes, but naval shellings often last several hours. Shells screaming in from overhead shake the ground and create a hellish condition. There is little one can do but take cover and cringe, wondering if the next incoming shell is going to hit nearby. Carson would later say that Guadalcanal was even worse than Pearl Harbor. He wrote, "During the day the [Japanese] ships would come in the harbor and shell us and we could do nothing but sit and take it like a bunch of defenseless fools . . . we would seek shelter in a fox hole or an air raid shelter."

In early November 1942, Carson was in a bomb shelter that took a direct hit from a shell. He happened to be standing near the entrance and was blown clear. The thirteen men inside were killed. He did not return to complete consciousness for a number of days, eventually finding himself in a hospital in New Hebrides. His records indicate that he gave a sworn statement to a navy official at Mare Island Naval Hospital in San Francisco in January 1943. Carson reported that Lieutenant Commander Dwight Hodge Dexter had authorized his advancement from seaman first class to coxswain in recognition of his services on Guadalcanal beginning August 7, 1942. In fact, a Higgins boat operator generally held the rank of coxswain. The navy accordingly advanced Carson.

Byrl Carson was honorably discharged on April 16, 1943, after stays in several naval hospitals. He returned home to Fairmont in April 1943. His brothers, the Marine POW and the bomber pilot, also survived and the family was reunited at war's end. Carson's closing statement in a short memoir he wrote just after returning home reads, "Was not needlessly wasted time or effort that I spent while in the service of this wonderful free country of ours." He married and he and his beloved wife, Gert, raised six children. He worked as a traveling printer for most of his career and spent a couple of years in Hawaii, but never once went to Pearl Harbor or Punchbowl National Cemetery. He had never failed to observe December 7, but the day was difficult for him. Carson did not speak much of the war for the most part, so his family was surprised when he expressed interest in going to Pearl Harbor in 1991 for the fiftieth anniversary of the Japanese attack. His family remembers him appearing anxious when they attended the observance with him, but the return at last gave him closure.

Byrl Carson passed away on February 18, 2004. He is buried at Fort Snelling National Cemetery in section 20-A, grave site 827. His family remembered him as a man who enjoyed heading off with the grandkids to go fishing, wearing his battered Pearl Harbor survivor cap and carrying his cane and pole. He once told a reporter, "People say it's not good to reminisce. I don't know. I don't regret it; I'd do it again. After I got discharged, I was asked to help commission some ships up at Duluth and at Savage. It was an honor and a privilege."

Donald V. Rose

Donald Rose was born and raised in Whalan in southeastern Minnesota, not far from Lanesboro. He was commissioned a naval officer at Pensacola, Florida, on April 17, 1942. Second Lieutenant Rose subsequently joined the Marines and was assigned to the First Marine Division. He went ashore on Guadalcanal alongside his fellow Marines in the fall of 1942.

The Japanese mobilized troops from throughout Asia to force the Americans off Guadalcanal or annihilate them. The Kawaguchi force, veterans of the war in China

U.S. Marines resting in the field before fighting on Guadalcanal. Photograph courtesy of the National Archives (80-G-20683).

and Burma, moved to Borneo at the time of the Japanese attack on Pearl Harbor. This six-thousand-man force was in the Palaus until late August 1942, when they began to move by night transport to Guadalcanal between August 29 and September 11. General Kiyotake Kawaguchi was ready to attack immediately. The Marines were on guard on their important foothold on the island, recognizing that Henderson Field was so important to control of the Solomon Islands that the airstrip was called an "unsinkable aircraft carrier." Marine intelligence had some sense of the growing Japanese presence on Guadalcanal. However, regular landings of the Imperial Japanese Army under cover of darkness, and the dense tropical jungle that provided them with cover once ashore, resulted in underestimates of Japanese strength.

The Marines were dug in on a grassy north-south-trending ridge just one mile beyond Henderson Field. Kawaguchi's veterans lay not far away, prepared to make their move on the night of September 12. The Japanese assault began after dark. They rushed the Marine line with fixed bayonets and the fighting was fierce. Official Marine reports state that gunfire was continuous throughout the night of September 12–13. The Japanese at one point broke through the Marine lines, but the dark, thick jungle prevented them from capitalizing on it. The Marines held through ten hours of hand-to-hand fighting before they could secure their position. Second Lieutenant Donald Rose was wounded sometime during this first night. He died the following day, not five months after receiving his officer's commission. Several hundred Marines died on what became known as Bloody Ridge before the Japanese ceased their massive night assaults. The Marines held, and Henderson Field allowed increasing American control, both in protecting U.S. landings and attacking Japanese landings and positions. The name Bloody Ridge on Guadalcanal resides in the honored annals of the U.S. Marine Corps.

Donald Rose was buried in the First Marine Division Cemetery on Guadalcanal. His remains were returned to Minnesota in 1948. His final resting place is in section B, grave site 315-N, at Fort Snelling National Cemetery.

Ernest B. Miller

The National Guard tank company in the quiet lake resort town of Brainerd, Minnesota, must have felt far removed from the fighting in Europe and Asia in 1940. None in the local Guard could have imagined the role they were to play in the history of American military heroism. The likelihood of U.S. involvement in the war had become increasingly apparent, and the army constituted various National Guard units from across the country into the 194th Tank Battalion on September 1, 1940. The Brainerd unit was designated Company A, 194th Tank Battalion. Captain Ernie Miller commanded the company, which consisted of his friends and neighbors. The men of the 194th Tank Battalion were inducted into federal service from December 1940 to the beginning of March 1941 and ordered to Fort Lewis, Washington, for training. They shipped out for the Philippines in September 1941, earning the honor of being among the first U.S. troops to go overseas.

Ernest Brumaghim Miller joined the Minnesota National Guard in St. Paul as a bugler at the age of fourteen. He was a sergeant with the Guard in 1916 in pursuit of Pancho Villa along the Mexican border. Miller saw action in France in the First World War with the Second Division and was awarded the Purple Heart for wounds received. He moved to Park Rapids, Minnesota, in 1921 and became an engineer and surveyor for Hubbard County. He joined the local Guard unit and later became commanding

Lieutenant Colonel Ernest Miller of Brainerd, Minnesota, with his son Richard in 1946. Richard, a senior at Brainerd High School, went on to West Point and retired from the army as a lieutenant colonel. The 1946 Ford, a gift of Mills Ford (predecessor of Mills Fleet Farm) in Brainerd, was believed to be the first new car in the state of Minnesota after the war. Photograph courtesy of the Minnesota Military Museum, Camp Ripley.

officer. Miller became chief engineer of the Minnesota National Guard's Camp Ripley Military Reservation in 1930. He moved to Brainerd, Minnesota, in 1936 to be closer to Camp Ripley and in that year formed the National Guard tank company in Brainerd.

President Franklin D. Roosevelt had sent General Douglas MacArthur to the Philippines in 1935 to organize its defense against the Japanese. MacArthur was retired from the U.S. Army and serving as military adviser to the Philippines when Roosevelt recalled him to active duty in June 1941 in preparation for invasion. When MacArthur requested additional troops, the army increased his command of American military men from twelve thousand to twenty-two thousand from July to October 1941.

MacArthur's total command, which was heavily Filipino, consisted of 135,000 soldiers. He also had at his disposal a sizable air force, including 175 fighters, of which 107 were P-40s.

The 194th Tank Battalion sent to augment MacArthur's force comprised fifty-four light tanks (M-3 Stuarts), nineteen half-tracks, and approximately four hundred soldiers. The army also sent the 192nd Tank Battalion; like the 194th, the 192nd was made up of Guard units from various states, as well as several coastal artillery units and an ordnance unit. While the American military force in the Philippines was still not substantial in December 1941, it was much more so than it had been just months earlier when MacArthur assumed command. The reality was that American intelligence did not expect the Japanese attack until sometime in 1942.

Japanese warplanes struck American military bases in the Philippines on the day after the surprise attack on Pearl Harbor. The Japanese again caught the American military unprepared, despite a warning nine hours in advance. They destroyed half the U.S. combat aircraft in the Philippines on the first day. The U.S. Asiatic Fleet left the Philippines following the destruction of its naval facilities. It became only a matter of time for the Japanese to take the Philippines once they established air and naval superiority. The Japanese began amphibious landings soon after the air strikes, with the main landing on Luzon taking place on December 22, 1941. Japanese forces pressed toward Manila within days.

The original strategic defense plan had been to concentrate the combined American and Filipino forces in central Luzon and deny the Japanese navy the use of Manila Bay for its armada. The fallback plan was to withdraw to Bataan Peninsula in the event of failure to prevent or defeat Japanese landings. Control of Bataan would allow the American-Filipino forces to continue to control strategic Manila Bay. However, MacArthur strenuously objected and ultimately obtained authority from Washington to disperse his forces so as to defend all of the islands of the Philippines. Consequently, most of the American-Filipino forces were unable to withdraw into the Bataan perimeter, despite the sacrifice by General Jonathan Wainwright and his North Luzon force to hold off the Japanese advance as best they could. The 194th Tank Battalion played an important role in covering the withdrawal into the Bataan Peninsula. The battalion was under fire throughout January 4 and 5, pulling back one tank at a time while under attack. The 194th decimated an enemy force estimated at eight hundred strong on the afternoon of January 5.

Those American and Filipino forces that did withdraw were within a defensive perimeter on Bataan by January 6, 1942. However, food and medical supplies, as well as ammunition and weapons, were critically low from the beginning of the siege due to the frantic and rapid withdrawal. Soldiers were put on half-rations immediately.

Headquarters Provisional Tank Group issued General Orders Number 5, awarding the Silver Star to Lieutenant Colonel Ernest Miller, commanding officer of the 194th Tank Battalion (L), with the following citation:

> During the Operations in the period from December 8, 1941, to January 7, 1942, Lieutenant Colonel Miller executed command from his tank in the fighting echelon . . . he personally fought his own tank, thereby contributing to the morale of his men and the efficiency of his section.

The Japanese pressed the attack on Bataan on January 9. The Americans and Filipinos fought with determination and inflicted heavy casualties. The Japanese poured in reinforcements, fearful that prolonged American resistance might expose the illusion of invincibility. Overwhelming Japanese forces finally forced American-Filipino forces to withdraw from their first line of defense on Bataan on January 25. The 194th Tank Battalion again covered the withdrawal. The tanks under Colonel Miller set up a killing zone and destroyed a considerable Japanese force as it attempted to press the withdrawal. Still the Americans and Filipinos held on, starving, exhausted, and diseased.

Colonel Miller and the sixty men of Company A from Brainerd were among the determined American soldiers on Bataan. The combined American-Filipino force held through February and into March. Soldiers weak from starvation and disease, particularly malaria, still held out. They became known as "the Battlin' Bastards of Bataan":

> The Battlin' Bastards of Bataan,
> No Mama, No Papa, No Uncle Sam,
> No aunts, no uncles, no cousins, no nieces,
> No pills, no planes, no artillery pieces,
> And nobody gives a damn!
> (Frank Hewlett, 1942)

The last major Japanese push on Bataan began on April 3, Good Friday. Miller wrote: "They poured into this sector a vast deluge of high explosive shells. All their efforts were directed at this one sector. At the same time, Jap bombers also concentrated on the area. Our line was, absolutely and literally, blown right out of the ground." The gallant defenders were overwhelmed within a week. The Japanese took prisoner nearly twelve thousand Americans and sixty thousand Filipinos. American nurses were among those captured.

The prisoners already were in a weakened state from the deprivations of the siege, but their condition worsened when the Japanese ordered a forced march up the Bataan

Peninsula to a former Philippine army camp sixty-five miles to the north. The agonizing journey became infamous as the Bataan Death March. Colonel Ernest Miller later wrote that his captors "were very brutal and needed only the slightest provocation to display that brutality. . . . I will never know how that march was completed. . . . Those who could not keep up were simply killed by clubbing, shooting and bayoneting. . . . The Death March was conducted strictly at the point of a bayonet." Miller further described the camp into which the prisoners were forced as "probably the worst scene, of anything I have ever witnessed in my entire life." There was no protection from the blazing sun and the men were packed shoulder to shoulder. Over six hundred Americans died on the march, and more than fifteen hundred Americans died at the camp in the first forty days of its existence. Another three thousand American survivors of the Bataan Death March died after transfer to the prison camp at Cabanatuan in June before they were sent to Japan. As many as ten thousand Filipinos died in the Death March and another twenty-five thousand in the camp.

The American command and its garrison held out on the island fortress of Corregidor, off the coast of Bataan, until May 6. General MacArthur had made his controversial escape by submarine to Australia on March 12, leaving General Wainwright to surrender. Partisans and irregulars in the jungle were the only resistance to the Japanese in the Philippines after May 6. Some were Americans who refused the order to surrender.

Colonel Ernest Miller survived the Bataan Death March and endured merciless imprisonment at the hands of the Japanese for three years and five months. Anna Miller learned in August 1943 that her husband was alive. The residents of Brainerd were outraged in January 1944 when the U.S. government released a carefully documented report, pieced together from escaped prisoners, that an estimated one-third of American fighting men captured in the Philippines had died at the hands of the Japanese while prisoners. Sorrow and revenge were competing emotions. The *Brainerd Daily Dispatch* quoted Anna, wife of the commanding officer: "The news is very discouraging. I still feel my husband is OK. . . . I am not ready to give up."

Ernie Miller wrote of his liberation in 1945: "That was the moment—the end of an era of hell—the beginning of an era of hysterical joy! . . . Prisoners screamed and danced and wept and prayed. . . . It was stark pandemonium. . . . And through it all was the common expression that leaped from prisoner to prisoner: 'Boy, we made it! We made it!'" He weighed 115 pounds, having lost over 65 pounds during captivity. The liberated prisoners shipped from Japan to the Philippines on September 12. Miller's joy was short-lived. While in Manila he learned that his oldest son, James, had died on Anzio beachhead in Italy.

James Brumaghim Miller left home to enlist in the army the day after the Japanese attack on Pearl Harbor, even as his father faced the Japanese in the Philippines. He fought against the Germans in North Africa with the First Armored Regiment, First Armored Division. The First Armored Division went ashore at Anzio, Italy, on January 23, 1944. Private First Class Miller had turned twenty years old just a few days earlier. The Allied force quickly ran into fierce German resistance. The Allied offensive to break out of the beachhead and take the strategic town of Cisterna took place on January 30–31. The Germans held and inflicted heavy casualties on the Allies. The War Department advised Anna Miller of the death of her son, "who died 31 January 1944 as a result of wounds received in action that date." The Allies were not able to break out until late May. James Miller's remains were returned to the United States and reinterred in section C-3, grave site 7786, at Fort Snelling National Cemetery on December 10, 1948.

Colonel Ernest Miller returned home to Minnesota with a contingent of survivors on the USS *Goodhue,* a landing ship named for Goodhue County, Minnesota. He was one of twenty-nine of the sixty-one soldiers of Brainerd's National Guard unit to survive combat and imprisonment and make it home.

The Minnesota American Legion made Ernie Miller its state commander in 1946 by acclamation. He subsequently traveled across the state, speaking of the need for military preparedness. Miller included this sentiment when he wrote and printed his war memoirs in 1949. A man of strong principle, he resigned his commission so as not to compromise his strongly felt views. *Bataan Uncensored* was published in 1949. Ernie Miller never fully recovered from his sufferings as a prisoner of war. His health problems led to troubles with personal finances. Miller's son Tom convinced Senator Hubert H. Humphrey to persuade Congress to reinstate Miller's commission and secure a pension for the war hero. Tom later enlisted the help of *Minneapolis Tribune* columnist George Grimm to publicize Miller's plight and sell the large number of copies of his book, which were stacked in a warehouse. Minnesotans responded and the family was inundated with orders. Orders continued to flow in even after the last book was sold. Tom and his mother, Anna, returned a number of checks, but many people sent the checks back to them to honor one of the state's greatest heroes. The state-of-the-art armor range at the Minnesota Guard's Camp Ripley is named for Ernest Miller.

Ernie Miller died in 1959 at the age of sixty. He is buried in section B-1, grave site 373–1, at Fort Snelling National Cemetery, not far from the grave of his son James.

The loss of the Philippines to the Japanese was a major defeat for the U.S. Army, one of the worst in American history. While the GIs fought splendidly against great odds, MacArthur's lack of preparedness led to disaster. He would have his chance to make amends.

Richard E. Fleming

The Japanese seemed invincible through early 1942 following their overwhelming victory at Pearl Harbor. In May 1942 they approached Australia as their large task force steamed into the Coral Sea, bound for Port Moresby. Two American aircraft carriers were all that stood in their way. The Battle of Coral Sea began May 7, 1942, and lasted for two days. The battle was fought entirely in the air. The USS *Lexington* was sunk and the USS *Yorktown* damaged, while American warplanes sank one Japanese carrier and badly damaged a second. The battle itself was perhaps a draw, but the Battle of Coral Sea was a major strategic victory for the Allies as they successfully turned back the Japanese.

Japanese and American naval and air task forces clashed again just a month later farther north. A Japanese task force was intent on occupying the strategic American military base at Midway Island, northwest of Hawaii. Their initial objective was to destroy the American fleet sent to confront them. The ensuing battle, like the Coral Sea, was a colossal air battle fought off the decks of aircraft carriers.

Captain Richard E. Fleming of St. Paul, Minnesota, flew from Hawaii to Midway Island just ten days before the Japanese onslaught. The University of Minnesota graduate already had a reserve commission in the army by virtue of his ROTC program while attending high school at St. Thomas Military Academy. He declined the commission and signed on as an aviation cadet. Fleming received his wings at the Naval Air Station at Pensacola, Florida, in December 1940 and joined the Second Marine Aircraft Group in San Diego. The squadron to which he belonged was Marine Scout Bombing Squadron (VMSB) 241. They flew the SB2U-3 Vindicator, a somewhat obsolete plane covered mainly with fabric. This construction limited the steepness of a dive, causing detractors to refer to the plane as the "Wind Indicator." VMSB-241 was augmented by the arrival at Midway of sixteen SBD-2 Dauntless dive-bombers, a new plane with strong performance characteristics.

For his gallantry, Captain Richard Fleming of St. Paul was posthumously given the only Medal of Honor awarded in the decisive Battle of Midway. Photograph courtesy of the Noel Allard Collection.

Catalina PBY reconnaissance planes spotted the approaching Japanese fleet on the morning of June 3. VMSB-241 took off with twenty-seven planes. Fleming was in a Dauntless. He flew wing to the squadron commanding officer, Major Lofton Henderson. Henderson, for whom the airstrip on Guadalcanal was named, went down in the early minutes of combat with a squadron of Zeroes. Fleming assumed command and led the attack. He flew his Dauntless to just four hundred feet above the water to release his bomb at close range on the Japanese carrier *Hiryu,* but he missed. Both he and his gunner were wounded and there were 179 holes in his plane, but he was able to fly back to Midway. Eight of the sixteen SBD-2 Dauntless were lost in the attack. Six of the eleven Vindicators were lost. Fleming and the others remaining refueled and returned to the air in search of a carrier damaged by another squadron, but were unable to locate it. The pilots were exhausted after two long-distance, over-the-sea missions.

The Midway pilots were awakened after less than four hours of sleep to again go after the Japanese fleet. Four Japanese heavy cruisers were on a night raid to bombard Midway's airfield when two collided. Both the *Mikuma* and the *Mogami* suffered damage, but the *Mikuma* in particular suffered critical damage such that its speed was limited. The two cruisers headed west with two destroyers in hopes of escaping the American planes. VMSB-241 took to the air at 6:00 a.m. The *Mikuma* was not difficult to find, leaking oil as it was. Captain Fleming flew an SB2U-3 Vindicator, leading five others. They accompanied six SBD-2 Dauntless. The Japanese antiaircraft fire was intense and accurate. The SBD-2 dive-bombers went in first, but the best they scored was a near miss. Fleming knew that he could not make a true dive-bomb attack on the *Mikuma,* so he chose his approach as a glide bomb run at about four thousand feet, coming at the cruiser with the sun behind him. The Japanese did not miss Fleming's attempt to slip in at the cruiser. Antiaircraft fire ripped through the engine of Fleming's Vindicator, setting it on fire. Some observers felt that Fleming might have been able to pull out of his dive and parachute into the water, but the truth will never be known. Instead, the intrepid Marine kept his flaming plane on course. The bomb he released missed the ship, but Fleming flew his Vindicator into the aft section of the *Mikuma.* There was a tremendous explosion from the Vindicator's fuel flowing down into the cruiser's engine room. The *Mikuma* was finished. American aviators the next day finished off the gutted hulk of what was once the *Mikuma* and sent her to the bottom of the sea.

The Battle of Midway was the most decisive naval victory in American history. The Japanese lost four aircraft carriers, as well as a heavy cruiser, 275 planes, and thirty-five hundred men. More important, they lost their offensive initiative for the remainder of the war. The Americans lost one carrier and a destroyer, half as many planes, and slightly more than three hundred lives. The United States honored Minnesotan Richard Fleming posthumously with the Medal of Honor for his heroism. His was the only Medal of Honor awarded for the Battle of Midway, a crucial victory marked by extreme heroism. Admiral William Halsey paid a visit to Fleming's mother, Mrs. Michael Fleming, on November 13, 1945, during a high-profile visit to the Twin Cities.

There were no remains to be buried, but a marker in Fort Snelling National Cemetery memorializes Captain Richard Fleming of the U.S. Marine Corps. The marker is in section F-1, grave site 111. South St. Paul's Fleming Field was named in honor of this local hero.

Admiral William "Bull" Halsey Jr. greeting Mrs. Michael Fleming, mother of Captain Richard Fleming, during his much-celebrated visit to the Twin Cities in November 1945 after victory over Japan. Photograph from the November 13, 1945, edition of the *St. Paul Pioneer Press*, courtesy of the Minnesota Historical Society.

Fleming left a letter for his fiancée, Peggy Crooks, with flight surgeon Dr. Forrester to be delivered in the event of Fleming's death. He realized that the clash off Midway would be costly in terms of lives. A portion of the letter, dated May 30, 1942, follows:

Letters like this should not be morbid or maudlin and we'll let it suffice to say that I've been prepared for this rendezvous [with death] for some time. I hope that you will not entirely forget me, but I also hope that you don't let this cause you any lasting sorrow. You're the finest girl I ever knew and I know that the future years hold much for you. This is something that comes to all of us; we can only bow before it . . . we really had something. Always regard it as such and don't let any of it cause you sorrow. All my Love, Dick

Peggy Crooks never married.

Eugene Arthur Michael Trowbridge

The Grumman F4F Wildcat was an ugly plane, its wings set well forward on the fuse-lage. While this configuration gave the Wildcat very high lift to allow for the quick takeoffs and slow landings necessary for duty on smaller escort carriers, the design resulted in slower air speed. In fact, the Mitsubishi Zero outclassed the Wildcat not only with greater speed, but also with a faster climb rate and superior turning ability. Marine Lieutenant Colonel Joe Bauer told his Wildcat pilots in the Pacific theater: "A Zero can go faster than you can, it can climb faster than you can, and it can out-maneuver you. Aside from these things, you've got a better plane." Further, while the American pilots lacked combat experience at this phase of the war, the Japanese pilots were seasoned veterans and generally considered to be among the best in the world. Yet in the end, the brilliant tactics of the American squadron commanders and the grim resolve of their young pilots made the difference. As the legendary American ace Joe Foss wrote, "It's not the crate, it's the man sitting in it. If it were not so, the Grumman Wildcat would have been a flying coffin."

Eugene Trowbridge, a graduate of St. Paul's Cretin Military Academy and the Min-nesota College of Music, composed a number of pieces for band and orchestra and played in several bands in the Twin Cities. Trowbridge's second love was flying—he had talked of flying since the age of twelve—and he joined the Minnesota National Guard in February 1938. He began training to become a Marine pilot in the spring of 1941 as war appeared imminent, and he earned his wings at Corpus Christi Naval Air Station in March 1942. Trowbridge was at San Diego for a short time before shipping out for Hawaii at the beginning of May. Pearl Harbor was still a devastating sight.

The Marine Corps transferred all but its five oldest pilots to Midway Island just two days after their arrival in Hawaii. Trowbridge was among the five remaining pilots who would organize a new squadron. He followed with concern the news of the Battle of Midway in early June, knowing as he did that his friends were "short on experience in the new F4F-3 and F2A-2." Trowbridge wrote of June 8, 1942: "A sorry day as the casualty list has been posted and I have lost some of my best flying partners. . . . God rest their souls as they tried and lost but gave their lives for their country. They will be avenged."

Lieutenant Trowbridge was a member of Marine Fighter Squadron VMF-223 by August 2, when he boarded the converted Essex-class escort carrier USS *Long Island*. He was not quite twenty-four years old. VMF-223 flew F4F Wildcats. The *Long Island* transported VMF-223 and another Marine squadron from Hawaii into the South

Marine First Lieutenant Eugene Trowbridge of St. Paul was a member of the original Cactus Air Force on Guadalcanal and one of the early ace pilots in the war. Photograph courtesy of Eugene Trowbridge Jr.

Pacific. The United States took the offensive in the Pacific in August 1942 in the aftermath of the victories at Coral Sea and Midway. The First Marine Division landed on the island of Guadalcanal in the Solomon Islands on August 7. The Japanese responded quickly, determined to drive the Americans off Guadalcanal. Thus began one of the bloodiest campaigns of the war, a struggle that lasted into February of the following year. The fighting was fierce in the jungles of Guadalcanal, in the straits around the island, and in the air above it.

An airstrip at Lunga Point, which the Japanese had not completed, became the key to the battle for Guadalcanal. Each of the planes of the two Marine squadrons was catapulted off the carrier as the deck was too short for takeoff. It was a "new experience," said Trowbridge. The pilots landed at newly named Henderson Field on Guadalcanal on August 19, less than two weeks after the Marine landing. Wrote Trowbridge: "We are really welcomed by the troops as the Japs have been taking their time bombing them and they figure we will help them quite a bit." The navy code name for Guadalcanal was "Cactus" and the small band of gutsy Marine aviators soon became known as the Cactus Air Force. The dark blue ball caps they wore became their trademark. The pilots and crew lived in tents along the edge of the field in a camp, which became known as Mosquito Gulch. There were not enough cots to go around at first, but even the cots sank into the mud. Meals prepared over open fires consisted mainly of canned hash, Spam, and dehydrated potatoes. The controlled perimeter was so small that Japanese snipers were a daily threat to the residents of Mosquito Gulch. Pilots at times had to crawl to their planes while under fire.

Henderson Field was the key to holding Guadalcanal. The Marines in the jungles would be under intense daily aerial attack without protection from the Wildcats of the Cactus Air Force. The American defense of Guadalcanal against the daily air attacks suffered from periodic crises in aviation parts and fuel supply. The primary advantage the American fliers had was the great distance the Japanese bomber squadrons had to fly from their base six hundred miles away at Rabaul. This forced the Japanese to fly a more or less direct route to Guadalcanal to make the most of their fuel. (It also made the timing of their arrival predictable, a situation further strengthened by coast watchers with radio transmitters on islands along the way. The Japanese planes generally hit Guadalcanal at noon.) The Japanese armadas also generally flew at lower altitudes to conserve fuel, which allowed a tactical advantage to the Marine fliers. Captain John Lucien Smith, who commanded Marine Fighter Squadron VMF-223—the unit in which Second Lieutenant Eugene Trowbridge flew—recognized the one advantage of the Wildcat relative to the Zero. The wings of the Zero could not withstand the force of a

USMC F4F Wildcats over Guadalcanal. Photograph courtesy of Eugene Trowbridge Jr.

vertical dive to the extent a Wildcat could. Smith would lead his squadron into the sky to await the arrival of the daily Japanese bombers and escort fighters. When the Japanese appeared, the Wildcats rolled into vertical dives and raced through the Japanese formation with their .50-caliber machine guns blazing in the hope of hitting the gas tanks of the enemy planes. The Japanese guns could not train on the Marine planes, and no maneuvering could escape the attack or break up the formation. The skill and tactics of navy and Marine pilots made up for any shortcomings of the plane. Daily ambushes by the two Marine squadrons slowly bled the Japanese air corps of its best pilots.

Gene Trowbridge saw his first action on August 21. His squadron leader was Captain Marion Carl, one of the few Marine fighters to survive the Battle of Midway, where he had scored his first kill. Trowbridge was grounded the next day because of a cold. As a result, the young Marine pilot experienced on the ground what he was trying to prevent from the air. He wrote in his diary, "Never again—It was terrible." He was determined to get his first kill. Trowbridge was back in the air on August 23 and shot down his first Zero. Despite a submarine shelling them that night and disrupting sleep, fourteen Marine pilots scrambled early the next morning to provide protection for the Cactus dive-bomber squadron. Their target was a convoy of two large Japanese troop transports with a cruiser and a couple of destroyers. The SBD dive-bombers scored direct hits on the cruiser and transports. The Wildcats returned to the airfield and fueled up for the regular noon bombing raid. Trowbridge shot down two more Zeroes for three kills in two days. Sleeping conditions were no better that night as the submarine returned. There was more shelling the next night as well. However, this time the sky was not so dark. The SBDs found three destroyers and sank two. The Japanese were learning respect the hard way.

The Cactus Air Force was running low on Grumman Wildcats. The Marines' number of kills was extraordinary, but the lack of spare parts rendered damaged planes unusable for the time being. Meanwhile, the Japanese had a seemingly endless number of expendable pilots and planes. The Marines were down to ten fighters when they went up on August 30. The battle for the control of the airspace over Guadalcanal became a war of attrition with neither side quite sure how long they or the other side could last.

Trowbridge got his fourth Zero on August 26, but a burst knocked out his engine. Fortunately, the dogfight was over Guadalcanal. He managed to recover from a spin and right the plane to crash-land on the runway. He walked away from the plane unscathed. The Cactus Air Force was dwindling to nearly nothing with no sign of the much-hoped-for fighter squadron. Trowbridge shot down one bomber on August 31, two more on September 3, another on September 9, and two more on September 10.

Japanese cruisers and destroyers nightly shelled Henderson Field throughout this period. The "Tokyo Express" made nightly runs of troops and supplies to the Japanese forces on Guadalcanal. They also lobbed a few shells on the American forces before heading home. One night a round from a cruiser killed two pilots and wounded a third.

The numerous landings of infantry always left open the threat of being overrun by an unexpected superior ground force. The Marines aggressively sought out the enemy and destroyed these units before they could accumulate sufficient strength to retake the all-important airfield. It was only through determination that the Americans held.

September 10 was a big day on Guadalcanal. VMF-5 flew into Henderson Field off the carrier USS *Saratoga*. Only five of the original nineteen F4F-4 Marine fighters were still flying. The expected Japanese raid was sizable, with twenty-six Betty bombers and twelve Zeroes. The Marines put forty-five fighters in the air. The massive numbers of U.S. fighters caught the Japanese off guard and only ten enemy planes managed to escape.

Trowbridge scrambled to get in the air in response to an alert on September 14. A new fighter strip had just been opened two days earlier. He hit an oil barrel while taking off through a large cloud of dust, but kept his plane flying. Another fighter suddenly appeared, coming directly at him from the other end of the runway. The two collided, although not exactly head-on. Trowbridge's Wildcat flipped and bounced some two hundred yards. He was evacuated to Great Lakes Naval Training Station in Chicago for recuperation. The navy promoted Eugene Trowbridge to first lieutenant while he was under hospital care. He had ten kills to his credit, and the Marines included him in an early 1943 "Aces for Victory" promotion, which featured nine Marine pilots with ten or more kills.

The Cactus Air Force struggled on without one of its original members. The need for more pilots, planes, spare parts, and fuel continued, but the daily midday scramble went on. The U.S. Navy established control of the seas around Guadalcanal in time. The long and bloody campaign for Guadalcanal did not end until February 1943. One more step toward Tokyo and final victory had been taken.

The navy awarded Lieutenant Eugene Trowbridge of St. Paul the Navy Cross for extraordinary heroism in the air over the Solomon Islands from August 20 through September 16, 1942. His citation reads:

Throughout that strenuous period when the Guadalcanal airfield was under constant bombardment and our shore establishments in the area were menaced by the desperate counter thrusts of a fanatical foe, Second Lieutenant Trowbridge repeatedly patrolled hostile territory, strafed enemy ships and intercepted persistent bombing flights. With bold determination and courageous disregard of personal safety, he pressed home numerous attacks against heavily escorted waves of invading bombers and, in five vigorous fights against tremendous odds, shot down a total of six Japanese planes. His superb flying skill and dauntless initiative were in keeping with the highest traditions of the United States Naval Service.

Eugene Trowbridge married in December 1942. He taught fighter tactics at the Naval Air Station in Jacksonville, Florida, for a time while still recuperating. He was promoted to captain in November 1943. He returned to combat in 1945 and finished the war with a total of thirteen kills. He served with Air Support Command in Hawaii–Okinawa from February 1945 to August 1946 before returning home with thirty-two months of foreign service. His service in this period included a stint in mainland China as the commanding officer of the headquarters squadron of Corsairs in Peiping (now known as Beijing) in late 1945. Trowbridge ultimately retired from the U.S. Marine Corps with the rank of major.

Eugene Trowbridge returned to his "other" love, music, after his retirement from the Marine Corps. He taught band at Cretin High School in St. Paul and at Robbinsdale High School, in the Twin Cities. He moved to Evanston, Illinois, and earned a master's degree in music from Northwestern University. He earned a second master's in school administration from Michigan State University. Trowbridge returned to Minnesota and taught music at the junior high level in the Edina school system for more than twenty-five years until his retirement in 1980. Numerous people and newspaper articles confirm that he was not one to bask in glory. He rejected offers to appear at air shows or to be honored at banquets. He would not talk about the war, preferring to discuss the band he was directing or the upcoming state music competition.

Eugene Arthur Michael Trowbridge died May 12, 1994, and is buried in section 2, grave site 202, at Fort Snelling National Cemetery. The Minnesota Aviation Hall of Fame inducted Eugene Trowbridge after his death.

Chapter 2

North Africa and Italy

Gilmore J. P. Lundquist

Gilmore Lundquist attempted to join the Army Air Corps in 1936 upon his graduation from North High School in Minneapolis, only to learn there was a five-year waiting list. Lundquist worked at Hamm's Brewery, loading trucks on the dock by day while playing sax and clarinet in a quartet in the evenings. He began studies at the University of Minnesota a year and a half later while continuing to work at the brewery. He received notice of an opening in the Army Air Corps in the fall of 1939 and left the university with an associate's degree. Lundquist graduated from advanced training and was commissioned a second lieutenant with wings in June 1940. For a time he flew as a copilot for Northwest Airlines while on military pay to learn instrumentation. He taught what he learned to fellow pilots in his squadron. Lundquist was promoted to first lieutenant and upgraded to flying B-25 bombers just one month before Pearl Harbor. The army promoted each of these pilots to a command position two weeks after the surprise attack. Gilmore Lundquist became a captain in late December 1941.

The bomber group based out of southern Louisiana and gained extensive practice navigating over long stretches of water by flying from Louisiana to Tampa, Florida, and back. The group shipped out for North Africa in early May 1942, assigned to support the British Eighth Army in Egypt and the Western Desert. They flew to Brazil and crossed the South Atlantic to Ascension Island. Fifty-one of fifty-four B-25s made it to the island, most with no more than ten minutes of fuel reserve. The group air executive was among those who were lost en route. The squadron commander assumed

Lundquist's position, and Lundquist was promoted to major in command of a squadron. He had been in the service less than two years and, at the age of twenty-three, was the youngest major in the service.

The bomber group crossed the sub-Sahara to Egypt, where they met camel caravans that had traveled for six weeks carrying fuel. Major Lundquist flew many bombing missions and helped drive the Germans out of North Africa. The group was reassigned to the U.S. Armed Forces when the Americans and British linked up in North Africa. He later served with his B-25 squadron in Sicily and Italy, including during their involvement in the battle of Monte Cassino. He later flew over the "Hump," the Himalayas, in the China-Burma-India theater.

Lundquist continued his service to the nation after the war, working in military intelligence in Berlin from 1953 to 1956. He was chief of overhead reconnaissance for air force intelligence during the 1962 Cuban missile crisis. He retired from the air force in 1965 and built a successful aviation operation in Faribault, Minnesota, which he managed until his retirement in 1983. Gilmore Lundquist died in 1987 and is buried in section V, grave site 3523, at Fort Snelling National Cemetery.

Edward Micka

General George Patton called it "about as desperate a venture as has ever been taken by any force in the world's history." While the Marines fought to hold Guadalcanal in the Pacific, British Prime Minister Winston Churchill and President Franklin D. Roosevelt took the first step toward taking back the European mainland from Nazi Germany. Operation Torch, the Allied landings in North Africa, began in the early hours of November 8, 1942, with three simultaneous landings at Casablanca in Morocco and at Oran and Algiers in Algeria. General Dwight D. Eisenhower was in charge of what was the largest amphibious landing up to that time, eclipsed only by the Normandy landings in June 1944.

The USS *Ranger* was the only large aircraft carrier in the U.S. Atlantic Fleet. She was more than ten years old, the first ship of the navy to be built from the keel up as an aircraft carrier. The *Ranger* and three small escort carriers provided air cover for the landings at Casablanca. So many of the navy pilots were inexperienced that no practice takeoffs and landings from the carriers were allowed on the passage across the Atlantic for fear of losing pilots and planes and hurting morale.

The success of the November 8 invasion depended on the pre-landing air attack by the carrier planes. The *Ranger* launched her squadrons before dawn and met with anti-

Lieutenant Edward Micka of Gayuga, North Dakota, was posthumously awarded
the Navy Cross for his gallantry during the invasion of North Africa. Photograph
courtesy of Violet Micka Katana.

aircraft fire from Vichy French pilots, who scrambled to engage the Americans in
dogfights over Casablanca. The Americans dive-bombed their assigned targets along
the coast while trading machine-gun bursts with the pursuing French fighters.

Lieutenant Edward Micka, a native of Gayuga, North Dakota, flew a Grumman
F4F Wildcat and commanded a four-plane section in Lieutenant Commander John

An F4F Wildcat on the deck of the USS *Ranger* off North Africa in November 1942. Lieutenant Edward Micka flew a Grumman F4F Wildcat and commanded a four-plane section in Lieutenant Commander John Raby's VF-9 Squadron off the *Ranger.* Photograph courtesy of the Department of the Navy.

Raby's VF-9 Squadron off the *Ranger.* Fighting Squadron 9 had the best-trained pilots in the *Ranger*'s Air Group. Ed Micka was twenty-seven years old on the eve of the invasion of North Africa. He enlisted in the navy in 1934, but received his discharge just one year later to accept an appointment to the U.S. Naval Academy. He graduated in June 1939 with the commission of ensign and served on the USS *Minneapolis* until detached in December of that year. He served on the new destroyer USS *Clemson* until mid-1941, when he transferred to the Naval Air Station at Pensacola, Florida. Ensign Micka was at Pensacola when the Japanese attacked Pearl Harbor. The navy commissioned him a lieutenant (jg) that same month. He was assigned to advanced carrier training at Norfolk, Virginia, and earned the rank of lieutenant on June 15, 1942.

Fighting Group 9 attacked the airfields at Rabat, Rabat-Sale, and Port Lyautey on the morning of November 8. Flying conditions were very poor with a low ceiling, steady rain, and limited visibility. Micka led his section in and participated in the destruction of twenty to thirty enemy planes. The next day, VF-9 scrambled to attack enemy planes at the airfield at Medouina. Flying conditions were much improved, with a ceiling of ten thousand feet and good visibility for ten miles or more. Micka led the Fourth Section into attack. The squadron action report states, "Heavy antiaircraft and machine gun fire was encountered." The report further says that Micka was on his fourth or fifth strafing run, "flying fast and low," when his plane was hit. One of the pilots in his section reported that "it looked as though the plane fell apart and immediately crashed to the ground and caught fire." Lieutenant Micka was reportedly shot down by antiaircraft fire, but one pilot reported him "shooting up a bomber on the ground when his plane received the full force of that bomber exploding." The attack on Medouina airdrome resulted in the destruction of all of the enemy planes, a total of fifteen fighters and six medium bombers.

The sacrifice of stalwart men like Lieutenant Micka allowed the North African landings to be successfully executed. This set the stage for the Allied advance across North Africa and the subsequent landings on Sicily and on the Italian peninsula at Salerno. Micka was posthumously awarded the Navy Cross for his valor. The citation reads:

> Leading a section of four planes in vigorous raids against hostile airdromes at Rabat-Sale and Port Lyautey, Lieutenant Micka, grimly pressing home his attacks in the face of relentless fire, contributed materially to the destruction of seventeen enemy planes on the ground and the silencing of three machine-gun emplacements. Later, he participated in a series of hazardous, low-altitude strafing runs on the airdrome at Medouina, persistently striking at his target through bursting shells of anti-aircraft fire until, on his fifth run, he was finally shot down. His superb airmanship and inspiring devotion to duty, maintained at great personal risk in the face of grave danger, were in keeping with the highest traditions of the United States Navy. He gallantly gave up his life in the defense of this country.

James Forrestal, acting secretary of the navy, signed the citation on behalf of President Roosevelt.

The U.S. Navy further honored Lieutenant Micka in May 1943 when it named destroyer escort *DE-176* in his honor. His wife launched the destroyer escort at the Newark, New Jersey, shipyards, shattering a bottle of champagne against the hull. The *New York Times* featured a photo of Evelyn Micka and her ten-month-old daughter at the christening on August 23, 1943. Edward Micka's remains were brought home after the war and buried in Fort Snelling National Cemetery, section C-1, grave site 7489.

Albert Anton Svoboda

Albert Svoboda's age at the outset of World War II exempted him from military service. The thought never occurred to the forty-eight-year-old farmer from Jackson, Minnesota, despite the urging of his wife. The son of turn-of-the-century immigrants from the Austro-Hungarian Empire had been a second lieutenant on occupation duty in Germany after World War I, and he remained active in the Minnesota National Guard after the war. "Scoob," as he was known, became a captain, commanding Company E (composed of men from Jackson) of the 135th Infantry Regiment. Svoboda was promoted to major and was serving as executive officer of the regiment's Second Battalion when the Japanese attacked Pearl Harbor. The battalion consisted of Minnesota men from the towns of Owatonna, Jackson, Hutchinson, and Austin. Washington federalized the National Guard, and the Minnesota Guard became the 135th Infantry Regiment of the U.S. Thirty-fourth Division. The Thirty-fourth, made up of National Guard units from Minnesota, the Dakotas, and Iowa, featured a bovine skull in red on their shoulder patch and became known as the Red Bull Division.

The Thirty-fourth was the first American division to be deployed overseas and shipped out to Northern Ireland in January–February 1942. Intensive training and maneuvers in the rugged terrain occupied most of the remainder of the year. A change in the army's "age in grade" ruling resulted in Svoboda, a lieutenant colonel by this time, being too old to command an infantry battalion. The army transferred him out of the regiment and made him provost marshal of the base. "Scoob" Svoboda was faced with the prospect of sitting out the war in the rear while the men he had trained went into battle. That changed when Colonel Lester Hancock, his longtime friend, was promoted to command the 135th Regiment on the eve of the invasion of North Africa. Hancock pulled the necessary strings to return the experienced Svoboda to his rightful place as executive officer for the regiment.

The North African campaign began with relative ease. The major British victory over German field marshal Erwin Rommel's Afrika Korps at El Alamein in early November led to a major German withdrawal eastward. The American forces landing in North Africa joined the British in the Allied advance across Tunisia. However, Rommel was far from whipped. He launched a fierce armored onslaught at the inexperienced Americans. The resulting battle at Kasserine Pass, a two-mile gap in the Dorsal Chain of the Atlas Mountains, was a disastrous loss for the Americans. Fortunately, Rommel disengaged.

The Americans regrouped but with morale low. General Eisenhower overhauled the units, giving officers more authority to make command decisions in the field. General Patton arrived and assumed command of the U.S. II Corps. The Americans began to recover and prepare. The motto of the Thirty-fourth Division became, "Attack! Attack! Attack!" The men lived by these words throughout the remainder of the war.

Patton's II Corps moved into position in late April against a strong German defensive position protecting strategic Fondouk Pass. The attack was across a five-mile open stretch before the Germans' elevated position. The first attack failed. A second assault was made and casualties were high, but the men of the Thirty-fourth Division were determined. The British were beginning to malign the American fighting spirit. The Thirty-fourth took the enemy position after dark, the 135th breaking through the left flank.

The next German position was even more formidable. Djebel Tahent was a complex of interlocking hills, with Hill 609 the dominant feature. The adjoining Hill 531 and Hill 461 allowed for murderous cross fire on any advancing troops. It was necessary to take these smaller hills before the final assault could be made on Hill 609. Machine-gun nests, mortar posts, and artillery observation posts made the enemy position strong and nearly impregnable. Patton assigned the Thirty-fourth Division the task of taking the Hill 609 complex.

Division command assigned Hill 461, which was to the northwest of Hill 609, to the Second Battalion of the 135th Regiment. Lieutenant Colonel Svoboda was in command by virtue of the wounding of his commanding officer. The assault commenced on the morning of April 28 behind a rolling artillery barrage. A German counterattack forced back the Americans, who reorganized and made a second attack, although with considerable loss. There was little cover as the regiment worked its way up the slope in the face of heavy enemy fire. The fighting was hand-to-hand and fierce as the two sides closed. The Germans held, and the attacks on the second day were also costly and unsuccessful. The Americans were determined to take the complex on the third day of fighting.

The division held off a determined counterattack the following day. General Omar Bradley's report describes the action: "A strong enemy attack was repulsed. Fighting all day was intense and bloody. The enemy was engaged with bayonets and grenades and there were many cases of outstanding bravery." Several of Svoboda's men remarked that he was carrying an '03 Springfield bolt-action rifle through the battle. This was standard issue in the National Guard before federalization and the issue of modern

Albert Svoboda (center) receiving the Minnesota Medal for Valor from the adjutant general of Minnesota on December 7, 1950. He was brevetted brigadier general in the Minnesota National Guard on this same day. Photograph courtesy of Herb Schaper, 135th Infantry Historical Files.

weapons. Svoboda is said to have replied, "Hell, it wasn't my job to kill Germans. It was my job to direct my men."

The U.S. Army awarded Lieutenant Colonel Svoboda the Distinguished Service Cross "for extraordinary heroism in action on 30 April, 1945." The citation reads in part:

> Under heavy enemy machine gun and artillery fire, he personally led his heavy weapons platoon into position against the enemy. He then moved forward to the leading elements of his battalion and utterly disregarding his own safety, directed their action and fire. His courage, bravery and coolness under fire inspired his men, contributed greatly to the accomplishment of his objective and stand as an example of the highest traditions of the Service.

The Second Battalion took Hill 461 and the other regiments of the division took their objectives. Even the British press praised the fighting spirit of the men of the Thirty-fourth Division.

The taking of Djebel Tahent resulted in the breakout of Patton's II Corps. The Germans had no opportunity to regroup. The commander of the German Fifth Panzer Army surrendered on May 9 and enemy resistance ended four days later. Casualties for the entire Tunisian campaign were more than four thousand. The Thirty-fourth Division played a major role in the victory in Tunisia. The men were veterans and would prove their value as combat troops time and again in subsequent battles up the Italian peninsula.

A victory parade was held in Tunis on May 20. U.S. Army headquarters selected the 135th as one of ten regiments to represent the U.S. forces. Lieutenant Colonel Albert Svoboda and his comrades in arms of the 135th Regiment marched proudly down Boulevard Galliene. "Scoob" Svoboda was transferred back to the States at the conclusion of the North African campaign. His men went on to fight with indomitable spirit up the Italian peninsula. He was assigned to a training regiment.

Svoboda was relieved of active duty on July 22, 1946. He returned home to Jackson. The state honored him with the Minnesota Medal for Valor in 1950. The award, instituted in 1927, has been given only six times. Brainerd's Colonel Ernest Miller of Bataan fame was the first. Svoboda was the second.

Albert Svoboda died on September 22, 1984, after a long bout with heart problems and cancer. A published history of the Thirty-fourth Division described him as "a man of rugged exterior, kind heart and great courage" and a leader who "held his men in position under tremendous enemy fire." There is, of course, no epitaph on his grave marker, but the men who served under him revere his name. Albert Anton Svoboda is buried in the DS section of Fort Snelling National Cemetery in grave site 80-S.

Leonard Vong

The Third Division, under the command of Major General Lucian Truscott, was among the American infantry units landing in North Africa on November 8, 1942. Truscott's Third Division was again in the forefront on July 10, 1943, when the Allies, having secured North Africa, invaded Sicily. The Third landed, crossed the island, and took Palermo after three days of hand-to-hand fighting. The division's next orders were to move east and capture Messina. This would complete the Allied conquest of Sicily. However, Messina was heavily defended by four German divisions, which were well entrenched in rugged terrain.

The veteran German Twenty-ninth Panzer Grenadier Division held the town of San Fratello, not far from the seacoast. German positions around San Fratello blocked any advance upon Messina. Their carefully laid defenses were incorporated into the rugged San Fratello Ridge, which was dominated by twenty-two-hundred-foot Monte San Fratello on the east bank of the Furiana River. Allied forces began a series of attacks on San Fratello on August 3. The attacks were unsuccessful and resulted in heavy casualties as there was little cover for the advancing soldiers.

Leonard Vong, a resident of St. Paul, served as a corporal in the Medical Detachment of the Thirtieth Infantry Regiment, Third Division. Vong won the Silver Star for gallantry at San Fratello. His citation reads:

> During the attack on the high ground near San Fratello, Sicily, Corporal Vong, while being subjected to heavy machine gun, machine pistol and mortar fire, rendered first aid to a wounded man in full view of the enemy machine guns located about 200 yards away. Ignoring his own safety, Corporal Vong made his way to the wounded man, rendered first aid with bullets striking all around him and moved the wounded man 150 yards to the cover of a defiladed area.

General Patton finally ordered an amphibious landing to flank the Germans at San Fratello. The landing by the Second Battalion of the Third Infantry, three miles behind San Fratello, caught the Germans by surprise. However, the trap did not close and the bulk of the German forces escaped to the Italian mainland. The Germans' withdrawal from their seemingly impregnable position at San Fratello prevented further casualties. Allied losses on Sicily amounted to nearly twenty thousand casualties in thirty-eight days. Sicily belonged to the Allies by August 17, 1943. The Italians removed dictator Benito Mussolini from power on July 25, 1943, even before the Germans began withdrawing from Sicily across the Straits of Messina. Italy formally withdrew from the war and the defense of Italy fell to the Germans.

Leonard Vong later also won the Bronze Star, as well as the Purple Heart, while serving the nation in the Second World War. He died on July 9, 1959, at the age of forty-three. He is buried in section H, grave site 4865, in Fort Snelling National Cemetery.

Arlo Olson

The Allies landed on the coast of Italy at Salerno just one month after securing Sicily. The Third Division again led the way. The Germans withdrew one week after the Allied landings to formidable defensive positions along the Volturno River. The Allies consolidated forces and began the second phase of the Italian offensive on the morning of October 13, 1943. Assault troops of the Allied Fifth Army waded into the raging Volturno River in the face of intense fire from German soldiers entrenched on the opposite bank. Arlo Olson, from Toronto, in Deuel County, South Dakota, was a captain in the Fifteenth Infantry Regiment of the Third Division and his company spearheaded the regiment's advance. Olson led from the front, making his way to the far shore at point-blank range to kill an entire machine-gun crew with two well-thrown hand grenades. When a second machine gun opened fire on his company, Captain Olson took out that nest, killing five German soldiers at close range with his pistol. He continued forward to the next machine-gun position and, again at close range, took out his gun and killed nine more Germans. Olson similarly led his company in the point position for two full weeks of continuous contact with the enemy. The American foot soldiers were pushed beyond the limits of endurance, fighting up ridges and across open zones of fire against well-established German positions blended into the terrain.

Captain Olson led his company in an attack on yet another enemy machine-gun position on October 27. He crawled to within twenty-five yards and charged, single-handedly killing the entire crew with his pistol. He led his company to the summit of Monte San Nicola, attacking in the face of strong enemy fire to drive off the German units facing him. Olson was wounded while making a reconnaissance for defensive positions on the summit. He refused aid until his company was established in defensive positions and all of his men had been taken care of. He died as his men carried him down the mountain.

The Allied Fifth Army drove the Germans from their entrenched positions behind the Volturno River by mid-November. The cost in lives was terrible. The Fifth Army suffered nearly ten thousand casualties, 2,699 of which belonged to the U.S. Third

Captain Arlo Olson of the Fifteenth Infantry Regiment of the Third Division
was posthumously awarded the Medal of Honor for his repeated heroics during
the crossing and early days of fighting along the Volturno River in Italy in
October 1943. Photograph courtesy of Jerry Cunningham.

Division. Captain Arlo Olson was one of the brave. The United States honored him
posthumously with the Medal of Honor "for conspicuous gallantry and intrepidity at
the risk of his life above and beyond the call of duty." His remains were returned to
the United States and buried at Fort Snelling National Cemetery in section C-24,
grave site 13787.

Chester Moeglein

The Thirty-fourth Division fought alongside the Third Division in the Fifth Army from
the North African landings, in Sicily, and in the Italian campaign. The Allies crossed
the winding Volturno River three times during October and November 1943, finally
forcing the German army to withdraw from the Volturno to the mountain defenses of
the Gustav line. The men of the Fifth Army were worn out from campaigning. The
rugged terrain, rain, and mud all made life difficult at the front line and posed a serious
challenge to moving supplies to the front and evacuating wounded to the rear. Then
winter set in, increasing the difficulties and discomfort of the determined GIs.

Major General Chester Moeglein, veteran of World War II and Korea, served as adjutant general for Minnesota from 1961 through 1975 before retiring. Photograph courtesy of the Minnesota Military Museum, Camp Ripley.

There were no roads in many areas of the fighting, and the terrain was such that none could be constructed. The only way to move to and from the front was on foot or by pack mule. Military historians have written that the Italian campaign of the winter of 1943–1944 would have been impossible without mules, and the number of mules needed was overwhelming. Two hundred and fifty mules were required to support an infantry regiment at the front. That job fell upon the shoulders of a Minnesotan named Chester Moeglein.

Moeglein enlisted in the Minnesota National Guard after he finished high school in 1931. He was commissioned a second lieutenant in August 1939 and wore captain's stripes by 1941 as the Guard went off to war as part of the Thirty-fourth Division. Moeglein, as the Thirty-fourth's transportation specialist, moved the division's equipment to New York City on 980 railcars. He contracted malaria while coordinating the division's move across the desert of North Africa, but his greatest challenge was getting men and supplies through the rain and mud of Italy. The rugged Minnesotan was not about to give up because of some bad winter weather. Captain Moeglein loaded up the division on the backs of six hundred mules and moved forward. Every aspect was a challenge. GI packsaddles were too big for the smaller Italian mules. There was a shortage of halters and even mule skinners. "In Italy it was bad," Moeglein later recalled. "The roads were limited and we had to move on pack animals. To make matters worse, the mules we got didn't understand a word of English." Yet American initiative and determination overcame the obstacles and got the job done. In the battle of Cassino in early 1944, the resupply of the frontline units involved a fourteen-hour round-trip by mule. The ammunition was tied onto the mules with quick-release knots to allow them to quickly drop off the ammo while under fire and evacuate the danger zone as quickly as possible.

Captain Moeglein was awarded, among other honors, the Distinguished Service Medal. He later commanded an ordnance battalion at Pusan during the Korean War, and in 1961 he became the adjutant general for Minnesota before retiring as a major general in 1975. He passed away in 1984 and is buried in section DS, grave site 20-S, at Fort Snelling National Cemetery.

Harold Beasley

The U.S. Army remained segregated during World War II. The debate as to the so-called combat worthiness of African American citizens still raged. Many African Americans thus served their nation as stevedores unloading ships, as truck drivers moving supplies, or as laborers serving in various assignments.

Harold Beasley, a native of St. Paul, was part of a large African American family of four boys and three girls. Beasley was twenty-six years old and married when he enlisted in March 1941. He took part in the landings in North Africa and the drive toward Sicily. On November 19, 1943, the *Minneapolis Spokesman,* the city's African American newspaper, reported his death with the headline "First War Casualty." A photo on the front page showed a smiling, sharp-looking man in uniform. Its caption read, "Sergeant Harold Beasley is First Minnesota Negro to Lose Life in World War II."

The adjutant general's office in Washington notified Sergeant Beasley's wife that he had died in North Africa on October 22. The Germans in North Africa had surrendered by this time and the war had advanced to the Italian peninsula. North Africa remained important in terms of supplying the advancing war effort. Harold Beasley died in the service of his country and is buried in section A-6, grave site 852, at Fort Snelling National Cemetery.

Harold Gohman

The Fifty-seventh Fighter Group distinguished itself in North Africa, Sicily, and Italy. The Sixty-fifth Fighter Squadron of that group was the prototype for Milton Caniff's comic strips "Terry and the Pirates" and "Steve Canyon." The Fifty-seventh's "Palm Sunday massacre" of April 18, 1943, was one of the great aerial victories of the war. The fighter group came across a large convoy of one hundred Junker transport planes, escorted by fifty Messerschmitt fighters, attempting to withdraw a large number of German troops across the Mediterranean Sea from Tunisia to Italy. Fighter Group Fifty-seven downed seventy-four Axis planes and claimed an undetermined but significant number of enemy lives. FG 57 moved from its base on Sicily to the Italian peninsula in September 1943 just one week after Italy surrendered and withdrew from the war. The enemy in the Italian campaign became the German military machine.

Harold Gohman was born in Minnesota in 1919. He was residing with his parents in Clear Lake, Minnesota, when he entered the military service on April 30, 1942. Lieutenant Gohman served with the Sixty-fifth Fighter Squadron, Fifty-seventh Fighter Group, as a P-40 pilot. The Fifty-seventh was based near the southern tip of the Italian peninsula at Amendola, near Foggia, from October 1943 through March 1944. General James Doolittle himself visited the famed unit that October. The first P-47 Thunderbolts arrived on November 11, 1943. American pilots suffered severe losses early in the North African campaign while flying the obsolete P-40s against superior German fighters. Wrote Wayne Dodds in his *Fabulous Fifty-seventh Fighter Group of World War II*, "This new plane was huge compared to the [P-40] Warhawk.... Although originally designed for high-altitude escort fighting, the ship was to be initiated as a low-altitude fighter and dive bomber. The Fifty-Seventh pioneered in this regard."

Most of the Fifty-seventh's missions in December were flown over Yugoslavia in support of the partisans and along the Yugoslav coast against German shipping. January 1944 came in as a tempest, with one-hundred-mile-per-hour winds sweeping across the base. The airfield became one huge mud puddle. The bad weather continued for well over a week. The veteran pilots were still adjusting to the P-47 from the P-40. The powerful P-47s were encountering a new concept in aviation: compressibility. The P-47s were capable of incredible speeds in a dive, so much so that the localized airflow over the wing approached transonic velocity. The resulting shock wave could lock the elevators on the wings. The learning curve for a pilot on a P-47 was far steeper than on previous fighters. Pilots were literally flying P-47s into the ground.

More P-47s arrived on January 12. Dodds wrote, "Training in P-47s underway for several days." A telegram dated the same day and sent to Gohman's parents in Clear Lake read: "The Secretary of War asks that I assure you of his deep sympathy in the loss of your son First Lieutenant Harold R. Gohman. Report states he died Twelve January in Italy as a result of an aviation accident. Letter follows." A subsequent report of burial gave the cause of death as "plane crash" and place of death as "Amendola landing ground near Foggia, Italy."

All sixty of the Fifty-seventh's P-40s—"the faithful Warhawks"—were replaced by the P-47s and shipped out by the end of January. The group continued its heroics. *Thunderbolts,* a color documentary film shot in 1945, chronicled the fighter group. The sequences are among the most spectacular ever filmed of air combat.

The U.S. government returned Harold Gohman's final remains to Minnesota at the end of 1948 and laid them to rest in section C-3, grave site 7788, at Fort Snelling National Cemetery. A letter from the War Department to his parents stated that he was due three more Oak Leaf Clusters for his Air Medal. His death serves as a reminder that flying has its risks, that learning a new, more powerful plane has its challenges, and that aviation accidents claim lives in times of war and peace.

Sylvester Hunter

The initial success of the Allied landings at Salerno in southern Italy never translated into the quick drive north for which Allied planners had hoped. The Italian capital of Rome remained a distant objective. The Minnesota men of the 135th Regiment of the Thirty-fourth "Red Bull" Division fought their way across the Volturno River with the rest of the U.S. Fifth Army. The Gustav line, built into the rugged terrain of the Italian peninsula and tenaciously defended by veteran German soldiers, prevented the Allies

First Lieutenant Sylvester Hunter, shown here with an example of Fascist sculpture, saw considerable action in the Italian campaign. Photograph courtesy of Gary R. Hunter, Sandra J. Gettys (née Hunter), and Susan J. Zipfel (née Hunter).

from advancing farther north. Monte Cassino, a massive, centuries-old monastery, anchored the Gustav line. The Battle of Monte Cassino was actually a series of battles from January through May 1944. General Mark Clark, commander of the Fifth Army, referred to this as "the most gruesome, the most harrowing and in one aspect the most tragic, of any phase of the war in Italy."

The first Battle of Cassino commenced on January 31, 1944. This involved an attack by the U.S. Thirty-sixth Division across the Gari River and a thrust by the Thirty-fourth Division into the mountains north of Cassino. The 135th Regiment of the Thirty-fourth was assigned the first major objectives on the massif Monte Castellone and the Colle Maiola. German Field Marshal Albert Kesselring committed major reinforcements to the sector. The 135th destroyed two German battalions in hand-to-hand fighting on February 2 and 3. Five German counterattacks by elite German paratroops failed on February 3 and 4, but fresh German forces began to get the upper hand on February 5. The regiment was only eight hundred yards short of the monastery, but unable to proceed.

Second Lieutenant Sylvester Hunter commanded a rifle platoon in Company G of the 135th Infantry Regiment. He was a southern Illinois farm boy whose family eked out a living on their forty-acre plot of land. He learned to shoot while hunting squirrels with a single-barrel, twelve-gauge shotgun. At the age of thirteen, weighing not much over eighty pounds, Hunter saved his mother's life when he fought off an attacking cow with his shotgun. *Prairie Farmer,* a national magazine focused on rural Midwest America, featured the young man in an article and placed him on their Hero Roll. It was an auspicious beginning. But Hunter's life resumed a normalcy. He grew up, moved to St. Louis to live with his aunt, and found work as a copyboy for the *St. Louis Globe–Democrat.* His life changed, as did the lives of all Americans, as the inevitability of U.S. involvement in World War II loomed. Hunter joined the service in 1940, applied for Officer Candidate School, and received his commission in December 1942. He returned home to marry his sweetheart, Margaret, that same month. Lieutenant Hunter shipped overseas and served in North Africa before the Italian campaign.

U.S. Fifth Army command assigned Company G the objective of taking Hill 593, just east of Monte Cassino Abbey. Veteran German soldiers of the crack First Paratroop Division held the position. Hunter led his platoon up the rocky slopes "in the face of murderous enemy machine gun and mortar fire" on February 6. The Germans drove back the first assault. Hunter regrouped his men. The platoon was at half-strength with eighteen men remaining. He and seven infantrymen survived the subsequent assault and made it to a stone wall, five hundred yards up the hill along the crest,

General Mark Clark, commanding officer of the U.S. Fifth Army in Italy, presents First Lieutenant Sylvester Hunter with the Distinguished Service Cross for extraordinary heroism in action at Monte Cassino. Photograph courtesy of Gary R. Hunter, Sandra J. Gettys (née Hunter), and Susan J. Zipfel (née Hunter).

where they took cover. They were subjected to continual machine-gun and mortar fire for two days and fought off numerous savage counterattacks against their position. The firefight was often at point-blank range. Ammunition carriers brought the eight Americans forty thousand rounds in just one night of combat. These men carried ten bandoliers of rifle ammunition and as many hand grenades as they could carry up the hill to the stone wall position.

A newspaper account quoted one of Hunter's men:

Well, sir, they threw everything at us from their side of that wall and every half hour or so they'd come over the top yelling and throwing grenades under smoke protection. But nobody ran off. We stayed there and fought 'em. We watched 'em come and shot back and killed 'em. We didn't know what they were hollering but we hollered back a lot of stuff you can't print in the papers. One time six of them got over the wall and started to set up a machine gun. They got it up but by that time we had wiped 'em out. Hunter told us there was nothing to do but stay. We did.

The small band of heroes accounted for approximately fifty Germans killed or wounded. One account claimed eighty Germans dead, "piled up on their side of the wall." Major Ray Eriksen of Minneapolis, who arrived with reinforcements to relieve Hunter and what remained of his platoon, reported that he found them "down to a bandolier of rifle ammunition apiece, out of grenades and piling up rocks to throw at the enemy."

The U.S. Army awarded Lieutenant Sylvester Hunter the Distinguished Service Cross "for extraordinary heroism in action," citing his "bold leadership and aggressive spirit" that inspired his men and "exemplifies the highest traditions of the Army of the United States."

The Americans were unable to pry the Germans from their position on Monte Cassino, despite heroism up and down the line. The attack of the Thirty-fourth Division on Monte Cassino became famous. Fewer than five hundred exhausted fighting men were all that remained out of three thousand. One account described them coming off the front line with "blank, staring eyes. The men were so tired that it was a living death . . . such a depth of weariness." Military historians described the assault as suicidal and the feat of the men of the Thirty-fourth Division as incredible. One penned, "Physical limitations, not lack of courage, denied them their victory." A desperate Allied command, fearful of losing more men, made the decision to destroy the historic monastery from the air on February 15. Thus began the second Battle of Cassino. Three major air attacks obliterated the monastery. Still the German paratroopers held their positions. It would not be until May that the Allies broke through at Cassino and advanced north toward Rome.

Hunter, having been promoted to first lieutenant, again distinguished himself during the northward advance after the taking of Rome. The retreating Germans dug in at Rosignano and put up a fight, which cost the 135th Regiment one hundred men. The Germans had been pulling frequent "spoiling attacks," in which they made small, sudden advances in the early evening with tanks. The 135th waited out the enemy thrust until it had fully developed, then passed through the German assault troops into the rear and established a strong position. Hunter directed the successful maneuver of his company, leading to the destruction of the German units.

The Thirty-fourth Division, including more than three thousand Minnesota Guards who landed in North Africa, fought in Italy through the taking of the Po Valley in May 1945. The division's record of 517 days of continuous frontline combat was unmatched by any other division in the European theater. Battle casualties for the division throughout the war totaled 3,737 killed, more than 14,000 wounded, and 3,500 missing in action. Soldiers of the Thirty-fourth earned ten Medals of Honor, ninety-eight Distinguished Service Crosses, and more than one thousand Silver Stars.

Sylvester Hunter was discharged from the army in late 1945, only to be recalled in 1946 and sent to Winter Warfare School. He subsequently applied for and was accepted into Army Flight Training School and became an army aviator. He was in Osaka, Japan, with the Twenty-fifth Infantry Division when the Korean War broke out. The Twenty-fifth was involved in the breakout from the Pusan perimeter, the advance across Korea to near the Yalu River, and the bitter fighting as the American forces withdrew in the face of the massive onslaught of Chinese troops. Air superiority played an important role in the war. Lieutenant Hunter flew more than 250 combat missions over Korea as a spotter in an L-5 observation plane, supporting Twenty-fifth Division ground troops. His extensive experience leading men and employing tactics on the ground made him invaluable in the air. Hunter earned the Distinguished Flying Cross with four Oak Leaf Clusters and the Air Medal with seventeen Oak Leaf Clusters. He returned to Japan as a captain.

Hunter returned to the States in 1952 and earned rotary pilot certification in helicopter flight training at Fort Sill, Oklahoma. He spent the next three years at Fort Sill as a flight instructor at Helicopter Training School. Hunter served from 1955 to 1958 in Berlin, where he was a command aviation officer for the army. He moved to Minneapolis in 1958 and was the aviation officer of the XIV Corps until his retirement in 1961 with the rank of major. He taught for two years at St. Thomas Academy in St. Paul. Sylvester Hunter died in 1979 at the age of sixty-one. He is buried in the DS section of Fort Snelling National Cemetery in grave site 19-S.

Clarence Spreigl

The Allied Fifth and Eighth Armies closed on the German army's Gustav line, which crossed central Italy, in early January 1944. The impregnable stronghold of Monte Cassino anchored the German position, and the Allies were unable to gain even a foothold on the north bank of the Rapido River near Cassino. The Allied command in January came up with a bold move to break the German stranglehold on the Italian peninsula. Fifty thousand men of the U.S. VI Corps landed up the Italian coast at Anzio to the north of and in the rear of the German Gustav line. The plan was to force a German withdrawal by landing well behind the line and threatening Rome.

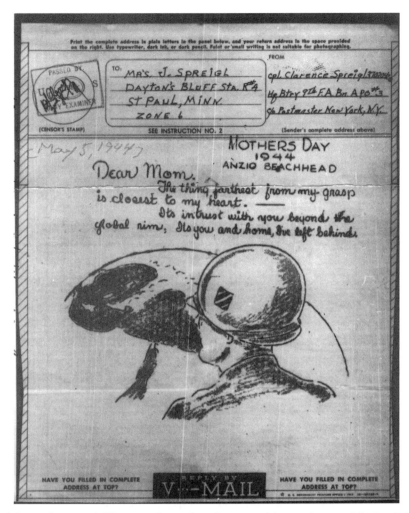

V-mail from Corporal Clarence Spreigl at Anzio to his mother on Mother's Day, 1944. Image courtesy of the Minnesota Historical Society.

The Third Division was in the forefront once again. Corporal Clarence Spreigl of St. Paul was among the soldiers who waded onto the beach. Spreigl, serving with the Third Infantry's Ninth Field Artillery Battalion, was a veteran of the successful invasions of North Africa and Sicily, having participated in the initial landings in both. He was wounded in Sicily and awarded the Purple Heart, but returned to action in time for the landings at Anzio. Spreigl wrote his brother from Anzio:

March 25, 1944. Anzio. Hello Herb. I believe I told you where we are—well you can see by the heading of this letter. Whenever you hear of a landing being made you can bet your last dollar that the Third Division is in on it. Do you know I was never afraid of the Luftwaffe until after this landing. We were just coming into the beach about seven-thirty in the morning when the sun came up and we all knew by experience that Jerry would start his dive bombing and he sure did. I went through two attacks before my turn was to get off. The first time they bracked [bracketed] our LST. You should have seen my field jacket all full of powder so you can imagine how close they were. My helmet flew about three feet in the air. They sure are cute little missed five hundred pounders. But Jerry sure paid in full. I have seen some good dog fights. . . . I have all the confidence in the world for our fliers.

March 28, 1944. Gosh I have seen some awful sights and some of the fellows in my outfit that I knew for a couple of years are gone but a fellow gets used to it and expects it.

Unfortunately, General John P. Lucas, commanding VI Corps, did not push forward from the Anzio beachhead. While the landing force consolidated, German reinforcements rushed to Anzio and contained VI Corps. The Anzio landing did not cause the German army to fall back from the Gustav line. Allied troops instead found themselves in two difficult situations—one at Anzio in the north and the other along the Gustav line to the south. Clarence Spreigl remained within the confines of the Anzio beachhead for months. He wrote home just before the breakout:

May 18, 1944. Anzio Beachhead. You told me of [brother] Ted being in the Navy. Well that's a hell of a lot better than the Army. They always have their living quarters and everything is clean and the Navy is a lot safer. In the Army you sleep any place, a lot of times in mud, and no place to dry off, just stay wet and dirty.

Spreigl fought through the Italian campaign, took part in the invasion of southern France in August 1944, and by March 1945 was in Germany, where he remained until that country surrendered in May. His veteran division was a reliable force, which the Allied command looked to time and again. He was a staff sergeant and a veteran soldier by the time he left the service in July 1945 and returned home to St. Paul. Clarence Spreigl died July 7, 1984, and was laid to rest in grave site 2228 of section Q in Fort Snelling National Cemetery.

John J. Rice

The First Special Service Force was among the troops that hit the beach at Anzio alongside the Third Infantry Division. At first the name of the unit confused German intelligence; they knew that Army Special Services provided entertainment for the troops. The Special Service Force, on the other hand, was a unique unit of Canadian and American volunteers, from whom the toughest and most rugged were selected for intense training in Montana. The intent was to send the Special Service Force into enemy-controlled territory for commando raids, but that never happened. The U.S. Fifth Army command instead threw the force into the line at the Anzio beachhead. When Allied troops found themselves unable to advance for months, the First Special Service Force held a quarter of the Allied line, the right flank. Twelve hundred men held an eight-mile front—an average of one man per eleven yards. The First Special Service Force used their training to regularly make nighttime raids deep beyond the German line. Their weapons of choice were M-1 Thompsons and bazookas, but the commando knife was frequently used to get the job done. Their preference for silently cutting the throats of the soldiers of the elite German units that opposed them instilled fear and respect in the arrogant enemy soldiers. It was customary for the night raiders of the First Special Service Force to leave stickers on the walls of buildings and even on the foreheads of dead German soldiers. The sticker consisted of the image of the unit shoulder patch—a stone Native American spearhead with the words "USA" and "Canada"—and the words *Das Dicke Ende Kommt Noch!* ("The worst is yet to come!"). The Germans named the men of the First Special Service Force *Schwartzer Teufel*—the Black Devils—for the black they wore on their faces in their regular night raids. *The Devil's Brigade,* a 1968 movie starring William Holden and Cliff Robertson, later memorialized the First Special Service Force.

John J. Rice, born in Walker, Minnesota, was twenty-four years old and living in Minneapolis when he entered the service. He answered the call for volunteers for the First Special Service Force, which made clear its challenges: "Vigorous training, hazardous duty." The force trained in the mountains of Montana. Rice's girlfriend traveled from Minneapolis to Montana to marry him in March 1943. He went overseas with his unit in June as part of the Fifth Company of the First Regiment. The First Special Service Force was deployed to Anzio in the beginning of February 1944. The Germans, determined to drive the Allies from the beachhead, launched a major offensive against the Allied position in February. At least two German battalions were cut to pieces in the first two weeks of March before the fighting stalled again. The night patrols and outposting became even more active and aggressive in the aftermath. As the historian of the First Special Service Force wrote, "The lines drew much closer during the hours of darkness." Night ambush patrols were common. On the night of March 19, a German patrol trying to slip through the outer barbed wire was discovered and

USA CANADA

DAS DICKE ENDE KOMMT NOCH!

A "death sticker" used by the First Special Service Force during nighttime commando raids at Anzio. The sticker, which translated "The worst is yet to come," was left on the foreheads of dead Germans as a means of intimidation.

cut down by machine-gun fire. Two nights later, the same machine-gun nest was attacked. The Germans used hand grenades, killing John Rice and severely wounding two others.

Private John Rice died at Anzio on March 21, 1944. The letter from the adjutant general to his bride apologized for being able to offer "only the briefest details as they are prepared under battle conditions and the means of transmission are limited." His remains were returned home more than four years later and laid to rest in Fort Snelling National Cemetery in section B-1, grave site 370-N. John Rice helped to establish the tradition of elite special forces that is carried on today in the U.S. Army.

George Thomas Krasevac

George Krasevac was the type of rugged outdoors individual for whom the U.S. Army was looking when it formed the First Special Service Force in 1942. He grew up on the western slopes of the Sierra Nevada in California's Gold Country. His father supported a wife and seven children by working for a mining company. George, the second-youngest sibling, went off to Virginia City, Nevada, as a young man to work some gold leases with his uncle. He was twenty-six years old when the Japanese attacked Pearl Harbor in 1941, at which time Krasevac enlisted in the military service at Reno, Nevada. Krasevac became a lieutenant in the Fifth Company, First Regiment of the First Special Service Force—the same company to which Private John Rice was assigned.

Krasevac, like Rice, found himself huddled on the Anzio beachhead in early 1944. The Allies, after enduring months of merciless shelling, mounted a major offensive in May and broke through the entrenched Germans in the hills overlooking the Allied position around Anzio. The Allied command debated at the time of the breakout how best to cut off the German forces to the southeast and also capture Rome. The Third Infantry Division, with an armored task force and the First Special Service Force, was assigned to advance to the northeast, seize Artena, Italy, and cut off Highway 6 at Valmontone. Highway 6, the major north-south highway in the region, was the main line of supply and the line of withdrawal for the German Tenth Army still in defensive position to the south.

First Lieutenant George Krasevac was leading his infantry company across three hundred yards of open land near Artena on May 28, 1944. He and his company moved against a strong enemy position "composed of three heavy machine guns, two 20mm flak wagons and approximately sixty riflemen in well prepared positions." Krasevac was the first member of the company to be wounded when the enemy opened fire on the attackers. His citation reads, "He was staggered by the impact of the bullet but grimly kept at the front of his men, knowing that if they were pinned down, the company would be annihilated without accomplishing its important mission." Krasevac continued the advance, shouting encouragement to his men, even as he was hit again and again by enemy fire. He was struck for the sixth time as he came to within a few yards of the enemy line. This serious wound to the leg brought him down. Despite severe

First Lieutenant George Krasevac of the First Special Service Force was awarded the Distinguished Service Cross for his leadership and heroism near Artena, Italy. Photograph courtesy of Virginia Krasevac.

wounds in his arms, legs, and feet, Krasevac refused first aid and ordered the deployment of his men into the enemy positions. The inspired men under his command rushed past their officer and took the enemy position, "wounding, killing, or capturing all of the enemy who remained." First Lieutenant George Krasevac was awarded the Distinguished Service Cross for his personal example, which "so inspired his men and officers that they were instilled with an aggressive spirit which insured the success of the attack against great odds."

Krasevac survived his wounds and the war, also winning the Bronze Star and six Oak Leaf Clusters. He settled in Minneapolis, where he studied drafting at Dunwoody College. He married and became a building contractor. This man whom bullets could not stop died tragically: he drowned while fishing in Lake Superior in 1959. He was buried in Fort Snelling National Cemetery. He never spoke about the war with his wife, whom he met after his return. As a result, she was surprised to receive a call from Fort Snelling just two weeks after the burial and to learn that her husband, as a winner of the Distinguished Service Cross, was entitled to be buried on DS row, the main drive in the national cemetery. The final remains of George Thomas Krasevac lie in grave site 69-N.

William Harold Brown

William Harold Brown wanted to become a U.S. Marine. His brothers Alfred and Howard were serving in the navy and army, respectively. The Waseca, Minnesota, native enlisted in the Marines only to die during training at Camp LeJeune, North Carolina, on May 10, 1944. Private Brown was buried at Fort Snelling National Cemetery on May 16 with full military honors. Sergeant Edward Armistead, a former schoolmate of Brown's from Waseca, served as the Marine escort for his remains. Six seamen from Wold-Chamberlain Naval Training Station in St. Paul served as pallbearers. The Phyllis Wheatley Male Quartet sang and representatives from both Phyllis Wheatley House and the Johnny Baker Post of the American Legion delivered tributes. Brown's brother Alfred attended the funeral; his brother Howard was unable to attend as he was serving with the army somewhere in Italy.

By the time of William Brown's death, America was facing up to the reality that African Americans were as combat-ready as any other Americans in the fight for freedom. The exploits of the Tuskegee Airmen in the European theater were well known. Other African American units also proved themselves. Next to the front-page article on the burial of William Harold Brown in the *Minneapolis Spokesman* was an article about a new film, *The Negro Soldier*. The Americanism Committee of the Johnny Baker Post of the American Legion, an African American veterans post, arranged to have the film shown for a week at the Newsreel Theater at Eighth Street and Hennepin Avenue in Minneapolis. The Legion committee urged each Negro citizen to ask one white person to see the picture.

U.S. Marine Corps Private William Harold Brown is buried in section A-3, grave site 379, and is believed to be the first soldier of World War II to be interred at Fort Snelling National Cemetery. The remains of those who died in that conflict generally were not returned home from overseas for several years after the conclusion of the war.

Raymond Maxfield

He had been given up for dead. No one recognized him at first when he calmly walked into the headquarters of the Ninety-fourth Fighter Squadron on September 29, 1944—certainly not with the handlebar mustache and the goatee he sported. Moments later, everyone was rejoicing. Lieutenant Raymond Maxfield had been missing from the squadron since his P-38 Lightning fighter was hit by flak and went down west of Bologna, Italy, on June 5.

The twenty-three-year-old from Mankato, Minnesota, was flying his twenty-fifth combat mission and strafing targets when antiaircraft bullets set both his engines afire. Maxfield's sister, Mary Lou Ballman, remembers him saying he had just finished shooting up a column of trucks and was headed for the lead vehicle, which was trying to make a run for it, when his plane was hit. The P-38 skimmed the treetops of an orchard and crash-landed. His comrades in the air could do little but momentarily circle overhead. They could see no sign of the pilot and, in any case, were unable to retrieve him, so they reluctantly left their downed friend and headed back to base. Lieutenant Raymond Maxfield was listed as missing in action, although few imagined ever seeing him again.

Maxfield knew he should have died in the crash. He managed to drag himself from the wreckage and slip into the forest before the German search patrols converged. He came upon a village and, desperate for help, knocked on a door. Maxfield later learned that only two houses in the village were involved with the Italian Resistance and he had picked one of them. He told his family after the war, "God must have been watching over me." The Germans knew there was a pilot in the immediate area and searched feverishly for him, but the Italian family successfully hid him. He became close to the family during this period.

Lieutenant Raymond Maxfield (right) survived his P-38 crashing behind enemy lines and fought alongside Italian partisans before returning to his fighter squadron. Photograph courtesy of the Raymond Maxfield family.

The P-38 pilot became a partisan. Maxfield spent several months with his new Italian friends, accompanying them in their efforts to do whatever damage they could to the occupying German forces. They blew up railroad bridges, destroyed communication lines, and attacked small German units whenever the opportunity presented itself. He went through the entire period without conversing with anyone in English. The *Mankato Free Press* of November 28, 1944, heralded the return home on leave of Lieutenant Maxfield and stated, "What happened in that intervening period since he crash landed his plane in the Italian orchard remains for the most part a military secret." He told the hometown paper of the Italians, "They surely treated me well," and added a note of hope to the families of all missing soldiers, saying, "Tell the parents not to give up. There's always the chance that they'll come back okay." The Mankato paper proudly announced that three of Raymond Maxfield's brothers were also in the service of the nation.

Maxfield originally received military training as a member of the Minnesota National Guard. His great-grandfather was among the first settlers in Mankato, settling there in 1852, and the family was well established in that southern Minnesota town. One of Maxfield's relatives was the commanding officer of the local National Guard unit, so it seemed only natural for the young man to join. The twenty-year-old Maxfield went to Alaska in 1940–1941 as part of the mobilization of the 215th Coastal Artillery. Kodiak, Alaska, was the site of an important naval air station, established in 1941. Its excellent harbor also served as a base for light cruisers and submarines. The 215th Coastal Artillery's 90-millimeter antiaircraft guns were part of the defenses for this important American base. There also was an army air base at Kodiak. Private Raymond Maxfield became determined to fly. He transferred to the Army Air Corps in December 1942 and received his commission in Arizona in December 1943.

Maxfield was in North Africa with the Ninety-fourth Fighter Squadron by March 1944. The Ninety-fourth, known as the "Hat in the Ring" Squadron, originated in the First World War with the legendary Eddie Rickenbacker and was one of three squadrons in the U.S. First Fighter Group. The group was proud to have been the first to fly missions over enemy territory and the first to down an Axis aircraft in the European theater. Lieutenant Maxfield was in action by April 1944, escorting bombers over France, Germany, and the Balkans. He saw considerable action over the Ploesti oil complex in May 1944. The First Fighter Group lost eighteen pilots in the course of escorting bombers into that strategic target. They earned a Presidential Unit Citation on May 18, taking part in a vicious twenty-minute dogfight while trying to protect a B-17 formation. Maxfield earned one kill that day for bringing down a German fighter.

Raymond Maxfield earned the Purple Heart and the Air Medal with Oak Leaf Clusters during his military service. He survived the duration of the war and returned home to Mankato. He continued with the Air Force Reserve until departing in 1957 with the rank of captain. He went to work in the glass business and later moved to the West Coast, where he became involved in the construction of skyscrapers in Los Angeles. Maxfield retired to St. Peter, Minnesota, just north of Mankato. He died in 1991 at the age of seventy and is buried in section Q, grave site 2197, at Fort Snelling National Cemetery.

John Mork

It was the work of the Catalina PBY planes to rescue pilots who went down in the water. Captain John Mork of south Minneapolis was described by the Twelfth Air Force as "one of the crack pilots of the 1st Emergency Rescue Squadron of the 12th Air Force." Mork patrolled the Adriatic Sea off the east coast of Italy. PBY pilots and crews had to be tough. They were well aware that their big, slow planes were easy targets for fighters and antiaircraft fire. They also knew that their missions never were called off due to bad weather.

Captain John Mork, one of the crack pilots in the First Emergency Rescue Squadron, rescued downed American fliers off the coast of Italy during the war from his Catalina PBY plane. Photograph courtesy of the Minneapolis Public Library, Minneapolis Collection.

Captain Mork and his crew were in search of a downed B-24 crew one morning. The weather was bad and they flew just below the stormy clouds and just above the thrashing seas. They spotted four men in a small dinghy being tossed around by the sea. Mork, recognizing the danger of setting a Catalina down in such waves, radioed for a rescue launch. The sea was so rough that the launch overturned. A destroyer was sent out while Mork continued to circle his PBY over the dinghy. The destroyer successfully plucked the airmen from the waters and quickly headed for the safety of the port. As Mork turned his PBY for home, a crew member sighted a man in a Mae West jacket bobbing in the waves. Mork knew the risk but did not hesitate to land his plane and rescue the lone airman. It was impossible for the PBY to take off under such conditions, so Mork taxied his plane through the rough seas for eighteen hours to reach port.

Mork was awarded the Distinguished Flying Cross for this mission. At this point in the war, he had flown more than fifty such missions, eleven of which were actual rescues. His other heroics included flying in directly under German shore batteries to rescue a downed flier. Mork made the U.S. Air Force his career after the war. His assignments included the Fourth Rescue Squadron at March Air Force Base in Riverside, California, and the 2156th Air Rescue Unit at MacDill Air Force Base outside Tampa, Florida. He later served in Korea and Vietnam and rose to the rank of lieutenant colonel in the U.S. Air Force. He died in 1976 at the age of sixty years and is buried in section P, grave site 3625, at Fort Snelling National Cemetery.

Donald Duane Johnson

Donald Duane Johnson was twenty-eight years old and living in rural Montana when he was inducted into the U.S. Army in January 1944. He underwent basic training in Texas and, after taking leave to return home, he shipped out to Naples, Italy, in July. The Allied progress up the Italian peninsula was slow and costly as the mountainous terrain afforded the entrenched German army every advantage. The U.S. Fifth Army, enduring severe losses of men, approached the strategic Po Valley in October 1944. Replacements regularly were rushed to the front to fill vacancies. Private Johnson traveled two days and nights by train from Naples and then rode by truck to the Replacement Depot, located about thirty-five miles from Florence.

Johnson was assigned to Company G, 351st Infantry Regiment, Eighty-eighth Division. The Eighty-eighth Division, consisting almost entirely of draftees, entered the combat zone in Italy at the beginning of March 1944 and, as such, was the first "draftee division" to do so. The Eighty-eighth fought fiercely to break the Gustav line in May and was among the first Allied units to enter Rome on June 4, 1944. German prisoners noted the fighting spirit of the men of the division, who adopted the nickname "Blue Devils"—the blue taken from the division's shoulder patches. They demonstrated that the American citizen-soldier was every bit a match to the vaunted veterans of Germany's Wehrmacht.

G Company of the 351st was off the line for a three-day rest when Private Johnson reported. He wrote, "The company had taken an awful beating, so there wasn't much the men wanted to talk about." He determined, "I've got to do something to help win, even if it's just a little so the war would be over." The Eighty-eighth Division's objective was the Po Valley and the city of Bologna. Monte Grande was the last dominating mountain before the Po Valley. The 349th Regiment took Monte Grande on October 20 with heavy support from air and artillery. The 351st moved up on October 22 to secure the flanks. Company G was given the task of taking the town of Vedriano.

The plan was for Company G's Second Platoon to lead through enemy lines, with the First and Third Platoons following up. Company F was to occupy buildings as they were taken. Company E was held in reserve. Johnson wrote: "We were supposed to have three machine guns and three mortars with our platoon, but they never showed up so we had to go without them. . . . The place we were supposed to take was about three or four miles ahead." Private Johnson describes a hellish march in the darkness with the occasional scream and explosion of an artillery round. "It was awfully dark out at this time and hard to keep track of the man ahead of you . . . the only way we kept together. . . . We didn't dare lose contact as we were only a company of men and needed every man for the attack." Company G was advancing in staggered formation on either side of the road when a machine gun opened up on them, killing the point man and wounding several others. They endured intense artillery fire from 2:00 a.m. to daybreak. However, as Johnson wrote, "none of us was awfully scared but we were determined to do our job and make the best of it. Screaming meemies and 88s came at us so heavy we had to leave the road."

The company started its climb to the summit of the hill at dawn on October 24. The weary GIs took more than forty Germans prisoner during the advance. Private Johnson was assigned to guard two German officers. Company G dug in to hold their position, but the Germans spotted them and began shelling. The men had to keep low. Johnson remembered sand being thrown in his face by bullets, which just missed: "I had to keep pretty close watch as the Germans were crawling up on us and weren't more than fifty yards away." The German command recognized the importance of what was happening and committed elite paratroopers to retake the position. An intercepted radio message from the First (German) Parachute Regiment to the Fourth Parachute Regiment stated, "Attack Vedriano. Vedriano is decisive!"

Private Johnson noted, "At about 9 a.m. and for the rest of the day, we had enough noise so we couldn't hear a fellow 10 yards away, except for short whiles. From now on we would have plenty of casualties." He added, "I said a lot of Our Fathers and Hail Marys and thought I would never live through the day." American warplanes strafed the advancing Germans around noon to no avail. The commanding officer called for help and was told that two companies had tried to reach them but were pinned by strong German counterattacks. His men, surrounded by large numbers of Germans, were exhausted after the long advance and the continuous shelling. The commanding officer surrendered at 3:30 p.m. Johnson felt that "if we would have had to stay until dark, chances are we all would have been killed." The eighty men remaining of the original force of 165 had advanced farther than any other unit in the U.S. Fifth Army. They were less than five thousand yards from the Po Valley's main highway when forced to surrender or die. A radio message intercepted later that day in the afternoon stated, "Vedriano retaken. Eighty Americans captured."

The Germans marched the prisoners steadily for twelve hours. Those not wounded tried to assist and carry the injured. Three men fell by the road, unable to go farther. Gunshots later suggested that the German guards finished them off. The prisoners went two days without food. Private Johnson later wrote, "The Jerries are no damn good. If I ever pity any of them at any time, I hope they shoot me."

Efforts to exploit the Monte Grande salient failed in the face of fierce counter-attacks up and down the line. The Allied command called off the offensive on October 26. The offensive was not renewed until April 1945, the following spring. By May, the war in Europe was over.

Prisoner of war Donald Johnson was transported by boxcar to Stalag 7-A near Munich after his capture. He won a diary in a lottery held by the International Red Cross in the POW camp and recorded his experiences before and after his capture. He wrote, "I never dreamed I would be taken prisoner. I thought I might be killed, but mostly I thought I would be wounded—I guess." He and his comrades suffered deprivations of food, heat, and clothing during their imprisonment. They served as forced laborers on the railroad. Living conditions improved somewhat when the Germans transferred Johnson to a camp near Amberg, Germany. An illness in February 1945 nearly proved fatal.

Liberation came on May 1, 1945. Johnson proudly noted that the first GI he saw was a Montana boy, like himself. The POWs were trucked to an airfield and put on transport planes for Reims, France. He was back in the United States by May 11. Johnson's wife, Catherine, had been pregnant upon his departure overseas. He returned home to a new family.

Donald Duane Johnson died in 1993 at the age of seventy-seven. He is buried in section S, grave site 2289, at Fort Snelling National Cemetery.

The Allied success in North Africa and Italy was costly, but tied up many elite German units. The attack on the "underbelly" of Hitler's Fortress Europe led to the Allied success and breakout at Normandy and, ultimately, to the end of the war. These are a few of the men of the Upper Midwest who played a role in these historic campaigns.

Chapter 3

Bombers over Europe

Robert Locky

The Allied success in North Africa allowed a new base of operations for heavy bombers attacking targets on the European continent. The Ploesti oil complex in Romania, the single most important source of fuel for the German war machine, was one of the foremost targets. Allied planners were determined to knock out the refineries with the first large-scale, low-level bomber attack of the war against a heavily defended target. The distance traveled by Americans during the mission was also the greatest in the war up to that time. Operation Statesman called for 170 B-24 Liberator bombers to simultaneously hit targets in five refineries within the complex. The task force included two bomber groups based out of North Africa and three groups out of England. The B-24 Liberators had a range of more than two thousand miles and could carry substantial payloads. Planners went so far as to arrange two full-scale practice missions to work out the final details.

The date set for Operation Statesman was August 1, 1943. It seemed that everything that could have gone wrong did go wrong. The lead plane for the first group, carrying the primary navigator for the mission, crashed on takeoff. Eleven other bombers aborted after takeoff and returned to base. Radio silence made adjustments to flight commands impossible, so the groups became separated early on. Heavy cloud cover caused further separation and disorientation. The various groups thus entered the target area from all different directions and simply selected whichever targets of opportunity they discovered. Their training had been in high-altitude bombing, but

Marjorie Locky receiving the Distinguished Flying Cross on behalf of her husband, Staff Sergeant Robert Locky, a POW in Germany. Photograph from the March 6, 1944, edition of the *St. Paul Dispatch,* courtesy of the *St. Paul Pioneer Press.*

they had to fly in at a low level. The low-level tactics also made the B-24s extremely vulnerable to antiaircraft fire from the ground. Further, enemy fighter strength was significant, some estimates being as high as four hundred in the area.

Staff Sergeant Robert Locky of St. Paul was a waist gunner on a B-24 named *Pudgy* in the 330th Bomb Squadron of the Eighth Army Air Force's Ninety-third Bomb Group. The Ninety-third was known as "Ted's Flying Circus" in recognition of commanding officer Colonel Ted Timberlake. The group was based near Benghazi, Libya.

Major Ramsey Potts led fifteen of the thirty-six bombers of the Ninety-third on the strike. Their objective, code-named "White III," included the Standard Petrol Block and the Unirea-Spiranza refinery. Locky and his crewmates faced fierce antiaircraft fire from the ground. Fifty rounds nearly sheared off *Pudgy*'s tail as it flew past an antiaircraft battery. The plane crashed in a cornfield and exploded into flames. Six of the crew members died on impact, while five others, including Sergeant Locky, survived. A crowd of Romanian peasants rushed to the burning wreckage. The peasants at first thought the flight crew were Russians. When the peasants learned the men were Americans, one man came forward to shake their hands, saying he had flown with the British Royal Flying Corps in the First World War. A beautiful young woman, the local doctor, made her way through the crowd and tended to the wounded, but enemy soldiers soon arrived and took the six crew members prisoner.

Pudgy was one of forty-four planes lost in combat over Ploesti. Another seven that were damaged limped to Turkey, where they were interned for the war. The loss of fifty-two of 177 bombers launched, including the one that crashed on takeoff, was catastrophic and the mission was a major disaster.

The March 6, 1944, edition of the *St. Paul Dispatch* included a photo of Robert Locky's wife, Marjorie, accepting a Distinguished Flying Cross on his behalf. The decoration was awarded to every crew member who took part in the fateful mission. The caption reported that Locky "won't see it until the war is over. Sgt. Locky, who took part in the celebrated air raid on the Ploesti oil fields in Rumania last August, is a prisoner of war." Locky did survive his long experience as a prisoner of war. He returned to Minnesota and for a time served Duluth as city assessor. Robert Locky died on June 22, 1994, and is buried in Fort Snelling National Cemetery, section 3, grave site 684.

William E. Anderson

The U.S. Eighth Army Air Force's daytime precision bombing missions over Germany were critical to the Allied victory in World War II. B-17 Flying Fortress bombers flying for up to nine hours at an altitude of twenty-five thousand feet could deliver a four-thousand-pound bomb load deep into Germany. The Germans fiercely contested their airspace. Bomber crews, consisting mainly of young men in their early twenties, faced swarms of dangerous German fighters to and from the target and fearsome antiaircraft fire over the objective. On average, 10 percent of the Eighth's bombers did not return.

With hundreds of bombers flying on a given day, the daily loss in men and planes was appalling. The Eighth Army Air Force had forty-one heavy bomb groups in action over Europe at its peak from mid-1944 into the first few months of 1945.

William "Andy" Anderson of St. Paul was a twenty-four-year-old and a graduate of the University of Minnesota when the United States went to war. He had no aviation experience before entering training. Anderson graduated as a navigator and was assigned to the crew of Bill Riegler, who flew *Pistol Packin' Mama* in the 613th Squadron of the newly formed 401st Bomber Group. Copilot Tom Cushman, from Michigan, later wrote:

> Our navigator was a big "Swede" by the name of William Einer Anderson. He was built like a brick-you-know-what and I would have hated to skate against him in a hockey game. Andy, [pilot] Bill [Riegler] and I were joined by a hotshot bombardier who outranked us. He had seen action in the Pacific and was rumored to have sunk a Japanese ship without a bombsight! We were awed by this big burly Texan who acted like a typical Army master sergeant. His name was Durwood W. Fesmire. We just called him Fes.

Riegler's crew, along with the other crews of the 401st, went through intensive training at Geiger Field in Spokane, Washington, and then Great Falls, Montana. On October 18, 1943, the 613th Squadron flew out of Great Falls, bound for England. The planes were given a general flight plan, but did not fly in formation. Cushman remembered:

> Our route passed fairly close to Canton, Ohio, [pilot] Bill Riegler's hometown. (Navigator) Anderson agreed that no one should notice if we drifted a little off course and passed directly over Canton. I tell you, the people in Canton knew their favorite son was on his way overseas! We roared down the main street of Canton below the tops of the buildings while I ran the propeller pitches up and down. We would pull up, swing around, and make another pass. . . . Bill proceeded to buzz his home in the same manner. . . . Finally, with light heads and excitement in our hearts, we proceeded on.

And so the young men went off to war. Riegler's crew and *Pistol Packin' Mama* crossed the North Atlantic and joined the other members of the 613th Squadron at its base at Deenethorpe, England. The squadron insignia was a cartoon "punching bomb" drawn by a young man named Walt Disney.

The 401st Bomber Group was among the much-needed replacement crews and planes that arrived in the immediate aftermath of the disastrous Schweinfurt mission, in which the U.S. Eighth Air Force lost sixty B-17s and six hundred crew members while attacking the vast ball-bearing factories at Schweinfurt, Germany, on October 14,

Captain William "Andy" Anderson and his crewmates on *Pistol Packin' Mama,* their B-17 bomber. Anderson is third from the left in the back row and pilot Tom Cushman is on the far left in the back row. Photograph courtesy of Thomas R. Cushman.

1943. Another seventeen bombers that returned to base were damaged beyond repair. The staggering loss of more than 25 percent of the bombers and crews caused many to question the sense of the air strategy. Yet the daily bombing missions continued by necessity.

Conventional wisdom was that if a crew survived their first five missions, they would have learned enough about survival techniques—how to stay in close formation, for instance, and how to keep better track of where their course had taken them. The better their survival skills, the sooner they could complete the required twenty-five missions and be allowed to go home. Yet the dangers were such that the statistical likelihood of completing twenty-five safe missions was low. It was a gamble either way.

The crew of *Pistol Packin' Mama* flew their first combat mission on November 26, 1943. The addition of the 401st Group gave the First Bomber Division 505 bombers to put into the air that day against Bremen, an important German seaport. Luftwaffe resistance was fierce, with up to one hundred fighters slashing at the bomber formations. Antiaircraft fire was heavy over the target and twenty-nine Fortresses went down, but *Pistol Packin' Mama* returned safely to base.

While the young men in the bomber crews felt part of a great adventure, reality set in quickly. The first combat mission made clear to each new crew that the sheer terror of the experience was more than anyone had anticipated. Nor did anyone ever seem to get used to the danger. The call of "Bandits at twelve o'clock high!" sent adrenaline rushing. Luftwaffe fighters flew straight in, head-on at the bombers, hoping to cause inexperienced pilots to change course and pull out of formation. There was the intense shock of near-miss antiaircraft fire over the target. Although B-17s were remarkably durable, an explosion in the fuel tanks could turn a Flying Fortress into a ball of flames. Damage to an engine could prevent a bomber from keeping up with its squadron formation, at which time the German fighters would descend upon it like a pack of wolves. A well-aimed shot to the tail wing could send a Fortress into a downward spiral with such strong centrifugal force that no one could parachute to safety.

Anderson and crew had more than a week to prepare for their second mission on December 5 against Paris. Their third mission on December 20 was again against Bremen. The command allowed the crews to stand down on Christmas Day. The fourth raid was against the oil plant at Ludwigshafen on December 30 and cost the Eighth Air Force twenty-three bombers. The fifth raid against Kiel took place on January 4, 1944. No enemy fighters appeared, the flak was only moderate, and the crew of *Pistol Packin' Mama* completed their fifth mission. The crew might have breathed a sigh of relief, but they knew well that there was far more to come.

While Andy Anderson and his crewmates started out with *Pistol Packin' Mama,* the plane was often too shot up by flak from a raid to be ready for the next and the crew was assigned to another plane. They became known as Riegler's crew rather than *Pistol Packin' Mama.* Each time a plane was shot up and repaired, it lost a bit of its maximum speed. Cushman, like all B-17 men, has only praise for the plane, saying, "She could really take quite a beating." The B-17 had large wings and could remain in the air with shell holes in the wings and the tail all battered up. Cushman added that a man never really got used to the antiaircraft fire; it was always terrifying with other B-17s exploding all around them. "The plane was always full of holes . . . I saw what flak could do." Those who made it often asked themselves how they survived when the group lost so many planes.

Riegler's crew was on their sixth mission over Germany on January 11, 1944. The objective was the German aircraft manufacturing complex at Oschersleben and considerable resistance was expected. The 401st Bomber Group led the First Bomb Division that day, with two other divisions accompanying them. The mission began poorly. A major front brought bad weather and caused most of the fighter escorts to return to base. The second and third bomb groups did likewise. Only the first bomb group continued toward the objective. The first was without any fighter support when more than two hundred Luftwaffe fighters attacked the bombers about fifty miles out from Oschersleben. The B-17s fought through the gauntlet with considerable loss and pressed on toward their objective. Extensive batteries of antiaircraft guns surrounded the aircraft manufacturing complex, and the Germans pounded the attacking planes with an intense barrage of flak. The Luftwaffe fighters waited outside the flak zone for another chance to pounce on the B-17s as they left their targets and began the long flight home.

Copilot Tom Cushman wrote of the terror of the journey back to base after the Oschersleben mission. He witnessed plane after plane from the 613th Squadron go down under the onslaught of the Luftwaffe fighters:

> "Red Dog Charlie to Red Dog Leader," came the frantic call. "Go ahead, Charlie." "Number four engine hit. Can't keep up." . . . As soon as he was alone, the fighters swarmed on him like a pack of angry bees. He bravely fought them off, but I saw him falter, waver. The big bomber went down with guns blazing. I could see no chutes. Tears rolled down my cheeks and froze on my oxygen mask. My vision blurred. For the first time in my life, I was scared, afraid I would never make it back home.

A lone P-51 Mustang suddenly appeared and plunged into the midst of an estimated fifty attacking German fighters. The Mustang pilot shot down three German planes (probably five, but two were not confirmed), damaged several others, and scattered the rest. Cushman recalls, "That one Mustang sure was a miracle." The heroics, which the six remaining Flying Fortresses of 613th Squadron witnessed, earned Major James Howard, a Mustang pilot with the 356th Fighter Squadron, the Medal of Honor. Howard, who had been an ace with the American Volunteer Group in China known as the Flying Tigers, was the only fighter pilot in the European theater to be so honored.

The crew of *Pistol Packin' Mama* made it safely back to base. The entire air division that made that fateful run at Oscherslaben received the Presidential Unit Citation, and each of the men was awarded the Distinguished Flying Cross.

The 613th Squadron's participation in the bombing of Berlin on March 6, 1944, was the thirteenth mission for Bill Riegler's crew. The German capital held special significance for both the Germans and the Allies. Consequently, enemy fighter opposition was particularly fierce and aggressive. The Eighth Air Force lost sixty-nine bombers—the most downed in a single day—but Andy Anderson and his crewmates again survived.

Riegler's crew was often selected to fly lead for the 401st Bombardment Group and was assigned the plane that was in the best shape that day. This was, at least in part, due to the navigational expertise of Andy Anderson and the bombardier skill of Fes Fesmire. When their crew's name went up on the board in the morning briefing, everyone would moan, as that indicated it would be a particularly key target and a tough mission. Lead and deputy lead planes were the only ones with bombsights; the entire squadron and group would release when the lead plane did. German fighters knew that and made a special effort to take out the lead and deputy lead planes.

Riegler's crew was preparing for its seventeenth mission in May 1944 when they were assigned a new crew member, S. Fine. He was the operator for the Mickey (or H2X) system, radar designed for navigation through the seemingly ever-present European cloud cover. Mickey operators eventually pulled together a radar image map of Germany for navigation and bombing. The Mickey operator set up in the plane's radio room next to the navigator and bombardier. He measured distance to target and regularly passed this information to the bombardier, who fed information into the Norden bombsight. If the clouds broke, the bombardier took over manually.

As with the bombsight, only the lead and deputy lead planes of each bomber group had the Mickey dish, which replaced the gun in the ball turret of the B-17 bomber. They were at risk as the Mickey not only guided the bomber squadrons, but also highlighted the pathfinder plane on German radar on the ground and made that plane the primary target for the antiaircraft batteries. German fighter pilots also knew that the lead and deputy lead planes carried radar. Despite all of these hazards, Riegler's crew completed twenty-five missions, enough to go home on leave.

Andy Anderson went home in July 1944, but returned in October. He and his crew members felt they still had a war to fight. Fes Fesmire returned as bombardier. Tom Cushman replaced an injured Bill Riegler as pilot. The second tour of duty consisted of fifteen lead missions from October 1944 to February 1, 1945. Andy Anderson and his crew members went home in February 1945.

Long after the war, the men began to gather for Bomber Group reunions. Andy Anderson never came. Cushman wondered about his old friend and tried for a time to locate him, but there were too many Andersons in Minnesota. Andy Anderson had worked in the Twin Cities for Northwest Airlines as a navigator after the war. He had been in the hospital for three months in 1952 when he came down with pneumonia. He died five days later on June 2, 1952, at the age of thirty-three. He never had a chance to communicate with his old crew members. Captain William "Andy" Anderson is buried in section B, grave site 164-N, at Fort Snelling National Cemetery. It was not until this book was being written that Tom Cushman learned what happened to the husky lad from Minnesota who was one of the finest navigators in the Eighth Air Force.

John Silvernale

John Silvernale wanted to get a job as a Greyhound bus driver, "but since I was registered for the draft, they didn't want me. I then decided to become a pilot in the Air Corps." The Minnesota farm boy (Shetek Township in Murray County) went to Fort Snelling for his physical, only to be rejected because his teeth were not perfect. He refused to give up. When he learned there was to be a mobile recruiting station for the Army Air Corps in nearby Slayton, Silvernale enlisted in the Army Air Corps so he could "at least be near airplanes." He was sworn in at Fort Snelling on August 19, 1941, and was working as a supply clerk at Luke Field in Phoenix, Arizona, when news came of the Japanese attack on Pearl Harbor. America needed good men to fly warplanes and Silvernale remained determined to become a pilot. He passed the physical for cadet training and transferred to Kelly Field in San Antonio, Texas. He married his longtime sweetheart, Margery Howard, on September 4, 1942, in Lubbock and two days later received his wings. Silvernale later wrote that, after additional training, "we were now supposed to be combat ready." He was in New York in late August 1943, preparing to ship overseas, when Margery delivered their first child, a boy.

First Lieutenant John Silvernale piloted a B-17 bomber over Europe. Photograph courtesy of Margery Silvernale.

The Eighth Army Air Force assigned Second Lieutenant Silvernale to the 381st Bomb Group, based at Ridgewell in Essex. He later wrote: "When we arrived I was sure it was the end of the line for me as the morale of the group was very low. They had just flown the Schweinfurt mission in which they got very badly shot up." Thirty-nine percent of the planes sent to hit the strategic ball-bearing factories went down over Schweinfurt. Silvernale and his crew were assigned a B-17G in the 534th Bomb Squadron. He named the plane *Sugar.* They flew their first mission on November 3, 1943. He was awakened at 4:00 a.m., briefed an hour later, and took off at 8:00 a.m. It was a "milk run": that is, no airships were lost. Mission two, two days later, was the real thing, he later wrote: "We came under heavy fighter attack and the flak was thick as hell." Silvernale and his crew received the Air Medal after completing their fifth mission. Soon afterward, they learned that the first pilot of the 381st Group had completed his twenty-five missions and earned the right to go home. The group had lost nearly three-quarters of the original crews in only five months. No one took life for granted. One pilot crashed on takeoff and his plane exploded on what was to have been his twenty-fifth and final mission.

Silvernale's *Sugar* flew on raids over Bremen on November 26 and December 13, 16, and 20. The industrial center was well known for its heavy flak, and Silvernale wrote, "I don't know why we were hitting Bremen so often, but we were." The city's seaport was the target. On the last mission in which he flew over Bremen, Silvernale's eleventh, four crews went down. His crew was selected to be a squadron A team (lead) after nineteen missions, and from that time forward flew only when the 534th Squadron led the group. There were so few losses when Silvernale's crew led that his missions were called "Silvernale's Gravy Train." He later wrote: "I have to admit the Good Lord was with me." His twenty-fourth mission on March 20, 1944, was a terrifying affair. His crew was leading the entire First Combat Wing to bomb Frankfurt when they flew into heavy clouds and lost all visibility. Every airship had to fly on instruments while in close formation. They salvoed their bombs and turned around to head home, flying "for an eternity" until finally breaking into the clear. The navigator did not recognize any landmarks with his map and only a dozen bombers remained with *Sugar*. Lieutenant Silvernale thought to himself, "Boy, are we a buncha sittin' ducks for enemy fighters. As luck would have it we flew all the way back to England without seeing an enemy aircraft. I'll never know why." *Sugar* returned to base with barely any fuel remaining, as did many other airships. They lost only one crew that day.

John Silvernale's coveted twenty-fifth mission was flown on a beautiful, clear day. The target was an airfield in southern France. The chaplain of the 381st wrote: "As we sat this morning, March 27th [1944] in the briefing room, I observed one of our men sitting on the front bench listening intently. There was an air of confidence on his countenance. Yet, withal, a look of anxiety. John Silvernale's name was on the top of the flight board. He would be leading the high group for the First Air Division and it was his twenty-fifth mission—his last. He had been with us since September 1943. Six months of combat had left its strain. Notwithstanding, he sat there with assurance." Silvernale described the raid: "It was amazing. We didn't see a fighter on the way in. As we neared the IP [Initial Point], I put the airplane on auto pilot and Happy took over with the bomb site [sight]. We made a beautiful run and obliterated the target." Wing headquarters gave the crew a Certificate of Commendation and promoted Silvernale to first lieutenant shortly after his return to base. He earned the Distinguished Flying Cross for completing his twenty-fifth mission and could proudly state that he had never lost a crew member. He wrote, "It was a day I thought I'd never see

The B-17 Flying Fortress was a high-altitude heavy bomber, which saw extensive service in the war over Germany as the mainstay of the Eighth Army Air Force. The B-17 was well regarded for its excellent flight characteristics and its ability to sustain damage and return its crew of ten back to base. The larger, more powerful B-29 rendered the B-17 obsolete late in the war. Photograph courtesy of the U.S. Air Force.

six months before." The chaplain reported, "Silvernale was happy as a lark." He bid farewell to his crew with whom he had developed close ties, as they had yet to complete their twenty-five missions. He was saddened later when his flight engineer died when a bomber crashed on landing during engine testing.

First Lieutenant John Silvernale was processed home quickly. "I never saw the military work so fast," he recalled. He signed out of Ridgewell on March 31 and shipped out of Liverpool for New York City. He arrived back in "the good ol' USA!" and later noted, "I never forget the afternoon we pulled into NY harbor." The military processed Silvernale and sent him home for a week's leave at which time he met his son for the first time: "It was a wonderful homecoming. I will never experience such a wonderful time in my life." The army sent him to Lockbourne Air Base in Columbus, Ohio, where he noted, "I learned more about flying B-17s there than I did before I went overseas." He became a B-17 flight instructor until VE Day—Victory in Europe Day, May 8, 1945. Afterward, with the United States focused on Imperial Japan, Silvernale trained on B-29s in preparation for the Pacific theater. That ended with VJ Day (Victory in Japan) on August 15. He mustered out at Camp McCoy, Wisconsin, and went home. He remained in the reserves for a time and became a captain.

John Silvernale joined his former comrades at Ridgewell, England, for a 381st Bomb Group reunion in August 1982. He gave a speech in which he recounted the great sense of foreboding he felt upon arriving at Ridgewell in October 1943. "Suddenly I realized, this is what it's all about. Then the terrifying thought occurred to me . . . I am just another bit of expendable humanity in the great struggle for freedom." He went on to say, "I cannot but feel the hand of God was with me. . . . But you know, we had to have lots of faith in those days—faith in ourselves and our training, faith in our crew members, ground crews and armament, faith in our leaders and commanders, faith in our airplane, faith in our country and people back home, and, finally, faith in God." He closed by honoring those who paid the supreme sacrifice and asking his comrades, "Is there one among us who cannot say 'There but by the grace of God go I'?" John Silvernale died January 22, 1996. He is buried in Fort Snelling National Cemetery, section 5, grave site 101.

Herbert Bunde

Second Lieutenant Herbert Bunde of St. Paul, Minnesota, was described by one of his crewmates as "a quiet, unassuming, lanky fellow." His sisters wrote that Herb was "very caring and kind to everyone" and that he was "always making or building something." The fact that he was "always making kites" suggests an early interest in aviation. For while he loved hunting and fishing, Bunde gave that up to fly in the service of his country, being inducted at Fort Snelling on March 14, 1942. He underwent pilot training at Stockton Field in California and received his officer's commission on July 27, 1943. He was subsequently assigned to become copilot on a B-24H Liberator named *Crud Wagon* in the 712th Squadron of the 448th Bomb Group. The 712th was composed of twelve B-24s with fifteen crews. The 448th Group based out of Seething Airfield, nine miles southeast of Norwich, England.

Bunde and crew flew their first mission on December 24, 1943. The milk run drew not a single flak burst. The Eighth Air Force was just beginning the Crossbow Campaign to destroy German rocket sites along the French coast. More than seven

Second Lieutenant Herbert Bunde was shot down on a bombing mission over the Romanian oil complex at Ploesti and spent the remainder of the war as a German POW. Photograph courtesy of Dr. James Gerber.

hundred bombers took part. Bunde and his crew flew thirteen missions by the end of March 1944 as part of this campaign. Charles McBride, Bunde's pilot, noted, "We were still not to the midway point of fifteen missions in the combat tour. . . . There was nothing to rely upon except good fortune and blind luck in getting through the gauntlet to that far distant goal."

The 448th Bomb Group was heading back to base from a mission on April 1, 1944. It had been five hours since takeoff. The last bombing run over Pforzheim had finished well over an hour behind schedule. The group's flight to the English Channel was more than three hundred miles in the face of extreme headwinds. *Crud Wagon* was cruising at fourteen thousand feet when Lieutenant Bunde asked Sergeant Campbell to check the fuel supply. The entire crew heard Bunde say, "For God's sake, we haven't got enough gas to make it back." There was a momentary silence, then Bunde announced, "Copilot to crew. We're going to leave the formation to try to save our gas. Everyone stay alert." Everyone watched and waited. Within the hour, another announcement followed, which would be Bunde's last: "Copilot to crew. You can start bailing out. We haven't got any more gas." The B-24 was at an altitude of eleven thousand feet. The crew, including Bunde, jumped from *Crud Wagon* over St. Pol, France, in the Pas de Calais region. *Crud Wagon* was one of five bombers in the 448th to be lost for lack of fuel that day.

The crewmen of *Crud Wagon* experienced parachuting for the first time as they bailed from the plane. Strong gusts popped the chutes and caught the airmen in violent swings. The long sail down seemed unreal to the men. The rough landing was followed by rougher treatment at the hands of German soldiers, who rounded up the crewmen as their chutes hit the ground. The soldiers took the American airmen to town to be interrogated and processed as prisoners.

Second Lieutenant Bunde spent the remainder of the war in Stalag Luft 1 in Pomerania. The camp population exceeded five thousand. An American officer managed to escape and brought back to American lines the names of many of those who were in his camp. The *St. Paul Pioneer Press* carried an article announcing that at least five St. Paul men, including Bunde, were prisoners in a camp in Germany. Bunde spent more than a year in the camp. Herb's sister, Elaine Gerber, remembers well the day two uniformed men came to their door to tell the Bunde family their son and brother was a prisoner of war. Until then, he was missing in action and they feared he was dead. Nonetheless, "It was very hard on our whole family while Herb was a prisoner of war." She is certain that the International Red Cross kept her brother alive. Sister Ruth decided to write her brother as soon as she received his address. "You couldn't write

The B-24 Liberator was produced in considerably greater numbers during World War II than the B-17 Flying Fortress. The Liberator's wings were very long, which accounted for increased load capacity, improved ascent characteristics, and greater range than the B-17. This heavy bomber was used in Europe, but particularly in the Pacific theater. Photograph courtesy of the U.S. Air Force.

too much at a time because you had to use the required V-mail, which was censored. I hoped and prayed that he would at least receive some of the letters."

The POW camp that held Herbert Bunde was "liberated" by the Red Army in May 1945. The German guards fled upon word of the advancing Russians. The prisoners later found an order on the camp commandant's desk, instructing him to have the prisoners killed. The Soviets seemed to show little interest in the prisoners' well-being. Some Americans who went off with the Russians were never seen again. Bunde wisely chose to remain in the camp and was liberated by American forces a week later. He returned home to his family. Sister Elaine Gerber recalls that the family was "so glad when we heard Herb was liberated. We were even happier to have Herb come home to stay October 1945." Sister Ruth Aker was thrilled to learn that her brother had received a large number of her daily letters.

Herb Bunde settled down to a well-earned life in a free democracy after the war. He married and raised seven children with his wife Jeanette. Herb told his family that as a result of his POW experience he never again wanted to feel crowded by people on all sides of him. He always lived in a house on a corner lot. He worked at American Hoist and Derrick for many years as a pattern maker and enjoyed retirement. Bunde died Christmas morning, December 25, 1993, at the age of seventy-three. He is buried in Fort Snelling National Cemetery, section 14, grave site 1358.

George E. Radle

George Radle was living with his parents and younger brother and sister on James Street in St. Paul as war loomed. He entered the army in September 1941 at the age of twenty-three and became a gunner on a B-24 in the 706th Squadron of the 446th Bomb Group. American crewmen on bombers over Germany were privates earlier in the war. When it was learned that the Germans treated prisoners better if they were officers, all crewmen were made staff sergeants (noncommissioned officers). Staff Sergeant George Radle flew on a B-24J called *Luck and Stuff,* piloted by First Lieutenant Weems D. Jones. Radle was assigned to the ball turret as a gunner, a position very much exposed to machine-gun fire from enemy fighters.

Twenty-two planes belonging to the 446th Bomb Group prepared to fly a mission to Berlin on April 29, 1944. The group was "stood down" for two hours, waiting for the weather to clear over the target. *Luck and Stuff* was third in the squadron formation that day when the mission finally got under way. Nose turret gunner Charles Perry recalled, "It was a beautiful day up there." Records indicate that friendly fighter support was good into the target, with P-51 Mustangs escorting the group most of the way. Perry recalled a German fighter appearing and being shot down in flames.

Flak over Berlin was heavy as always. *Luck and Stuff* "caught it in No. 2 engine" on the bomb run and began to lose oil. There were other problems. The twenty-five-hundred-pound napalm bombs refused to release and the bomber headed home with its payload still in the bomb bay. All hell broke loose after the group began the return flight. German fighters often hung just outside the actual bombing zone to avoid being hit by the heavy flak being put into the air from below. They would pounce on the American bombers leaving the target area.

Luck and Stuff began to straggle behind the rest of the group that was homeward bound, and headwinds apparently delayed friendly fighter escorts from regaining contact with the bomber wing. Reports on that day's return flight state that between thirty-five and forty German ME-109s made "vicious and sustained attacks." Three ME-109s attacked *Luck and Stuff* from the rear. Enemy fire set the bomber on fire and injured seven of the ten crew members. The raging fire made communication impossible between the cockpit and the crew in the back. First Lieutenant Jones later reported that he and the crew members in the front bailed out through the nose-wheel door. Those in the back went out through the rear windows. Staff Sergeant Perry reported that as he free-fell to just above the clouds before opening his chute, *Luck and Stuff* had already blown up. Upon landing, he was surrounded by several hundred civilians armed with axes, hoes, and clubs.

Staff Sergeant Radle was hit by heavy-caliber fire in the knee. He made it out of the plane, but was dead when radio operator Arnold Kaminsky later found him lying on the ground. He likely bled to death on the way down. Two other crew members died and the remaining seven were taken prisoner on April 29, 1944. A Western Union telegram to the Radle family, dated September 6, 1944, stated:

> Report now received from the German government through the International Red Cross states your son Staff Sergeant George E. Radle who was previously reported missing in action was killed in action on twenty-nine April over Germany. The Secretary of War extends his deep sympathy.

The U.S. government returned the remains of George Radle to Minnesota after the war. He is buried in section A-22, grave site 5466, near Gate 2 at Fort Snelling National Cemetery.

Walter P. Shimshock

The Soviet Union's Joseph Stalin was determined to control Poland and Eastern Europe in general in the postwar period. The Poles remembered only too well the 1939 invasion of Poland by the Soviets following Stalin's nonaggression pact with Hitler. Nor had they forgotten the atrocities during the Soviet occupation, including the massacre of several thousand Polish officers in the Katyn Forest. The grim reality by the fall of 1943 was that the Red Army was driving back the Nazis and approaching Poland.

The Polish government in exile in London had every intention of running Poland for Poles after the war's end. The nationalists recognized the importance of showing strong resistance to the German occupation force to legitimize their claim to their homeland after the war. The Warsaw Uprising, organized by the Polish Home Army, the resistance arm of the Polish government in London, began on August 1, 1944, even

Staff Sergeant Walter Shimshock was tail gunner on a B-17 bomber. The son of Polish immigrants died in combat on a mission over Warsaw on September 18, 1944. Photograph courtesy of the 390th Memorial Museum, Tucson, Arizona.

as advance units of the Red Army approached Warsaw. The light weapons of the Poles were inadequate against the German army units they faced in the streets of Warsaw, much less against the strongly fortified positions of the German army throughout that city. When the Warsaw Uprising became reality, the Red Army ceased its advance westward and went on the defensive. It was generally assumed that the Soviets were content to let the Nazis remove the threat of Polish nationalists to facilitate the eventual Soviet takeover of Poland at war's end. Polish nationalists, aware of Stalin's heinous plans, begged the West for assistance, both political and military.

Roosevelt and Churchill desperately wanted to help the Poles, but there were few realistic options. The best of these was to drop supplies to the Poles from the air. American B-24s and British Halifaxes flew out of bases in Italy throughout August and into September to Warsaw. The long flight from Italy (1,750 miles round-trip), the long exposure to enemy fighters, and the dangerous low-altitude airdrops over Warsaw combined to account for high bomber losses. Churchill and Roosevelt approached Stalin as to allowing American and British bombers to use Ukrainian airfields for rest and refueling after dropping supplies into Warsaw. Stalin refused for days until he OK'd clearance for the Americans September 9.

Walter Shimshock was born Wladek Szymczak on April 28, 1925, in Minneapolis. He was drafted in 1943 not long after graduating from DeLaSalle High School. Shimshock went overseas on July 6, 1944, flying with his nine crewmates on *I'll Be Seeing You/'Til We Meet Again,* a B-17 bomber. Shimshock was their tail gunner. The new crew was assigned to the 568th Bomb Squadron of the 390th Bombardment Group. The 390th had been in action over Europe since August 1943. The Eighth Army Air Force was sustaining serious losses every day and wasted little time getting replacement crews and their new planes into action. Shimshock and his crewmates flew their first combat mission on August 8, 1944, over France. Their ninth combat mission, flown on August 27, was over Berlin. They flew five more missions over Germany from September 9 through September 18.

On the morning of September 18, three bomb groups took to the air, headed for Warsaw. The Ninety-fifth, the 100th, and the 390th Bomb Groups totaled 110 B-17s. The Warsaw run was the fifteenth combat mission over Europe for Walter Shimshock and his crewmates. Each B-17 carried a dozen large supply canisters in lieu of the bomb loads. Warsaw was surrounded by considerable numbers of German antiaircraft batteries and airfields supporting German fighter squadrons. German fighters were so aggressive over Warsaw that they entered the flak zone over the city to attack the bombers. Consequently, three squadrons of American fighters—159 P-51s—escorted the B-17s. The plan was for approximately half of the fighters to continue the escort to the landing base in the Soviet Union.

The plan was to fly over Warsaw at less than half the altitude from which they typically released bombs over a target. The crews' lives were risked in the hope of getting as many supplies as possible to the Polish nationalists. In all, the three bomb groups dropped 1,284 containers of food, weapons, medicines, and supplies into Warsaw. Unfortunately, despite the low-altitude release, many parachuted containers drifted into German-controlled areas. Estimates were that only one-fourth of the material was delivered to the Poles. More supplies would have been delivered success-fully and the impact would have been far greater had the mission taken place sooner, when the Poles controlled more of the city. *I'll Be Seeing You* was hit by flak over War-saw and pulled out of formation with its number-four engine on fire. German fighters pounced on the wounded bomber, which exploded shortly thereafter. This B-17 was the only bomber lost in the mission to Warsaw. Two P-51s also were lost and nineteen B-17s suffered heavy damage. Another thirty bombers and three fighters were likewise damaged. Weather conditions, combined with Soviet political maneuverings, delayed another attempt until most of Warsaw was in German hands.

Only two of the ten-man crew were able to bail out of *I'll Be Seeing You*. Walter Shim-shock was not one of them. He died after serving in the air over Europe for just forty days, but he was a veteran of fifteen bombing missions. The telegram to his parents read: "The Secretary of War desires me to express his deep regret that your son Staff Sergeant Walter P. Shimshock has been reported missing in action." His family likely did not know at the time about the connection between their brave son's death and the Warsaw Uprising. Even to this day, the incident is not well known. When they did finally learn, they must have been proud of their son's contribution to their ancestral land of Poland.

I'll Be Seeing You went down near the village of Lomianki on the outskirts of Warsaw. German authorities ordered the eight crewmen buried in a collective grave. The Poles exhumed the bodies in 1946 and reinterred them in Powazki Cemetery. U.S. military authorities later removed the remains to the American military cemetery in Belgium. The remains of Walter Shimshock eventually were returned home at his mother's request and reinterred in Fort Snelling National Cemetery, section C-6, site 8406.

Long after the war, the Poles did not forget the efforts of those who came to their aid in the darkest of times. Shimshock has a street in Lomianki named after him, and the people of Lomianki built a monument to the American crewmen of *I'll Be Seeing You*. The monument has become a stopping place for American dignitaries. Marcus Shook, the radioman and one of the two surviving crew members of *I'll Be Seeing You*, participated with President George Bush in a memorial ceremony at Lomianki in 1987. This was in the time of Gorbachev's perestroika, a year before the Polish government legally recognized and began to negotiate with Lech Walesa's Solidarity movement and two years before the fall of the Berlin Wall. Vice President Al Gore paid his respects to the memorial in 1994 while in Poland for the fiftieth anniversary of the Warsaw Uprising. Minnesota Governor Tim Pawlenty paid his respects to the monument in June 2004 while on a trade mission to Poland. Walter Shimshock and the crew of *I'll Be Seeing You* are not forgotten.

Eldon Personette

Eldon Personette was born in Spencer Brook Township, Minnesota, in 1924. He was living in Cambridge in Isanti County when he enlisted in the service in July 1943 at the age of nineteen. He went overseas on September 3, 1944, and became part of the 701st Squadron, the 445th Bomb Group, based at Tibenham in East Anglia, England. Movie star (Captain) Jimmy Stewart served with the 445th Group.

Sergeant Eldon Personette became a waist gunner on Captain Tracey Ford's B-24 Liberator bomber. Personette made his first combat mission on October 7, 1944. The crew was in the air for eight hours to hit the motor-transport works at Kassel, Germany. They used five-hundred-pound and one-thousand-pound bombs to pummel the target, and mission results were declared "excellent." The crew flew every few days, taking part in six combat missions over Germany in October 1944.

After participating in a mission on a German air base at Hanau on November 10, the crew did not fly again for more than two weeks. They were assigned to join Group Mission 194 on November 26, 1944. Captain Ford was no longer the pilot, having been replaced by Second Lieutenant John Barringer. Eighth Air Force Command dispatched 1,137 bombers, accompanied by more than seven hundred fighters. Four hundred and six of those bombers dispatched were assigned the oil refinery at Misburg near Hanover, Germany.

Wing Wash, the paper for the Second Combat Bombardment Wing (to which the 445th Bomb Group belonged), wrote of that day:

> One of the great battles of the air war was fought over Germany today as the German Air Force opposed a relatively shallow penetration in greater strength than ever before! Before the hour long battle was finished, U.S. fighters had destroyed 114 enemy aircraft with a loss of only 14 to themselves and the bombers had accounted for another dozen Jerries.

Wing Wash reported that the 445th Bomb Group was to the low left of the lead and that, as a result, the group was the first to be hit by about twenty-five German fighters attacking low and from the rear. They shot down five bombers in that first pass.

> Lt. Barringer of the 701st Squadron and his crew were leading the "slot" element—low in the center and slightly to the rear within his squadron which, in turn, was the low left squadron of the 445th Group formation. They were therefore the first targeted by the Germans' orchestrated fighter attack. Their ship was seen to immediately drop from the formation, going into a slow spin to the left.

The plane crashed and exploded upon impact with all nine crew members aboard. Personette's life was over at the age of twenty years. Nearly one hundred American men were killed or missing in action on that single mission against the Misburg oil refinery. Despite the fierce resistance, the results of the attack were officially reported as "good."

Eldon Personette's remains were returned home and reinterred in Fort Snelling National Cemetery on April 26, 1950, in section C-9, grave site 9129.

The magnitude of the Eighth Army Air Force effort and sacrifice over Germany is difficult to convey. This colossal armada of airpower played a key role in winning the war with Nazi Germany. The price was huge. The men of the Mighty Eighth suffered more than forty-seven thousand casualties, including more than twenty-six thousand deaths. Another twenty-one thousand became German POWs. More than sixty-eight hundred B-17s and B-24s and thirty-seven hundred fighters (P-47s, P-38s, and P-51s) went down. Of course, a vast support group on the ground, men and women both in Europe and back in the United States, kept the war machine going. It truly was an organizational effort of immense proportions.

Chapter 4

Normandy Invasion

Denzil Carty

Americans of all races and creeds joined in the effort to defeat totalitarianism. African Americans, treated as second-class citizens in their own nation, were for the most part assigned to labor details. Men who were prepared to fight and die for their country were judged inferior as soldiers on the basis of their skin color. Their labors were difficult and exhausting, and there were those who resented the nature of their duties, yet they performed work critical to victory in the war. The movement of supplies across the ocean and through the French seaports, for instance, was one of the single most important efforts in the defeat of Nazi Germany. Chaplains, such as Denzil Carty and others like him, worked tirelessly to buoy the spirits of the men with whom they served.

Denzil Carty was born in 1904 in the British West Indies. He immigrated to New York City, where he attended Washington Heights Evening High School and graduated as valedictorian. He went to work for the Tuberculosis Association in New York City. Carty graduated from the Episcopal Church's General Theological Seminary in Manhattan with a bachelor of divinity degree in 1934. He was ordained a priest in the Episcopal Church and served three African American parishes in New York in the late 1930s and early 1940s. He likely came into contact with Roy Wilkins, a 1923 graduate of the University of Minnesota, who worked at the National Association for the Advancement of Colored People (NAACP) in Harlem and was editor of its national magazine *Crisis*.

Reverend Carty entered the military service on January 2, 1944, and was commissioned a first lieutenant. He became a chaplain with headquarters of the 512th Port

Reverend Denzil Carty (standing, center), shown here with a young Dr. Martin Luther King Jr. in St. Paul during the Montgomery, Alabama, bus boycott. Carty became active in St. Paul as a civil rights leader after serving as a chaplain and captain in World War II. Photograph courtesy of the *Minneapolis Spokesman-Recorder*.

Battalion and shipped over to England with his unit on April 7, 1944. He later was promoted to captain.

The Allies had been gathering strength in England since late 1943 to prepare for the colossal invasion of Hitler's Fortress Europe. Immense quantities of supplies and vast numbers of troops crossed the Atlantic Ocean in the face of German U-boat attacks. This effort accelerated in early 1944 in anticipation of the June landings at Normandy. Much of the muscle that made this possible was African American. The Port of Southampton, England, for example, handled more ships and tonnage between D-Day and VE Day than any other port in the world during that period. Twenty-five of the twenty-seven port companies at Southampton were African American.

The inherent danger of working on port detail was driven home on July 17, 1944. Two Liberty ships at Port Chicago, California, near San Francisco blew up as they were being loaded with bombs and ammunition. Three hundred and twenty sailors lost their lives, including more than two hundred African Americans. Within two weeks of the tragedy, surviving members of the port battalion were ordered to commence loading ships. They refused. The men were tried for mutiny, found guilty, and sentenced to prison. They were not released until January 1946.

The great majority of African American service units in World War II were assigned to ports, base sections, and supply depots. More than 350,000 African American soldiers were stationed in the United States and almost as many overseas in March 1944. Nearly half a million African Americans were overseas by December 1944 and fewer than 250,000 remained stateside as the Allies pressed into Germany. Seven hundred thousand African Americans were in the service of their nation by the end of the war. There was racial friction among American troops. The command emphasized the importance of carefully controlling this situation. The role played by officers, including chaplains, in managing this situation should not be underestimated.

Denzil Carty returned to the United States in September 1945. He was discharged from the service in January 1946 at Camp Llauche, Louisiana. He married his wife, Sylvia, in 1946 and earned a master's degree in clinical psychology from Wayne State University in Detroit. Carty moved to St. Paul, Minnesota, in 1950 to be rector of St. Philip's Episcopal Church. He became active in the civil rights movement, often serving as a spokesperson for the African American community. Reverend Carty preached, "The only thing worth doing is helping others.... You must do it selflessly, with your whole heart and soul." His broad involvement in the community included the Fair Employment Practices Commission, NAACP, St. Paul Urban Coalition, St. Paul Urban League, St. Paul Housing and Redevelopment Authority, the St. Paul and

Artillery equipment being loaded onto LCTs (landing craft tanks) at an English port in preparation for the Normandy invasion. Nearly half a million African Americans served overseas during World War II. Most were given noncombat assignments. Many served in port battalions and played an important role loading and unloading critical supplies for the war effort. Photograph courtesy of the U.S. Army.

Minneapolis councils on human and civil rights, and the St. Paul Opportunities and Industrialization Center.

A talk that Reverend Carty gave in 1964 offers insight into his direct style. He noted in "The Religious Basis of Equality in Education" that "there is no other arena left in which the problem of race can be discussed calmly and rationally, but that of religion." He chided those who worked to help blacks in the South but did little at home. Carty defiantly told his listeners, "In Birmingham so in Minnesota. Don't you dare speak of equality" and warned that "anything that tends to unnecessarily separate mankind is sinful." He admonished those who held to the "half-truth" that substandard schools were due in part to the neighborhoods in which they were situated and insisted they "admit that segregated neighborhoods have met with our blessing, because either consciously or unconsciously we have felt that certain of God's creatures were not worthy to be our neighbors." This was the fire that earned Reverend Carty the respect of so many in the Twin Cities community.

Reverend Carty's postwar efforts overshadowed the important role he had played as a citizen-soldier in the war to defend democracy. He was a member of the Attucks-Brooks American Legion Post 606 in St. Paul for many years.

He retired as rector of St. Philip's on June 10, 1975, after twenty-five years of service. He died just three months later on August 24. Denzil Carty's remains lie in section T, grave site 1655, at Fort Snelling National Cemetery.

Manford Jerome Christofferson

Although Manford Jerome Christofferson grew up in St. Paul, his Norwegian American family retained close ties to the family homestead in western Minnesota. Christofferson joined the Minnesota National Guard's 109th Observation Squadron in September 1940 at the age of twenty-five; 109 was the number designation allocated to support units of the Thirty-fourth Division during World War I. The 109th was the first state Guard aviation unit to be formed anywhere in the nation. They flew old army biplanes out of Holman Field in St. Paul.

When the United States abruptly entered the Second World War in December 1941, the army quickly deployed the 109th Observation Squadron to England aboard the ocean liner *Queen Elizabeth*. The 109th flew dangerous low-level photo reconnaissance missions over Nazi-occupied France. The squadron flew British Spitfires at first and later American-made P-51 Mustangs. The unit became known as the "Looker Squadron" for their duties, and they adopted the famous cartoon character Kilroy peeking over a fence as their mascot. Perhaps the most important role of the 109th involved photo recon missions in preparation for the June 1944 landings at Normandy.

Manny "Chris" Christofferson was an aircraft mechanic. These unsung heroes were an integral part of the American war machine. He and many others like him kept American warplanes in the sky in the best possible condition. He provided entertainment for his comrades in the off-hours by playing tunes on his accordion. The 109th and many other aviation units moved to France after the Allies broke out of the Normandy beachhead. The recon squadrons stayed close behind the front lines, flying recon missions to provide valuable intelligence to the Allied command. Men like Tech

The Republic P-47 Thunderbolt, known as "the Jug," was a reliable and extremely rugged plane, which endeared it to pilots such as Captain Thomas McGovern. Photograph courtesy of the U.S. Air Force.

Sergeant Manny Christofferson kept the Mustangs in the air, despite inclement weather. The 109th finished the war with more than one thousand completed combat operations, winning thirty-four Air Medals and more than two hundred Oak Leaf Clusters.

Christofferson returned home after the war, married, and raised a family. He served as a member of the Minnesota National Guard until his retirement in 1973. In his later years he entered the Minnesota Veterans Home and spent five years as a resident until his passing in 1992. His remains lie in section 15, grave site 3070, at Fort Snelling National Cemetery.

Thomas T. McGovern

In the two months before D-Day, Allied forces savagely pounded the coastal defenses and roads and rail centers to the rear. More than two thousand fighters and fighter-bombers, along with seven hundred light and medium bombers, made up an immense and invincible air armada. The fighter-bombers proved to be particularly effective in executing precision attacks, as well as evading Luftwaffe pursuit.

Captain Thomas McGovern participated in those tactical missions leading up to June 6, 1944, and was in the air nearly continuously on D-Day in his P-47 Thunderbolt over the beaches of Normandy. McGovern might have seemed an unlikely warrior to some. The St. Paul, Minnesota, native was a musician well known throughout the Twin Cities before the war. He was an accomplished piano player, orchestra leader, and arranger. He was the musical director for the Dorothy Lewis ice show, and helped write the "Aquatennial Swing" for that annual summer festival in Minneapolis.

After enlisting, McGovern became a flight commander of a fighter-bomber group of the Ninth Tactical Air Force. He completed his one-hundredth mission by October 1944. He finished the war with four Bronze Stars and an Air Medal with eleven Oak Leaf Clusters.

Captain Thomas McGovern died in 1982. He is buried in section W, grave site 1630, at Fort Snelling National Cemetery.

George Ziemski

> Individuals had to be capable of fighting at once against any opposition they met on landing. Although every effort was being made to develop the communications and techniques to permit battalions, companies, and platoons to organize promptly, we had to train our individuals to fight for hours and days, if necessary, without being part of a formal organization. . . . we sought to train the Paratroopers to the highest peak of individual pride and skill.
>
> — *General James Gavin, commanding the Eighty-second Airborne Division*

Such wisdom and training gave American paratroopers the edge they needed to survive and to achieve their assigned objectives time and again. George Ziemski of St. Paul, Minnesota, was drafted in April 1942 and volunteered for the Airborne Division with four of his buddies from basic training. His height of six feet four inches should have disqualified him for the paratroops, but he scrunched down and managed to get in. Ziemski finished jump school and was assigned to Company F, 505th PIR (Parachute Infantry Regiment) of the Eighty-second Airborne Division. General Matthew Ridgway commanded the Eighty-second and Colonel James Gavin commanded the 505th PIR. Ziemski recalled in later years, "When you go to parachute school, they instill in your mind that you are the greatest that ever was and nothing can stop you. They instilled that in us and everybody believed it."

Private George Ziemski of the Eighty-second Airborne jumped into Ste. Mère Eglise with his comrades on the early morning of D-Day. Photograph courtesy of the George Ziemski family.

Paratroopers preparing to jump. Photograph courtesy of the Library of Congress, Prints and Photographs Division, FSA-OWI Collection, LC-USW33-000389-ZC DLC.

Private Ziemski was stationed in North Africa in May 1943. The division traveled across the Atlantic by troopship, landed at Casablanca, and then trucked to Tunisia. Their first combat jump on July 9, 1943, was part of the invasion of Sicily. The jump was successful as the paratroopers seized an airfield and held it until the First Infantry Division linked up with them. Ziemski's next combat jump with the Eighty-second was at night. The U.S. Fifth Army was stalled at Salerno beachhead in southern Italy. The 504th Regiment jumped on the night of September 13 and the 505th Regiment on the next night. The gritty paratroopers stopped a German counterattack intended to push the Americans into the sea. The Eighty-second fought its way to Naples alongside the Fifth Army before being pulled back to England.

The Eighty-second Airborne Division boarded C-47s on the night of June 5 to prepare to jump into Normandy as a prelude to the landings to commence the following morning. It took 378 C-47s to transport the 505th Regiment alone—one "stick" of paratroopers per plane. The paratroopers were loaded down, there being a real possibility that they might be isolated for days before lining up with infantry from the beach. Each man carried more than one hundred pounds of gear and rations. The weather was rough and the intense flak even worse. A red light inside the plane signaled the paratroopers that they were approaching the drop zone. Each man rose and lined up, hooked his static line on the overhead steel cable, and inspected the lines of the man in front of him. When the green light came on, the men jumped one by one into the darkness amid bursts of flak. The Eighty-second Division's first objective was to take the crossroads town of Ste. Mère Eglise, inland from Utah Beach. Their second objective was to prevent German troops from rushing to reinforce the beach.

Some of the Airborne Division landed in proximity to German units and were killed as they touched ground. Others drowned. After he landed, Ziemski joined fairly easily with about thirty other paratroopers, as most of the Second Battalion landed in the assigned target zone. The Americans seized Ste. Mère Eglise from local German forces at about four o'clock that morning, making it the first French town to be liberated. The paratroopers set up a perimeter and awaited the German counterattack. Ziemski's platoon was assigned to defend the north end of town. They took up position behind a stone wall and waited for dawn. The Germans counterattacked throughout the day with no success. The infantry from the beach linked up with the paratroopers at Ste. Mère Eglise and solidified the position. The 505th Regiment went on the offensive. Only 27 of 120 of Ziemski's company were free of wounds or injury by the time the men were relieved from frontline duty on July 8.

Ziemski made his fourth combat jump in Operation Marketgarden in Holland on September 17, 1944. The casualties were severe during the disastrous mission. Ziemski suffered his first wound of the war, the result of an exploding German tank shell. He recovered and rushed back to join his unit.

George Ziemski finished the war as a staff sergeant. He returned home to St. Paul, where he lived until his death on June 22, 2002. He is buried in section 16, grave site 460, at Fort Snelling National Cemetery.

Charles H. Parker

We were lowered down into the wild waters of the English Channel in our LCAs— Landing Craft Assault boats—about 10 or 12 miles away from Omaha Beach.... We were wet, shaking with chill and anticipation.... The seasickness was so bad that vomit covered the bottoms of many of the boats. . . . Machine gun fire, mortars and 88 artillery shells were coming in all around us. . . . Whole boatloads were blown up before they even hit the beach. . . . There were bodies laying all over the beach. There were bodies still alive in the water washing back and forth with the tide's waves. . . . We had no idea it was going to be this bad.

So wrote Charley "Ace" Parker of the landings at Omaha Beach on D-Day, June 6, 1944.

Parker was born in Hecla, South Dakota, in 1919, the son of a country doctor. He entered the service in 1941 and subsequently volunteered for the Army Rangers. In *Lead the Way,* Henry Glassman writes, "Men of the Rangers were average men, but with above average spirit." That description fit Parker. Army ground forces formed the Fifth Ranger Battalion in September 1943 as part of a special assault force for Operation Overlord, the Normandy landings. The battalion underwent intense physical conditioning and combat training before shipping out to Great Britain in January 1944. Once overseas, the battalion began amphibious and cliff training on a stretch of Scottish coast that matched the coastline of Normandy.

Military planners were focused on sending U.S. Army Rangers against the German gun emplacements at Le Pointe du Hoc, four miles west of the landing site code-named Omaha Beach. The Pointe du Hoc promontory afforded a sweeping killing field over the landing zone. It was necessary to take out these gun emplacements for the invasion to have any chance of success, and there was no certainty that naval and air bombardment could destroy the guns. At the same time, the steep cliffs at Pointe du Hoc made a successful infantry assault nearly impossible. This was an assignment for which the Rangers had trained.

First Lieutenant Charley "Ace" Parker led his Company A of the Fifth Ranger Infantry Battalion onto the sands of Omaha Beach on D-Day. They landed alongside the Twenty-ninth Division, which would cover itself with the mantle of glory as it fought its way across France and into Germany. During those critical early moments while pinned on the beach by enemy fire, Brigadier General Norman Cota, assistant division commander of the Twenty-ninth Infantry Division, told Lieutenant Colonel Max Schneider, commanding the Fifth Ranger Battalion, "Rangers, lead the way!" They did, and the phrase became the Rangers' official motto.

Parker's Company A landed on the left flank of the battalion. Units became confused and disorganized in the chaos on Omaha Beach. Lieutenant Parker managed to gather his company and get his squads in order. He kept in mind what he had learned in Ranger training: "To live, keep moving. If you stop, you may die." He had respon-

First Lieutenant Charles "Ace" Parker and the men of Company A, Fifth Ranger Battalion, loading for the invasion of Normandy. Photograph courtesy of Katherine Parker.

sibility for the lives of seventy-five men and he had a specific objective: to get off the beach and secure Pointe du Hoc.

The GIs who survived the landing huddled against a rock wall at the far edge of Omaha Beach, pinned down by enemy fire from positions above. Elaborate barbed-wire barriers laid by the Germans lined the entire beach and prevented advance. The Germans had spent years preparing the terrain and laying down machine-gun killing zones. The Americans began to organize. Special teams pushed bangalores—long torpedo charges—up to the barbed wire and blasted small holes, often one man wide. Columns of soldiers, one man at a time, scrambled through the openings into the minefield below the bluff. It was the only way out from the death and destruction on the open beach. The smoke from the artillery of both sides allowed some cover for the advancing Rangers and infantrymen.

The coxswains who brought Lieutenant Colonel James Rudder and three companies of the Second Battalion ashore landed them at the wrong place on Omaha Beach. The assigned mission of the Fifth Battalion and two other companies of the Second Battalion was to follow Rudder's force and climb the cliff if Rudder secured Pointe du Hoc, or move inland and swing around behind to take the point if they received no signal that it was secure. In the chaos of that bloody day, the Fifth Battalion was already moving inland, having received no signal by the time Rudder and his brave men made it to the base of Pointe du Hoc.

Lieutenant Parker led Company A up and over the bluff and to the edge of an open field, where they took some casualties from sniper fire. He led his men around the field by leading them single file along a three-foot-deep drainage ditch. Progress was slow as he used only hand signals to escape notice by the enemy. Parker and his men ultimately reached the first rendezvous, an inland chateau. Eight companies of Rangers were to rendezvous there, a total of 560 men. Parker had only twenty-three men of his company with him when they arrived at the chateau, and no other Rangers arrived at the rendezvous point. He remained focused on keeping moving, "so we took off." They worked their way through narrow lanes between thick, overgrown hedgerows, and exchanged periodic firefights with pockets of German soldiers. The small band of Rangers met with increasing resistance as they moved inland. When they realized they were surrounded, they fell back one hundred yards on the run. Parker led a patrol through enemy-controlled territory the next morning and located the rest of his battalion. His small command had penetrated farther inland than any other unit on D-Day.

D-Day was one of the most important days in U.S. military history. The Allies gained a foothold on the Normandy beaches and held on against counterattacks while reinforcements arrived. The Allies ultimately broke out of Normandy and in time drove across France toward Germany after the sacrifice of many good men.

First Lieutenant Charles H. Parker was promoted to captain and awarded the Distinguished Service Cross for extraordinary heroism in action on June 6, 7, and 8, 1944, in the Vierville-sur-Mer and Le Pointe du Hoc area. The citation reads:

> Lieutenant Parker led his company up the beach against heavy enemy rifle, machine gun and artillery fire. Once past the beach he reorganized and continued inland. During this advance numerous groups of enemy resistance were encountered. Through his personal bravery and sound leadership this resistance was overcome.

Like so many heroes of the "greatest generation," Parker wrote his parents to say he was not sure he deserved the medal. The men who served under him were certain.

First Lieutenant Charles Parker being awarded the Distinguished Service Cross for his leadership and heroism on D-Day. Photograph courtesy of Katherine Parker.

Staff Sergeant Wilbur Ingalls said, "I don't believe there was a better officer than Ace Parker. . . . He was fair, coolheaded, and down-to-earth. He was dedicated and he felt responsibility real strong. He cared about his men. He was just the kind of guy you followed." The Rangers, in following Parker, helped win the war and defend freedom and democracy. Charles Parker died in 1999 and is buried in section 6-C, grave site 417, at Fort Snelling National Cemetery.

Bernard M. Pepper

Bernard Pepper, a native of Minneapolis, entered the service in August 1942. The twenty-eight-year-old former shipping clerk volunteered for Ranger school after completing basic training. Pepper was a powerfully built man, standing six feet tall and weighing 220 pounds.

The U.S. Army created the Second and Fifth Ranger Battalions in preparation for the invasion of Hitler's Fortress Europe. The specific purpose of the Ranger battalions was to secure key road junctions and other strategic positions that were critical to the advance of the Allied landing forces off the beach. Pepper and his fellow Rangers underwent four months of strenuous training at Tullahoma, Tennessee. A Ranger wrote after the war of "our first Company Commander, Lt. Pepper" during training at Tullahoma and how Pepper "led the men of our company and jumped right into deep water. It was then it became apparent that he couldn't swim at all and they fished him out." The Rangers shipped out to England in January 1944 and the training continued on the other side of the Atlantic. Two months were dedicated to commando training in Scotland, followed by study and exercises at the Assault Training Center and rigorous cliff training at Swanage on the southern coast of England. Bernard Pepper was a lieutenant with Company B, Fifth Ranger Battalion, on the eve of the landings at Normandy.

Concentrated German firepower cut to pieces the first wave of Rangers—two companies of Second Battalion—on Omaha Beach on D-Day. The Fifth Battalion commander ordered the landing boats one mile east and then sent the entire Fifth Ranger Battalion ashore. The men of the Fifth re-formed behind the seawall and prepared for their first assault. The Rangers were ordered to infiltrate the German position and create deadly havoc as the Twenty-ninth Infantry Division came ashore. Squads and platoons made small gains here and there with other units pouring into the gaps that opened. Heroic individuals risked their lives to allow an opportunity for breakthrough, and others led men forward. Action reports indicate that Company B led the battalion inland through several enemy strongholds to a position not far from

Lieutenant Bernard Pepper led a company of Rangers ashore on D-Day and across Europe to final victory. Photograph courtesy of the Minneapolis Public Library, Minneapolis Collection.

its objective, Vierville-sur-Mer. The Fifth Rangers then took the little town, securing their right flank of the beachhead about a mile from shore. Lieutenant Bernard Pepper was awarded the Silver Star for his gallantry and heroism on June 6, 1944.

Companies B and E led the attack on Grandcamp-les-Bains on D-Day plus two. Several weeks of leave followed, most of which was occupied with further training. The Fifth Ranger Battalion returned to action at the end of August. The Allied objective was the Port of Brest, ringed by a complex of forts. The Fifth Ranger Battalion's first assignment was Fort Toulbrouch. The fighting was intense. A German counterattack necessitated committing the battalion reserve to stop the advance. Company B finally took the fort with the tactical support of the Ninth Army Air Force's P-47s. The Rangers followed just twenty yards behind the strafing runs and took the fort within minutes after the last pass. The fierce and bloody fight for Brest and the Le Conquet Peninsula lasted until September 18. Pepper was wounded on September 16, for which he was awarded the Purple Heart.

The Fifth Rangers were attached to General George Patton's Sixth Cavalry Group for the Saar Campaign in November–December 1944. The Fifth again found themselves in heavy fighting. Patrols led to contact with more aggressive patrols followed by serious combat action. In his autobiography, Victor Miller wrote of his Company E commander ordering him to make his way through the woods to locate Company B and their flank. Miller came across Lieutenant Pepper, Company B's commanding officer, who briefed him on the situation at hand. Company B distinguished itself on a raid on December 21, killing and wounding a large number of German soldiers and capturing a high-ranking officer for interrogation.

Late February was the time scheduled for the Fifth Rangers' perhaps last significant operation of the war. The Fifth Rangers crossed a footbridge over the Saar River under cover of darkness and made their way through German lines to a crossroad three miles beyond. Their orders were to hold the position for two days until an armored division broke through to them. The two-day mission became a desperate nine-day struggle to hold on and survive. The battalion suffered 47 percent casualties.

Bernard Pepper ended the war with the rank of captain. He had cheated death many times in the service of his country and distinguished himself. It was difficult for him to return home to his previous job as a shipping clerk, so he stayed in the army. Captain Pepper was serving with the First Cavalry Division in the occupation of Japan when North Korea invaded South Korea in 1950. The First Cavalry was part of the U.S. Eighth Army that was pieced together to stem the advancing North Korean army until reinforcements moved from the States. The Eighth Army fell back with great losses into the Pusan/Naktong Perimeter against overwhelming odds but managed to hold out against a series of fierce offensives. When General MacArthur's brilliant landing in the north at Inchon surprised the North Koreans, the Eighth Army broke out of the Naktong Perimeter on September 16 and began driving out the North Koreans. Bernard Pepper gave his life for his country on September 22, 1950, during this drive.

His remains were buried at Fort Snelling National Cemetery one year later on September 24 in section B, grave site 134-A.

Rex Kelsey

> There was a corpsman for each platoon. They didn't carry weapons, just little medical kits: morphine syrettes to inject subcutaneously, sulfa packs, bandages and gauze pads to stem the bleeding or plug a chest wound. Brave, brave guys doing their job under fire. A lot of them were wounded and killed.
>
> — *Dr. Joseph C. Flynn*

Rex Kelsey of Aitkin, Minnesota, was a private serving with Company B of the 104th Medical Battalion of the Twenty-ninth Division. Kelsey was not quite twenty-two years old when he entered the service on July 2, 1943. He went overseas in December of that year. The 104th consisted of a great many draftees from all over the United States.

Kelsey landed with the Twenty-ninth Division on Omaha Beach on June 6, 1944. The Twenty-ninth and the First Divisions were expected to carry out a frontal assault across an open beach against well-entrenched positions. They somehow succeeded, but the cost in human life was horrific. Each of the Twenty-ninth's three infantry regiments had an independent medical detachment to care for its wounded on the front line. Company B was assigned to the 116th Regimental Combat Team. Those who survived the landing were stunned and shaken and surrounded by dead men. All semblance of order was lost for a time until individual leaders stepped forth to regain control. The soldiers lay only barely protected by the slightest cover from enemy machine-gun fire while artillery and mortar shells rained down on them.

The Twenty-ninth Division's beachhead was only a few hundred yards deep by midafternoon. The 116th Regiment lost one-third of its men in the first few hours. Some rifle companies ceased to exist. Medics like Private Kelsey did all they could to tend to the wounded while under constant fire. Few medics were decorated for heroism as so many brave deeds were done that day. There were also few survivors to recount the bravery for citations.

Arnold Levin, a comrade of Kelsey's in Company B, wrote of the landings:

> We landed in the a.m. of 6 Jun with elements of the 116th RCT. Nobody landed with the designated element since the situation was so chaotic. Somehow we got the job done. . . . we were not armed and we did not have red crosses on our helmets since that made you a target. . . . For the D-Day landing our unit was split into about 10

Medics like Private Rex Kelsey risked their lives throughout each day of action, constantly moving into vulnerable positions to offer aid to and remove the wounded. Photograph from Heritage Photographs.

units among the infantry units for more support.... Our mission was to give medical support and locate a site for a station in the beach and we didn't get to do either. While later that night trying to site a station we ran into an ambush when seven of our party of 12 was taken prisoner.

Rex Kelsey survived the Normandy landings and the brutal five-week campaign to reach St. Lo. The Twenty-ninth moved south to attack the heavily fortified city of Brest, which did not fall until September 1944. The Twenty-ninth joined the Allied advance into Germany, officially referred to as the Rhineland Campaign (September 15, 1944, to March 21, 1945). November was a particularly costly month for the Twenty-ninth Division. The division suffered 2,099 casualties, including nearly 400 killed. Private Kelsey was killed in action on November 22, 1944, near Julich, Germany. Arnold Levin wrote:

> Kelsey was a member of Co. B, 104th Med Bn when he was killed. The after-action report for 1944 shows he was killed during the battle for Julich—one other member of our unit was wounded but later died as a result of those wounds.... He was probably evacuating wounded when the incident occurred.... We were part of the 116th RCT and took care of three battalions. There were medical personnel at the Bn Aid Station including an M.D. We evacuated by vehicle (jeep and ambulance) from access points near the aid station to our station where the primary job was TRIAGE (sorting as to severity of wounds).... Usually casualties at the point of battle are treated by aid men assigned to each unit of the infantry regiment and evacuated from access points by whoever is around to help. We traveled as part of the infantry from 6 Jun 44 to 8 May 45—we didn't operate in the rear.

Rex Kelsey's remains were transferred home after the war and lie in section C-3, grave site 7805, at Fort Snelling National Cemetery.

Donn R. Driver

The fragile lives of the wounded men scattered across Omaha Beach hung in the balance. Medics could do only so much; doctors were needed. Tending the wounded brought with it the constant risk of being killed by a sniper bullet or machine-gun strafe. One surgeon wrote, "In Normandy we saw tremendous trauma—awful wounds. We were taking the shrapnel—massive pieces of metal—out of people's hips and chests and there were many compound fractures.... up there, under fire, was where you learned about trauma."

Donn Driver graduated from St. Louis Park High School and Hamline University. After graduating from medical school, he joined the Army Reserve in Minneapolis in 1939 as a medical officer with the rank of first lieutenant. The army called him to active duty in early 1941. He laughingly related to the family that he would be gone "for one year, and then I came staggering home five years later." Driver went overseas with his medical detachment in December 1943. They trained for the invasion of Normandy and moved to the marshalling area. The detachment was assigned to the 457th Anti-Aircraft Artillery Battalion of the Twenty-ninth Division, the leading elements of which were among the first units to hit Omaha Beach on the morning of D-Day. The AAA battalion loaded onto an LCT—a landing craft tank—on June 6 with the plan to hit the beach twelve hours into D-Day. However, progress on the beachhead was behind schedule. Driver recalled, "The Germans were so entrenched on the bluffs that we had to send the navy up and down the coast and knock out those gun emplacements with their heavy guns or we would have never gotten ashore. We landed that night." The operator of the LCT was an experienced Brit who had taken part in the landings on Sicily, Driver recalled: "He got us right on the beach. I was in my 2 1/2 ton truck, we barely got our tires wet." The medical detachment got to the top of the bluff and spent the first night in France in foxholes.

A soldier of the 457th wrote, "Life for the Battalion in the Beach area never settled down to being merely routine living; incidents which occurred almost daily were too varied to fit one pattern." Military surgeons in the war zone work under tremendous pressure to save lives and there is little time to rest. One surgeon wrote, "The first doctors were at the battalion aid stations. They always looked tired and haggard."

Captain Driver settled into his bedroll, sheltered under a tree for cover from rain, and fell into a deep sleep. The 457th batteries were active that night of June 13 from midnight until four in the morning. German Junker JU 88s, fast dive-bombers with excellent night-flight capabilities, constantly harassed the beach and vicinity to disrupt the movement inland of men and supplies. Battery B shot down a JU 88 that night. The plane passed directly over the unit, literally breaking off the tops of trees, before crashing nearby. An officer awakened Driver "and told me to get out of there in a hurry. Seems like a German plane had jettisoned a canister and had gone right through the tree above me and landed just a few feet from me. Fortunately it didn't detonate. It was a block buster, a 2-kilo bomb." The "bomb" turned out to be packed with ammunition for nearby German troops. The nightly German air raids increased in intensity. A bomb exploded near the battery command post and severely wounded a soldier on

Captain Donn Driver (standing) served as battalion surgeon from D-Day until the German surrender. The man on the cycle was a German POW. Photograph courtesy of the Driver family.

June 15. There were six attacks on the night of June 16. Battery B shot down its share of planes, but also incurred continual losses of men.

Battalion surgeon Captain Driver and his colleague, Captain Roswell S. Mills, rushed to answer an urgent call for help from Battery D on the evening of June 20. Three soldiers from an adjacent AAA unit had wandered into a minefield—they were everywhere—and were severely wounded when they detonated a mine. The two surgeons and aid man Ralph Bailey carefully worked their way through the minefield for a distance of fifty yards. They reached the men, finding only one still living. They gave him medical aid and evacuated him.

Driver and his detachment were transferred to Patton's Third Army and took part in the breakout and subsequent drive across France at the end of July 1944. They did not stop until reaching the Saar region, at which point Patton could get no more fuel for his tanks. Driver saw action in the Battle of the Bulge and afterward was transferred to the Forty-fourth Armored Infantry Regiment of the Sixth Armored Division as battalion surgeon. He wrote:

We had aid men with troops up front. They would do whatever they could if anybody was injured and then they would evacuate them back to the battalion Aid Station. Then we would do what we could do, which wasn't very much, stabilize them and then evacuate them further back.

Driver was later transferred to the 104th Evac Hospital. He worked twelve-hour shifts in the triage area, evaluating casualties and deciding priorities. He returned home in September 1945. He remained in the service for many years, ultimately achieving the rank of brigadier general. He became commanding general of the 5501 U.S. Army Hospital, headquartered at Fort Snelling. Donn Driver passed away on November 26, 2002, at the age of eighty-seven. His remains lie in section 5, grave site 49, at Fort Snelling National Cemetery.

Robert D. Hanson

The Group was just reassembling and starting to set course for home after the first dogfight. My wingman, Lt. Zierlein, and I were sitting low at seven o'clock to the Group leader. I turned to the left to join Yellow Leader (Major Hedlund) and his wingman, who were flying alone, wide on the left. As I started to pull up on Major Hedlund's right wing, I saw three ME-109s pulling in at six o'clock level to him. I called a break and then followed the third ME-109, who pulled up to the right and over us, at which time I fired one burst at him. I fired another as my wingman and I followed a third E/A [Enemy Aircraft] down toward the deck on a course of approximately 150 degrees. He was right on the deck, going along a little river valley. We were slowly pulling up on him when I noticed he was leaving a trail of smoke—although I don't remember having seen any strikes up to then. I could not see flames or holes. We followed him along the deck for approximately four minutes. I was closing with him from directly behind. I fired burst after burst, with range approximately 300 yards closing to fifty yards. After I had almost run into him and fired a burst point blank, he pulled up and jettisoned his canopy. I pulled out to the left and just as I looked back, pilot was standing up in the cockpit . . . the pilot bailed out . . . landed in the woods nearby.

The account of combat by Lieutenant Robert D. Hanson of the 428th Fighter Squadron was part of the daily life of a fighter pilot over Europe in the months following the invasion at Normandy. This particular action took place on July 18, 1944, over France. The published history of the 428th states that the squadron came of age in July, the month after the Normandy landings, noting, "Unquestionably, July 18 was the day, of all days, that it happened." The mission targeted several railroad lines east and south of Evreux, France. One specific objective was a critical railroad bridge at Mercey, which had survived several aerial bombings and fighter-bomber missions. The original plan was for each of the group's three squadrons to split off for their assigned targets. However, the squadron controller advised that the Germans were vectoring a large number of fighters into their target area. The group flew en masse for the bridge at Mercey. Thirty German FW-190s flew out of the sun at the formation. There were dogfights across the sky. Just as the 474th Fighter Group seemed to get the upper hand, a second formation of FW-190s and ME-109s appeared. The determined Americans, most of them in only their third month of combat, prevailed. Their results for the day consisted of four enemy aircraft destroyed, another three likely destroyed, and six others damaged. The squadron also hit its ground target.

Robert D. Hanson of Montevideo, Minnesota, was one of the original pilots of the 428th Fighter Squadron formed for the invasion and retaking of Europe. The squadron originally based out of Warmwell, England. Their first mission over Europe was a fighter sweep on May 1, 1944. The squadron saw no enemy aircraft until their eighth mission, and that was off in the distance as an ME-109 shot down a U.S. bomber. May was a difficult time, waiting word of the D-Day invasion and anticipating a major confrontation with the vaunted Luftwaffe. The squadron flew its first combat mission alone on May 11. The flak was the worst yet encountered. Bob Hanson's P-38 took some hits, although he was able to keep flying. The second mission of that day finally encountered and engaged German aircraft. The pace picked up. German bombers hit the squadron's airfield three times in one twenty-four-hour period late in May.

The 428th flew tactical support missions throughout the early days of the invasion landings. The P-38 was well suited for bombing and strafing targets. While there was little interference from the Germans in the air, ground fire was a constant threat. Hanson took part in mission number thirty-three on June 7, in which the 428th destroyed a highway bridge at Carquebut. Their success hindered the movement forward of the German counterattack against elements of the Eighty-second Airborne holding that town. The following day's mission was a dive-bombing against six coastal guns at Pointe de Barfleur on the Cherbourg Peninsula. The P-38s released bombs from twenty-five hundred feet to fifteen hundred feet as they strafed on the way into the target. All six guns were hit. Lieutenant Hanson scored a direct hit and a near miss on locomotives on mission number forty, June 12, 1944. He led Yellow Flight the next day on mission number forty-one and the squadron commander recorded that he "did a top-notch job." The flight tallied quite a score along a rail line the next day. The pace during those days just after the invasion was hectic, but the pilots knew what was in the balance and flew in all kinds of weather.

The Lockheed P-38 Lightning—the "Forked-Tail Devil"—was a versatile fighter-bomber. Lieutenant Robert Hanson saw extensive combat action in a P-38 over France and Germany. Photograph courtesy of the U.S. Air Force.

The 428th moved across the English Channel in August 1944 to base operations out of Normandy. Hanson was leading squadron missions by the beginning of November. He headed home in December on a thirty-day leave and was in the States when word came of the massive German counterattack in the Ardennes Forest, which became known as the Battle of the Bulge. He returned with the rank of captain in the position of assistant operations officer for the squadron. He continued to fly his P-38 and take part in the destruction of the German infrastructure, strafing and bombing bridges, railroad tracks, river barges, and defensive gun positions. The 428th supported the American First Army's crossing of the Rhine, one of the major operations of the war.

The 474th Fighter Group was the first P-38 group to join the Seventieth Fighter Wing of the IX Tactical Air Command of the Ninth Air Force in April 1944. The 474th flew P-38 Lightnings throughout the war and was the only fighter group in northern Europe still flying P-38s at the end of the war. The men of the 474th considered themselves fortunate.

The 428th Fighter Squadron in which Bob Hanson flew lost many pilots through the course of the war. Hanson's own wingman was shot down and killed on March 2 as the war in Europe neared its end. The squadron lost two officers on that particular mission. Hanson survived the war as one of the 428th Squadron's original officers. He returned home to Minnesota after the war, where he married, raised a family, and became a well-regarded architect in the Twin Cities. A friend recalls of Hanson, "He was a very unassuming guy. He would rather talk about architecture than his heroics in World War II." Hanson joined the Air Force Reserve at Minneapolis's Wold-Chamberlain Field and served for many years. He retired in 1969 as a colonel and deputy commander for operations with the 934th Tactical Airlift Group.

Bob Hanson initiated the first reunion of the 474th Fighter Group, which was held in Minneapolis in 1975. He began working with former comrades on a recounting of the history of the squadron, which was published under John Steinko's name in 1986. Hanson and his wife, Marilyn, joined members of the 474th Fighter Group on a trip to Europe in 1984. They stopped to pay their respects at four American cemeteries, including the Ardennes cemetery near Liège. The Hansons stood at the grave of Captain Harold "Scotty" Scott, a Californian who had been one of the original pilots of the 428th Squadron along with Bob. The 428th Squadron lost Scott when twenty FW-190s pounced on them while over Germany. Bob Hanson recalled Scott's last words: "Hey gang, I've got about nine of them cornered up here in the sun!"

Robert D. Hanson passed away not long after the reunions got under way, dying in 1987 at the age of sixty-two of lung cancer. He left behind a family and the memory of a man who humbly served his nation. He is buried in section V, grave 7654, at Fort Snelling National Cemetery.

These are but a handful of the men of the Upper Midwest who risked and gave their lives in the Normandy landings. The Allies managed to land an estimated 130,000 men on the beaches at Normandy by the end of the first day. Over twenty thousand additional troops went in farther onshore by parachute or glider. The Allies suffered nine thousand casualties, including three thousand dead. This was the beginning of the end for Hitler's Fortress Europe.

Chapter 5

Pacific Theater

While the Allies fought their way onto the shores of Normandy and prepared to move across Europe toward Germany, American forces began a series of fiercely contested landings in the Pacific theater against the Japanese.

John Millet

The Japanese ravaged the Asian mainland for years before Pearl Harbor. Chinese General Chiang Kai-shek recruited Claire Chennault, a retired U.S. Army captain, as an instructor and adviser for the Chinese air force. Chennault, who advocated "defensive pursuit" against the massive Japanese bomber squadrons, went to Kunming in the Yunnan Province in 1938 to train a cadre of fighter pilots. The Yunnan Province lay on the southwestern edge of China on the border of Burma and French Indochina. Rugged mountains and impassable roads isolated Kunming and Yunnan from the rest of China and the world.

Chennault's repeated requests for fighter planes were finally answered when the United States secretly sold to China one hundred crated Curtiss P-40Cs that the British had rejected as obsolete. President Franklin Roosevelt signed a secret executive order on April 1, 1941, approving Chennault's recruitment of volunteers from active-duty U.S. military personnel. One hundred pilots and two hundred ground crew and support personnel became known as the American Volunteer Group. AVG ground crews painted the noses of their P-40s with a wide grin, flashing teeth, and the evil eye of the tiger shark. The AVG first drew blood December 20, 1941, less than two weeks

Members of the American Volunteer Group, who went to China to fight the Japanese before the United States entered the war in 1941, found an exotic land. Photograph by John Millet, AVG, courtesy of Margaret Millet.

after Pearl Harbor, shooting down four of ten Japanese bombers on the outskirts of Kunming in what was the first Allied victory in Asia in the war. *Time* magazine heralded the success of the "Flying Tigers" and the name stuck.

Kunming was the all-important terminus of the eleven-hundred-mile-long Burma Road along which the Allies delivered supplies to the Chinese. The Imperial Japanese Army cut off the Burma Road in March 1942, creating a crisis in the China-Burma-India theater. Supplies were the key to maintaining the resistance to the Japanese invaders in China, and they had little chance of being delivered without the AVG's air protection. The Allies brought in men and planes to fly the Hump (over the Himalayas) to continue the steady flow of supplies. Pilots fought to get their heavy loads to safe altitudes and to avoid extreme turbulence, severe thunderstorms, and the ever-present risk of icing on the wings. Tonnage flown over the Hump increased slowly, but kept the flow going.

The U.S. Army absorbed the AVG into its own ranks in July 1942. The volunteer unit had destroyed nearly three hundred Japanese planes and killed one thousand airmen in just six months. Their exploits marked the first time in five years that the

Japanese had been defeated in the air. Only five pilots followed Chennault into the China Air Task Force of the U.S. Army Air Corps.

John Millet entered the service at Minneapolis on September 17, 1940. He subsequently volunteered for the AVG and shipped overseas to China with the initial group. Millet was among the few original ground crew who remained with Chennault in the China Air Task Force. Millet and Harris Gibboney were radio operators assigned to Kweilin in July 1942. They served together at that base for nineteen months. After one worked a twenty-four-hour shift, the other relieved him. They manned a fighter control station approximately three miles from the air base. Their makeshift station consisted of a power generator and a radio transmitter hidden in one cave with the receiver in another cave one hundred feet away.

Chennault devised an intricate warning system for the Flying Tigers to allow his pilots time to meet the Japanese bombers. The Chinese term *jin-bao* means "to be alert." Americans unfamiliar with the Chinese language inadvertently modified the phrase to *jing-bao,* and that became the name of the AVG's warning system. The Flying Tigers established three concentric rings of observers to keep a lookout for approaching Japanese bombers. The observers called in sightings and confirmations to an interpreter, who then passed the information on to Millet or Gibboney. The radio operator on duty then contacted Kweilin by telephone via three miles of wire run through the jungle. The fighter pilots scrambled immediately to their planes and received further information and air assignments from the fighter control station once they were airborne.

The *jing-bao* warning system also communicated the condition of alert throughout the area via large black spheres or balls, two to three feet in diameter, hoisted on poles. One ball meant Japanese planes were approximately 180 miles away, at the outer edge of the network on the third ring of observers. A two-ball *jing-bao* alerted all to clear for action as the bombers were 120 miles away. A three-ball alert warned all to take cover immediately as the enemy was closing, only sixty miles away. Later, a black cube advised that the Japanese bombers were gone and the danger was over for the time being. The fighter control station also helped to locate downed pilots and coordinate rescue operations.

John Millet was assigned to a forward base after his nineteen months of duty at Kweilin. By this time, the China Air Task Force was constituted as the U.S. Fourteenth Air Force per special order of President Roosevelt in March 1943. Chinese army units provided protection. The Japanese commenced a massive offensive in southern China in October 1944 to recapture the air bases used by the Americans for staging air raids

Sergeant John Millet at the AVG base camp in Kunming, China. Photograph courtesy of Margaret Millet.

against them. Millet and the many other radio operators in forward bases evaded capture and returned to the safety of the main force. The Japanese took many of the Fourteenth's major air bases, including Kweilin, by mid-November. A combined American-Chinese effort halted the Japanese advance by May 1945, and the Allies took the offensive from that point through the end of the war.

John Millet spent five years in China. He learned to speak Chinese and made many friends by sharing candies, cigarettes, and silk stockings that he bought from the post PX (general store). He and his buddy, Joe Angelus, tried to raise pigs at one point, a venture that lasted about a month. Millet adopted a pet monkey, whom he named Riggs. Millet returned home and married in 1947. He and his wife, Margaret, were blessed with ten children. He graduated from the College of St. Thomas in St. Paul and taught high school English and drama in Waseca, Minnesota, for many years. Among his prized possessions from China was a red silk scarf with his name embroidered on it. The scarf was a gift from the Chinese people, presented by Madame Chiang Kai-shek herself. He had another beautiful silk scarf, which he won in a raffle at a banquet honoring the Flying Tigers during the war. Technical Sergeant John Millet died on January 10, 2003. He is buried in section Y, grave site 342, at Fort Snelling National Cemetery.

Helen Mary Roehler

Helen Roehler was born and raised in Fairmont, Minnesota, near the Iowa state line. She grew up between two brothers, Henry and Oscar, and worked alongside them on the family farm. Like many women, Helen was determined to join the fight to defend America and preserve democracy. She entered the U.S. Navy on July 3, 1942. She served first at Bethesda, Maryland, and later was assigned to Dutch Harbor, Alaska.

With the Japanese seemingly in control of the Pacific theater in the early stage of the war, the Imperial Navy moved against Alaska's Aleutian Islands. Admiral Yamamoto hoped to divert U.S. naval forces from the Central Pacific. He also recognized the psychological impact of Japanese forces taking American soil. The Aleutians campaign took place from June 1942 through August 1943. The campaign opened six months after Pearl Harbor as Japanese warplanes bombed U.S. Army and Navy installations at Dutch Harbor. Japanese ground forces first occupied Attu and Kiska, and later seized other strategic locations in the Aleutians. The U.S. Armed Forces recaptured Attu in May 1943 and Kiska in August 1943. Thereafter, the United States made efforts to solidify its hold on the "northern" approach to the United States.

Ensign Helen Roehler lost her life in a plane crash in the Aleutian Islands in 1944. Photograph courtesy of Henry Roehler.

Ensign Helen Roehler was a navy nurse assigned to the Aleutians for some time, according to her brother William. A National Guard unit from Fairmont, Minnesota, was on duty in the Aleutians and the boys were excited to have a visit from the pretty Minnesota girl. Ensign Roehler was flying aboard a PBY Catalina flying boat on April 23, 1944, as part of a hospital inspection tour. Their objective was a distant outpost in the Aleutian Island defenses. Visibility decreased and the pilot flew into a mountain on Umnak Island. There were no survivors. The official report states that Roehler was "killed in the line of duty in the Aleutian area." She was posthumously awarded the World War II Victory Medal. The government returned Helen Roehler's remains to Minnesota in late 1948, where they were reinterred in section C, grave site 7660, at Fort Snelling National Cemetery.

James B. Carter

James Carter was living with his wife and daughter on Girard Avenue in Minneapolis when the war began. He entered the service at the beginning of June 1942, enlisting at Fort Snelling. He became a part of the Ninety-third Division, an African American unit, which had just reactivated. The Ninety-third had seen action in France in the First World War and the men had distinguished themselves in combat. However, the old arguments from influential figures began to resurface in the 1940s, questioning whether African Americans could fight. The U.S. Armed Forces remained segregated. Further, the vast majority of African Americans in the military were assigned to load and unload supplies, bury the dead, drive supply trucks, and such. It seemed that no theater commander wanted African American combat troops. African Americans in the service totaled six hundred thousand by the end of 1943 and attained seven hundred thousand by the end of the war.

Australian politicians pressured General Douglas MacArthur to refuse to accept African American troops. MacArthur is said to have remarked that a man's fighting spirit could not be measured by his color. The Ninety-third performed well in training during the summer and fall of 1942 and in maneuvers during April through June 1943. Secretary of War Henry Stimson approved sending the Ninety-third Division to Hawaii to relieve a white division for fighting, only to be met with resistance. The army subsequently ordered the Ninety-third to the South Pacific on January 2, 1944. In fact, despite the considerable attention paid to the deployment of the Ninety-third Division, there was an African American regular army unit, the Twenty-fourth Infantry Regiment, already engaged in the South Pacific. Newspapers nationwide,

The Ninety-third Infantry Division on patrol in the Solomon Islands. Photograph courtesy of the Library of Congress.

including the *Washington Post* and the *New York Times,* reported on these developments for their readers.

African American troops were not permitted to donate blood when the war began. Necessity required the surgeons general of the army and navy to rescind that order in January 1942. However, medical personnel were still required to label each unit of blood. A physician serving in the field later wrote, "Once in combat, no one paid any attention to the labels . . . blood was just blood."

The Twenty-fifth Regiment and the 593rd Field Artillery Battalion, a medical and an engineering battalion of the Ninety-third Division, arrived at Bougainville in the Solomon Islands on March 29, 1944, after ten days of jungle training on Guadalcanal. While the Twenty-fifth was relegated to duty behind the front line, platoons from the regiment accompanied white units on patrol and began serving as backup troops on assaults. The first casualties took place in mid-April when a Japanese ambush of a patrol left four men of the Twenty-fifth Regiment dead. Some members of the Twenty-fifth accompanied the 148th Infantry Regiment pursuing Japanese up the Laruma River. African American Wade Fogge won the first Bronze Star in the division for knocking out three Japanese pillboxes with his rocket launcher. The command's plan to ease the inexperienced troopers into combat alongside seasoned veterans, rather than just throw them into dangerous situations, was successful.

However, one company from the Twenty-fifth, moving into action on its own, ran into Japanese machine guns and panicked. No one in the field thought it unusual that inexperienced troops lacking in jungle training would panic. Nonetheless, a report on the incident was passed from headquarters up the ladder to Washington, D.C. Too many desk jockeys were willing to use the incident to condemn all African American troops, making the situation sound worse with every telling. The entire Twenty-fifth Regiment was subsequently pulled off the line and ordered to report to staging areas in the rear.

The U.S. Army saw fit to award certain individuals who distinguished themselves on Bougainville. The *Minneapolis Spokesman,* the town's African American newspaper, carried a notice on the front page of the December 29, 1944, edition: "Sgt. James B. Carter Wins Bronze Star." The army honored Carter for his "meritorious service . . . while serving on Green Island and the Solomon Islands in the South Pacific."

Carter survived the war, settled in Los Angeles, and died in 1981. His remains were returned home to Minnesota for burial. James B. Carter is buried in section W, grave site 3580, at Fort Snelling National Cemetery.

Sheldon Gordinier

Lieutenant Sheldon Gordinier of Minneapolis had been flying his patrol bomber Martin flying boat on a reconnaissance mission for hours. The PBM Mariner is much less well known than the Consolidated PBY Catalina as a maritime patrol aircraft. In fact, the PBM was larger and faster and was used increasingly in the navy toward the end of the war. The PBM's maximum speed was only about two hundred miles per hour, but its range was twenty-five hundred to thirty-five hundred miles. The PBM squadron fanning out to the west had orders to fly hundreds of miles in search of a Japanese fleet.

The American landings on Saipan began on the morning of June 15, 1944. A formidable Japanese naval force, which included nine carriers and five battleships, rushed to the defense of Saipan. The Japanese high command wanted the Mariana Islands (Saipan, Tinian, and Guam) held at all cost. American B-29 bombers based on the Mariana Islands would be capable of routine bombing runs on the Japanese mainland. The Americans, for their part, relished the opportunity to engage the Japanese at sea. They had an even larger fleet with more aircraft carriers than their foe.

The Japanese fleet had 475 warplanes, which would be joined by their land-based warplanes from the Mariana Islands. The American fleet stood between them and Saipan. Japanese planes attacked the U.S. fleet on the morning of June 19, 1944. American pilots rushed to the fight and decimated the enemy. Only two American carriers sustained damage. Two more waves of Japanese planes met the same fate. Meanwhile, U.S. submarines got clean shots at the Japanese fleet and sank two carriers. The resounding victory on the first day of the Battle of the Philippine Sea became known as "the Great Marianas Turkey Shoot." The defeated Japanese withdrew and headed for home. Attempts at pursuit were futile. The Japanese fleet had disappeared. Reconnaissance planes were sent out to find them.

Sheldon Gordinier was a tenacious young man who had earned the nickname "Tuffy" as quarterback for the University of Iowa football team. His PBM and three others spread out and scanned the horizon, not certain of their own fate if and when they found what they were looking for. The search continued for hours. Lieutenant Gordinier sighted the Japanese fleet at about 9:30 p.m. on June 20. The ships were running without lights and Gordinier was directly over the armada at an altitude of only two thousand feet before he realized it. The Japanese had sent out well over three hundred planes that day to attack and the seamen on lookout apparently assumed that Gordinier's PBM was a returning Japanese warplane. There was no light to make out the shape of the plane until it was close. The fleet turned on its lights and lit up flares to guide the plane down to the deck of an aircraft carrier. The Japanese opened fire when they realized their error, but Lieutenant Gordinier flew his plane and crew out of the danger zone without being shot down. His PBM radioman sent the message that the admirals in the main fleet were so anxiously awaiting.

The Japanese fleet was nearly out of range. Nonetheless, more than two hundred U.S. warplanes launched and headed for one last chance to deliver a telling blow. They

Lieutenant Sheldon Gordinier in the cockpit of his PBM (patrol bomber Martin) Mariner. Photograph courtesy of the Gordinier family.

sank another carrier and damaged three others and shot down another sixty-five planes. Day two of the Battle of the Philippine Sea made the victory complete. The Japanese lost 395 planes, more than 90 percent, in the two-day battle. The American fliers were hard-pressed to return to the carriers. More than seventy planes ran out of fuel and were lost to the sea. Rescue planes recovered most of the pilots. Sheldon Gordinier was likely among those retrieving the downed dive-bomber pilots. Admiral Raymond Spruance ordered Gordinier and another pilot to report to his cabin after they returned to the fleet. "The men had a pleasant conversation with the admiral, who served them lemonade, coffee and cookies and commended them on the work they had done."

Sheldon Gordinier lived a long and successful life. He passed away on December 30, 2003, at the age of eighty-nine. He is buried in section 20-A, grave site 1049, at Fort Snelling National Cemetery.

Lawrence C. Lundberg

Lawrence Lundberg was fascinated with planes and flying from the time he was a boy. Barnstormers touring the country in the 1930s captured his imagination. Lundberg grew up in Albert Lea, Minnesota. His mother struggled to raise her children on her own. Lundberg graduated from high school and hopped a freight train to North Dakota State University, where he had earned a football scholarship. He transferred the following year to the University of Minnesota with another football scholarship. Since the scholarship covered tuition only, he stoked furnaces at a residence hall in exchange for board and waited on tables in exchange for food. He graduated from the University of Minnesota in 1940 with a major in physical education.

Lundberg was living on Forty-eighth Avenue in Minneapolis when he enlisted in the service on April 15, 1941. He went through basic training and then transferred to the Army Air Corps. He was a cadet at Ballinger Field in Texas when he wrote to his fiancée, "I really like this flying business. I guess it must have been the way I flew on Friday, but there is something about the smell of gasoline, a roaring motor, whistling wind and exhaust fumes. It just does something to you. . . . I love to swing the plane around and make it perform for me." That was on December 7. Cadet Lundberg wrote the following day: "This country is now at war with Japan and so I suppose I am now a war bird. . . . My life will depend on my flying ability, so I went up determined to fly perfect."

Lundberg and his fiancée, Dorothy Murdock, also of Minneapolis, traveled to San Antonio, where they married on April 27, 1942, and honeymooned just before he began flight school at Randolph Field, San Antonio, Texas. He graduated with Roger Manteuffel, a friend from Mankato, Minnesota, earning his wings and an officer's commission. The army sent Lundberg to Camp Davis, North Carolina, to gain experience flying P-39 Airacobras and to improve his flying skills. Lieutenant Lundberg was preparing for a landing one day when he discovered that the landing gear would not come down. No one in the squadron had any idea how to engage the gear backup system. Lundberg circled the field, anxiously watching his fuel gauge while the ground crew called the manufacturer and talked to the company engineers. They relayed instructions and he landed safely. Such situations were everyday in a nation rushing to war.

The Eighty-second Recon Squadron, Seventy-first Recon Group, to which Lieutenant Lundberg was assigned, shipped out to New Guinea in October 1943. They arrived a month later. He wrote home that he was sick of seeing nothing but ocean

First Lieutenant Lawrence Lundberg served with distinction in the South Pacific, piloting P-39 Airacobras and later B-25 bombers. Photograph courtesy of Larry Lundberg.

and that he was glad he was not in the navy. The pilots of the Eighty-second Recon Squadron were flying their P-39 Airacobras just two weeks after arriving. Recon had a different connotation than simply observation. Their missions were often search-and-destroy tactical efforts, hitting whatever targets they came across. Lundberg wrote on December 13, 1943: "We're getting in the groove now and are actually doing some good in this war down here." He wrote less than two weeks later: "Being in a reconnaissance outfit has its advantages. We know what's going on in the war, at least . . . we can see the results of our work and it makes us feel good." He observed: "It's pretty easy to tell the Allied territory from Jap. Trucks, men, ships, etc. are moving all over our lines. Nothing stirs behind Jap lines. That's what air superiority does."

General Douglas MacArthur was focused on retaking the Philippines in mid-1943. American control of the straits between New Britain and New Guinea would open the approach to the Philippines, as well as allow a drive westward along the north coast of New Guinea. The First Marine Division landed at Cape Gloucester on the western tip of New Britain on December 26, 1943. The campaign against the Japanese defenders, fought in the tropical jungle, lasted four months. The Albert Lea and Minneapolis papers both carried articles featuring First Lieutenant Lawrence Lundberg's role "reconnoitering at virtually zero altitude over the entire region" in his P-39.

January 24, 1943: "Out over enemy territory the other day I started dodging weather and ended up about 50 miles from a fairly big Jap base without much gas to get home on. I sweated out the return trip—just two of us, but nothing happened." While Lundberg included bits and pieces of the war that were vague enough to pass the censors' black pen, he wrote often to his wife about money, how she might keep their 1939 Oldsmobile (which he had named Arabella) running, and their plans for a regular life after the war. His letters in time began to address his growing concern about his health. He suffered from jungle rot, an affliction of the foot common to the South Pacific, which could become serious enough to cause loss of limb. Lundberg became overwhelmed with excitement after receiving the news that his wife was pregnant and due to deliver their first child in June. At the same time, it was difficult, as he knew that he was the only person who mattered to her, and he was halfway around the world from her, unable to help.

Lundberg requested a transfer to fly bombers. He waited throughout January with no word, but orders finally came through. He became a B-25 Marauder copilot and later pilot on a plane named *Dragon Myass.* He flew in the Seventeenth Recon Squadron, also within the Seventy-first Recon Group. Lundberg wrote on June 4, 1944: "I was at Noemefor Isle. I don't suppose you know where that is, but it's a Jap-held island on the other side of Biak. We found two barges full of Japs and strafed them. I suppose we killed 50 or so." Lundberg by this time had logged 210 combat hours with seventy missions in. He noted, "We're really close to the front lines now. I can hear machine gun and artillery fire most of the time." He closed his letter by assuring his wife, "I hope you don't worry when I talk about combat and stuff, because this B-25 is a rugged plane and has carried many a pilot through a rough mission."

The bomber squadron attacked Japanese harbor installations and supply depots along the north coast of New Guinea, but also any Japanese they happened to come upon, whether barges, planes, or troops on the ground. The fight for New Guinea, while a seemingly forgotten campaign, was essential to MacArthur's drive to the Philippines and, ultimately, Japan. Yet those in the fight sometimes had their doubts, given the general lack of coverage back home. Lundberg wrote, "I hope what we're doing here is making a difference in the war." In any case, the news of the Allied landings in Normandy was welcomed. "The invasion of Europe has boosted morale considerably over here," he wrote. News reached military personnel in the South Pacific quickly. *Guinea Gold,* an Australian four-page military newspaper circulated throughout the South Pacific by U.S. Army Air Force planes, often scooped the major publications.

"We had a little excitement the other night, but none of the broadcasts [Japanese radio propaganda] said a word. . . . As a matter of fact, we had quite a bit of excitment, *[sic]* but my fox hole is about 2 feet deeper than it was and has a roof over it."

The war climaxed for Lundberg on his twenty-third bombing mission. The standard operation involved a wave of bombers coming down, one after another, to drop their bomb load on the target. The antiaircraft fire was particularly intense that day. The relatively inexperienced bombardier in the plane ahead of Lundberg's dropped his load a bit prematurely. *Dragon Myass* was caught off guard and the pilot, copilot, and bombardier found themselves flying into a wall of fire and gas. The blast blew out the bombardier's window. Lundberg crawled down to check on him, but there was nothing he could do. The crewman was dead. The plane suffered severe damage and the crew began the long flight home. As if the situation was not bad enough already, Lundberg discovered that the hydraulics, necessary to lower the nosewheel for landing, were not working. He crawled down through the wreckage, wrested the severely mangled body of the bombardier from the controls, and attempted to hand-crank the wheel into position. He did all he could, but there was no way to get the wheel down. The long flight back to base was a quiet one, all of the crew realizing that their only hope was to land the plane on its belly. The pilot and copilot Lundberg managed to land *Dragon Myass* without further injury to the crew. Lundberg hung out his flak jacket to let the rain wash the bombardier's blood from it. It was years later before he could speak of the incident to his son. Lundberg had been smoking Old Gold cigarettes at the time he was struggling in the bombardier's pit and forever associated that memory with Old Golds. His son recalls that the veteran pilot could detect the distinctive smell of Old Golds in the midst of a crowd and would become uncomfortable.

Lundberg was in the hospital by the end of June, his jungle rot having developed into a serious matter. His inactivity added to the suspense as to whether his child had been born and whether it was a boy or a girl. He wrote on June 29, "Here it is 9 days

First Lieutenant Lawrence Lundberg (right) and friend at flight training.
Photograph courtesy of Larry Lundberg.

after I'm supposed to be a papa and I'm in the hospital with no prospect of mail for at least two days." He sent a telegram on July 14, desperate to hear something, but received no response. He passed the time by making a teddy bear. A letter, dated July 22, read: "I'm so glad it's a boy. I don't know when his birthday is or what color eyes and hair he has yet, but he's a boy. Larry [the infant's name] sounds mighty good."

Lawrence Lundberg shipped home to a military hospital in California. He had flown eighty-one combat missions and earned the Distinguished Flying Cross and two Air Medals for his part in World War II. He logged 205 flight hours in a B-25, 167 in a P-39, and more than 600 hours in observation planes for a total of 1,378 hours of pilot time in the service. Sixty-eight percent of that time was as first pilot. Lundberg received his discharge from the service on November 27, 1945, and returned home to Albert Lea to his wife and son, Larry. He taught physical education and coached high school for a year, but something was missing. Lawrence Lundberg was back in the air the next year. He worked crop-dusting jobs, became a flight instructor, and flew charters. He was the pilot for Hubert H. Humphrey during Humphrey's 1952 campaign for the U.S. Senate.

Larry remembers that his father "wanted to get his hands on a jet when the jets first came out," and that his dad told him, "The government taught me how to fly, so I feel I owe them some time." A pilot of Lundberg's experience had little trouble fulfilling that desire. The Ninety-seventh Squadron of the 440th fighter-bomber Group was activated at Minneapolis's Wold-Chamberlain Field (which we know today as Minneapolis–St. Paul International Airport) in June 1952. Lundberg joined the Air Force Reserve on May 6, 1952. He made captain in February 1955.

Larry Lundberg enjoyed hanging out with his dad, who took him flying and taught him a lot. He remembers Friday, October 12, 1956, "like it was yesterday." He was twelve years old. His mother told him that they would eat supper as soon as his father returned from his flight that day. The Air Force Reserve flew Lockheed F-80C Shooting Stars. The United States' first operational jet fighter saw action in the Korean War and, afterward, many were delivered to Air National Guard and Air Force Reserve squadrons around the country. Captain Lawrence Lundberg was practicing aerobatics and simulated flameout landings that day. The tower at Wold-Chamberlain Field gave Lundberg approval to make a simulated flameout approach at 3:50 p.m.

Larry returned from riding his bike to find a dark blue '52 Chevy parked in front of his house. He went inside to find his mother in the kitchen with two men in uniform, one a colonel and one a chaplain. She grabbed Larry without saying a word, pulled him into her arms, and held him. Larry knew something was wrong.

Captain Lundberg had been flying over the Twin Cities metro area when his jet began having trouble. He reported to base that the engine was sputtering and advised them that he was flying south, across the Minnesota River and away from the populated area.

"Minneapolis Tower, 806, I have an emergency, over."

"Roger 806, you're cleared to land any runway, advise, over."

"806, roger."

"Minneapolis Tower, this is 806. I'm ejecting over the river."

"OK, 806."

Witnesses said the jet began falling apart and then burst into flames. Lundberg managed to pull his seat ejector, but died from injuries from the jettison exit. His son remembers his father telling his mother that all F-80 pilots knew that there was a problem with the ejection mechanism, that the canopy could not be properly ejected unless it was fully closed. He jokingly added that he had a hard head and not to worry. The family understood that there had been smoke in the cockpit due to electrical malfunction, and that Lundberg had opened the canopy to clear the air. F-80s later were retrofitted so that a bar above the back of the seat would break the canopy.

Captain Lundberg's body was found three hundred yards from the wreckage. Air force officials stated, "Apparently it was another case of a pilot killing himself in an effort to save the lives of others." The accident was concluded to be from material failure. The *Minneapolis Tribune* reported that the crash was the fourth jet crack-up since June. The air force awarded Lundberg a second Distinguished Flying Cross for his courage.

The funeral was held at Fort Snelling National Cemetery on Tuesday, October 16, 1956. President Dwight Eisenhower happened to be in the Twin Cities for a motorcade. Ironically, the presence of the former five-star general resulted in the refusal of authorities to approve the aerial flyby over Captain Lundberg's service. Larry remembers well that one buddy of his dad's from the squadron, likely at great risk of being disciplined, roared overhead, despite the flight restriction, in a final salute to Lundberg. His remains lie in Fort Snelling National Cemetery, section B-1, grave site 151-1. He was a war hero who returned home and later found himself in the unique situation of again being a hero. The second time cost Lawrence Lundberg his life.

Larry Lundberg recalled that the University of Minnesota for a time honored his dad by presenting a graduating senior with the Captain Lawrence C. Lundberg Memorial Award. The award went to an air force ROTC student who partially supported his own schooling, was above average in scholarship and leadership abilities, and demonstrated excellence in flying. Larry remembers meeting those awarded and the honor that he and his mother felt. The award disappeared after a few years for lack of funding. To honor her husband's memory, Dorothy Lundberg kept a model of every plane he ever flew displayed in her home. There was little talk of the tragic death. It was not until research for this book that Larry Lundberg saw the obituary of his father's death, including a photo of the twisted wreckage. He commented that people too often focus on the deceased and forget there is a family left behind that struggles with the reality for decades. Captain Lawrence C. Lundberg's memory has remained intact through all these years with his son.

Ross Robinson

"First Strike at Manila" read the headline in the October 23, 1944, issue of *Life* magazine. The correspondent wrote the nation about being with the American task force in the Pacific, from which carrier-based planes struck Manila on September 21, 1944. The pilots returned to say the targets had been "a strafer's dream." They destroyed so many ships that it was believed to be "the most destructive day on Jap shipping in the entire war." The warplanes also destroyed a huge ammunition dump and claimed six Japanese planes in air combat. *Life* proclaimed U.S. Navy Fighting Squadron Two, the "Fighting Two," the hottest fighter squadron in the Pacific and cited numbers of 261 Japanese planes shot down in the air with the loss of only three pilots, another 200 planes destroyed on the ground, and fifty thousand tons of shipping obliterated. The article featured photos of each of the forty-four hotshot pilots. The caption under the picture of Ensign Ross Robinson read, "Handsomest man in squadron, shot down five."

Ross Robinson grew up in St. Paul and was working at the 7-Up Bottling Company when he enlisted in the service in July 1942. He became a Hellcat pilot based on the carrier *Hornet,* which left Pearl Harbor on March 15, 1944. The *Hornet* and its fighter squadrons were involved in seven weeks of intense combat in the Mariana Islands beginning in June. Robinson earned the Distinguished Flying Cross on June 15, 1944. He downed two Japanese planes in a morning raid on Bonin-Kazan. He had just returned to the deck of the *Hornet* when the alarm sounded that enemy planes were approaching. He scrambled back into the air and destroyed two more Japanese planes that same day. Five days later, on June 20, he was among a pack of Hellcats that attacked and sank the Japanese aircraft carrier *Shokaku* in the Philippine Sea. Admiral Marc Mitscher cited Robinson for an Oak Leaf Cluster for the Distinguished Flying Cross for this action. Ensign Robinson returned home to St. Paul in late November 1944 as part of a war bond tour. The *St. Paul Pioneer Press* featured his return and exploits on the front page. He ended the war with five kills to qualify as an ace. He was one of twenty-seven aces in VF-2.

After the war, Admiral Chester Nimitz ordered the formation of a Navy flight exhibition team. Demobilization had cut the navy air arm to an all-time low. Combat ace Lieutenant Commander Butch Voris was selected to build the team, which became known as the Blue Angels. Lieutenant JG Ross Robinson was among the initial eight pilots in the team.

Their first flight demonstration took place at their home base, Jacksonville Naval Air Station, in June 1946. The Hellcat-flying Blue Angels became famous overnight for their diamond formation. Two months later in August 1946, the Blue Angels transitioned to Grumman F8F Bearcats. On September 29, Lieutenant Robinson was flying one of the new Bearcats in a high-performance individual routine. Lieutenant Commander Voris described what happened next: "During the second half of a Cuban Eight with a roll and a half recovery, he appeared to hesitate due to restricted visibility, and pulled insufficient G's causing the breakaway of only one outboard wing tip, which

The USS *Hornet* (CV-12), home to the "Fightin' Two" fighter squadron and veteran of numerous battles in the Pacific theater. Photograph courtesy of the National Archives (80-G-469319).

in turn caused the aircraft to roll into the landing mat beyond the runway." Lieutenant Robinson was killed instantly. He is buried at Fort Snelling National Cemetery in section DS, grave site 5.

Harry Hesslund

Guam had been an American protectorate since the end of the Spanish-American War. The Japanese landed on Guam on the day following their surprise attack at Pearl Harbor. The brave American defenders consisted of two hundred Marines, some navy personnel, and an island defense company. The subsequent brutal Japanese occupation lasted two and a half years. The U.S. Navy arrived offshore in early July 1944, when the Japanese garrison was nineteen thousand strong. U.S. naval guns and carrier-based planes rocked Guam for seventeen days. The initial landings by the U.S. Marines took place on July 21, 1944. The Japanese put up a fierce resistance. More than one thousand U.S. Marines and more than seventeen thousand Japanese soldiers died before the island was secured on August 10.

The U.S. Navy established Naval Construction Battalions at the outset of the war. More than 325,000 men, commonly referred to as Seabees, served their country during World War II in 150 Naval Construction Battalions. Many were older, as the navy sought men with construction experience. Most Seabees served in the Pacific theater, often landing soon after the Marines had taken a foothold on the beach. The major-scale work of rebuilding the island as a base for subsequent operations commenced once the island was secured. Heavy equipment operators, blasting crews, survey crews, mechanics, and supply men all played an important role.

Harry Hesslund of Minneapolis was a storekeeper third class in the Forty-eighth Naval Construction Battalion. The battalion history, *Tradewinds* (published in 1945), described their arrival ashore:

> We climbed from our Higgins boat onto what was once a dock. Now it was nothing more than a jagged pile of coral reaching a short distance into the bay! What was left of destroyed Jap planes and boats could be seen everywhere in the water! Piles of rubble marked where buildings once stood and all that remained of a huge fuel-storage tank was a big, twisted pile of steel. The tall palm trees had been bomb-blasted into naked, charred stumps and huge shell craters pocked the landscape. Through this mess of destruction a bulldozer had cleared a path and trucks plowed back and forth to keep the supplies and men moving. . . . And so we were introduced to our new island! As the trucks carried us to our temporary bivouac area and we silently viewed the endless scenes of destruction, all of us were conscious of the odor that hung in the air—the odor of death! We had all expected conditions to be rough but few of us really expected such scenes as these!

The work was difficult, and the unit history records, "Despite the fact that we were miserable and living under the worst conditions, it was surprising to note the good spirit of most of us! We did a lot of wailing but we did a lot of laughing too!" Many suffered from dengue fever and dysentery. A navy photographer heard of a family reunion and captured the moment on film. Hesslund's two first cousins, brothers from St. Paul, also happened to be on Guam. It was the first meeting in more than two years between Seabee Harry Hesslund, Marine PFC Richard Crossley, and Army Private James Crossley.

Seabee Storekeeper Third Class Harry Hesslund (far right) of Minneapolis reunited on Guam with his cousins, Private First Class Richard Crossley, U.S. Marine Corps, and Private James Crossley, U.S. Army, both of St. Paul. Photograph courtesy of the Minneapolis Public Library, Minneapolis Collection.

The Forty-eighth Seabees and others feverishly converted Guam into a major air base by the end of 1944. As described in the history of the battalion, "We watched the war-torn island transform from a mass of wreckage to a thriving, orderly forward base. We entered on roads of mud and when we left we sped down modern paved highways... and we were proud that we helped make it possible." B-29 Superfortresses with a range of more than three thousand miles attacked the Japanese mainland throughout 1945 from this base until the Japanese surrender.

Harry Hesslund died in 1976 and is buried in section R, grave site 1501, at Fort Snelling National Cemetery.

Richard Edward Kraus

Umurbrogol is a name little known outside the U.S. Marine Corps. The series of ridges were the center of Japanese defenses on the island of Peleliu in the Palau Island group. Peleliu, east of the Philippines, was intended to serve as an air base for

General MacArthur's retaking of the Philippines. MacArthur and Admiral Nimitz were unaware how strongly defended Peleliu was. The Japanese had developed an extensive network of caves, bunkers, and tunnels through the high ground on the center of the island. Six thousand Japanese were well entrenched in the rugged terrain, their defenses of underground bunkers and shelters well covered by thick jungle growth. Three days of naval bombardment, which preceded the landing, were ineffective against these positions. The fighting on Peleliu involved weeks of intense combat, often hand to hand, in September and October 1944.

Operation Stalemate II was the largest amphibious operation in the Pacific theater up to that time. More than eight hundred ships and sixteen hundred aircraft took part in the operation. Three regiments of the First Marine Division landed on the western beaches of Peleliu on September 15. They faced enfilading fire across the beach and from the high ground above.

Amtracs, amphibious tanks loaded with infantrymen, moved ashore. Although there were veterans among the Marines, many were inexperienced draftees not long out of basic training. Richard Kraus was a graduate of Minneapolis's Edison High School. He entered the service in January 1944, just after turning eighteen, and went overseas on July 31, 1944. Private First Class Kraus was assigned to the Eighth Amphibious Tractor Battalion, Third Amphibious Corps. Peleliu was his first battle; he had been overseas for just three months. Isolated pockets of Americans faced determined Japanese counterattacks after the initial landing. The combat evolved to slow advance, measured in yards, as the Japanese fought to the last man. Amtrac Marines, in keeping with the Marine tradition "Every man a rifleman," served as infantrymen when not operating their vehicles. Kraus volunteered to evacuate a wounded comrade from the front line on October 5, 1944. His citation reads:

> Pfc. Kraus and three companions courageously made their way forward and successfully penetrated the lines for some distance before the enemy opened with an intense, devastating barrage of hand grenades which forced the stretcher party to take cover and subsequently abandon the mission. While returning to the rear, they observed two men approaching who appeared to be Marines and immediately demanded the password. When, instead of answering, one of the two Japanese threw a hand grenade into the midst of the group, Pfc. Kraus heroically threw himself upon the grenade and, covering it with his body, absorbed the full impact of the explosion and was instantly killed.

The Marines lost twelve hundred dead and over five thousand wounded on Peleliu. Kraus was one of eight Marines to be honored with the Medal of Honor for bravery

Private Richard Kraus was eighteen years old when he saved the lives of three fellow Marines on Peleliu by covering a grenade. The Marine Corps awarded him the Medal of Honor posthumously. Photograph courtesy of the U.S. Marine Corps.

on Peleliu. The *Minneapolis Times* headline read "Slain Minneapolis Marine, 18, Awarded Medal of Honor Posthumously" on July 20, 1945. The *Times* carried another article two weeks later on August 3, 1945, when Mrs. Edwin Olsen, Richard's mother, received his medal. She was invited to christen the destroyer *Kraus,* named in his honor, in March 1946. The remains of Richard Kraus were reinterred in Fort Snelling National Cemetery in 1948 and lie in section DS, grave site 61-N.

U.S. Marines received eighty-one of the 433 Medals of Honor awarded during World War II. Fifty-one of those eighty-one were awarded posthumously.

Robert Adair Meyer

"Old, low, and slow" was the name their pilots and crews jokingly used to refer to the planes. They flew at night to overcome these performance limitations. The planes were painted black to adapt to their necessary operating conditions. They had no bombsight and no bomb bay—the bombs were instead wired to the wings—as they needed to be able to set down in water and float. Their base was often a floating tender.

The Navy Black Cats proudly served in the Pacific theater and earned a solid reputation for delivering results. To get the job done, the U.S. Navy's VPB squadrons flew Catalina PBY-5 planes. (VPB came from V for roman numeral five and PB for patrol bombers). The PBY-5s were not the fastest planes, nor were they particularly well armed. Their long range made them well suited for doing recon patrol and search-and-rescue missions, but also for stalking the many inlets and straits of the South Pacific in search of transport and supply ships. It was in this predatory mode that the Navy Black Cats of the South Pacific developed their reputation. The standard load for a PBY-5 was two one-thousand-pound bombs and two five-hundred-pound bombs. A common approach was to attack an enemy vessel along its length to allow more room for error.

Bob Meyer earned his pilot's license while attending the College of St. Thomas in St. Paul. He took lessons at Minneapolis's Wold-Chamberlain Field, which offered civilian pilot training. He entered the navy in June 1943 and was sent to Iowa City for further pilot training. He married his wife, Ardis, during this period. Meyer was assigned to VPB-33 Patrol Bombing Squadron and connected with them at Naval Air Station Kaneohe on Oahu. The squadron was ordered to report to Perth, Australia, in October 1943. The squadron members took part in their first night bombings and VPB-33 "officially" became part of the Navy Black Cats. The Japanese who operated

Lieutenant Robert Meyer (front row, far left), Navy Black Cat pilot, and the crew of his Catalina PBY. Photograph courtesy of the Robert Meyer family.

on the sea in the Black Cats' area of operation feared the squadron's trademark sudden night raids.

VPB-33 jumped into the real war in the Pacific when navy command relocated the squadron to Samarai, New Guinea, in mid-February 1944. The squadron remained in the South Pacific for the duration of the war. Night search patrols and attack missions against enemy shipping in the Bismarck Sea were fraught with danger, as the Japanese had a strong military presence in the area. New Guinea and the Solomon Islands were the "front line." While the PBYs had three gunners in each crew of six, the guns were not powerful. VPB-33 relocated to a small island in the Admiralty Island chain. They performed numerous duties, including daylight searches, bombing missions, and air-sea rescue missions (known to the VPB crews as Dumbo missions). The squadron also provided coverage for the landing on Japanese-occupied Hollandia. U.S. forces took over the airfields on Hollandia on April 29, 1944. The squadron subsequently moved aboard a seaplane tender and conducted air-sea rescue over a broad area.

VPB-33 began what became a celebrated run at the beginning of September 1944. The squadron focused on night search-and-attack missions. Every PBY was getting kills, some pretty big. Lieutenant "Wild Bill" Sumpter destroyed a ten-thousand-ton seaplane carrier and two destroyer escorts on September 23. Lieutenant James Merritt ignored flak from five escort vessels and sank one troop transport and damaged a second on September 26. Sumpter sank a six-thousand-ton light cruiser on October 3. The navy awarded both Sumpter and Merritt the Navy Cross. The squadron combined for a total of forty-three ships sunk and another twenty severely damaged for a total of 157,000 tons. It was a record never met by another Black Cat Squadron. Declared General MacArthur, "No command in the war has excelled the brilliance of their operations."

VPB-33 was presented the Presidential Unit Citation on the basis of this performance. The citation reads:

> For extraordinary heroism in action against enemy Japanese forces in the Netherlands East Indies and the Southern Philippines Areas from September 1 to October 4, 1944. Operating dangerously but with bold aggressiveness in the most forward combat areas, the pilots and aircrewmen of Patrol Bombing Squadron THIRTY-THREE struck with devastating effectiveness at the enemy's vital merchant and combatant ships. Persistent and courageous in tracking hostile targets, they flew their perilous night missions through brilliant moonlight or foul weather, constantly braving intense antiaircraft opposition from major units, their escorts and shore installations to destroy or damage thousands of tons of enemy shipping. Ready to face all hazards and daring in combat tactics, Patrol Bombing Squadron THIRTY-THREE fought as an indomitable team in disrupting the Japanese life line of supply throughout a period of thirty-four consecutive nights, a record of valiant and loyal service which reflects the highest credit upon these gallant officers and men and upon the United States Naval Service.

VPB-33 performed daylight searches for enemy threats in the Philippine Sea at the time of the Battle of Leyte Gulf. Light duty followed, and VPB-33 was relieved of duty in February 1945.

The strong bonds formed in combat endure. Bob Meyer flew with one crew for more than a year and the six men in the crew developed camaraderie. He felt bad when their paths split, the crew remaining intact with the two pilots being assigned to new crews. A pilot feels a certain responsibility for his crew and Meyer was concerned. Just days later, the plane went down and none of the crew was recovered. The loss remained

A Navy Black Cat in action in the Pacific. Photograph courtesy of the National Archives (80-G-1022359).

with Meyer for years. He became inspired to look up the families of the crew members at the time of the fiftieth anniversary of D-Day. He had been particularly close to Leo Wilcox, the crew chief. Meyer hunted up the family, who had never had contact with anyone from the service who had known their brother personally. Twelve members of the Wilcox family attended the very next VPB-33 reunion. A second connection also worked and that family came to several reunions. They seemed to get some comfort, perhaps closure, for the loss fifty years earlier. Bob Meyer found it rewarding to be able to do this for the men's families, and he himself felt some closure with an issue that had lain dormant for fifty years.

Robert A. Meyer had a successful career as a Lincoln-Mercury auto dealer in Bloomington, Minnesota, following his return home to St. Paul. He and his wife, Ardis, raised ten children. He passed away on May 29, 2002, and is buried in section F-1, grave site 945, at Fort Snelling National Cemetery.

The Marine assault on Betio Island in the Tarawa atoll in 1943 was the first fully opposed landing on a fortified atoll. The Japanese had constructed an imposing defensive network intended to stop any invasion on the beach. More than one thousand Marines paid the ultimate price. Corporal Lawrence Johnson survived Tarawa only to die on a later island assault. Photograph courtesy of the U.S. Marine Corps.

Lawrence R. Johnson

The U.S. Marine Corps focused on Tarawa in the Gilbert Islands following their success on Guadalcanal. Tarawa was the first of many bloody atolls on which so many brave Americans lost their lives. The primary objective was the fortified island of Betio, on which the Japanese had built an important airfield. Betio was less than three hundred acres of surface. In fact, no part of the island was as much as three hundred yards from the beach and almost every foot was defended. The entrenched positions were well planned and manned by capable veteran Japanese troops.

The attack on Betio began November 20, 1943. The first waves of Marines had LVT amtracs, amphibious tractors, to maneuver over the coral reef to the beach. Resistance was fierce, with rifles and hand grenades of little use against the dug-in Japanese. The weapons of choice became flamethrowers and TNT. Five thousand Marines went ashore by the end of the first day, but almost one-third of them had been killed or wounded. Medical corps personnel worked tirelessly to evacuate the wounded from the beach under fire.

Corporal Lawrence Reuben Johnson of St. Paul took part in the initial assault as squad leader of a light machine-gun unit. He was a veteran of Guadalcanal, having taken part in the landings of August 7–9, 1942, and the long fight for that island through January 1943. In the fight for a toehold on the beach at Betio, a Japanese unit attempted to infiltrate Johnson's unit on the right flank. He risked exposing himself to enemy fire to better understand their movements and direct the fire of the men of his command. His commanding officer reported in the citation for the Bronze Star awarded to Johnson, "He accomplished this mission so effectively that the enemy troops were destroyed or routed and his unit's flank secured. It was high skill and devotion to duty."

The Pacific campaign was bitterly fought and each victory led to yet another costly landing against fierce enemy resistance. Johnson took part in the landings on the beaches of Saipan in the Mariana Islands on June 15, 1944. He was with Company I, Third Battalion, of the Second Marine Division. He was wounded in action on June 16 and died of wounds later that day.

Lawrence Johnson's remains were returned to Minnesota after the war and re-interred at Fort Snelling National Cemetery. He is buried in section C-1, grave site 7517.

William Carl Hoffmann

William Hoffmann of Dent, Minnesota, enlisted in the U.S. Army in 1925. He was a true "mustang," serving proudly as an enlisted man for fifteen years before being commissioned a captain of infantry in 1940 as war clouds gathered. When General Walter Krueger formed the Sixth Army in January 1943, he ordered Lieutenant Colonel Hoffmann to report to him from the Third Army to serve on his staff. Hoffmann wrote after the war, "Nothing so boosted my morale and I am sure I became a different person, being assigned to a 'fighting outfit' in a 'fighting theatre of operations' on the other side of the world." He added, "Down through the years we of the SIXTH ARMY felt we were the cream of the crop!" Hoffmann's voyage from San Francisco to Brisbane, Australia, was marked by two heavy encounters with Japanese submarines.

Colonel William Hoffmann (right), shown here with Major General Roscoe B. Woodruff, served with the U.S. Sixth Army in New Guinea and the Philippines. Photograph courtesy of the Hoffmann family.

The Sixth Army was designated a field army. Its first operation was against the Japanese base at Rabaul in New Britain. Subsequent operations involved moving up the coast of New Guinea, "slugging it out through the jungles under the very worst conditions," Hoffmann wrote. He was shocked during this time by the death of a friend, killed in action, the first of many. Sixth Army headquarters coordinated five military operations that summer of 1944, "all of which kept everyone in perpetual sweat." Hoffmann at one point found himself in "THE MACARTHUR headquarters with lots and lots of RANK" to make a presentation. But the major focus of the staff was the top secret plan to land in the Philippines.

Lieutenant Colonel Hoffmann stood out to sea on October 11. One hundred thousand men of the Sixth Army were to land on the beaches of the island of Leyte. The Japanese command was expecting MacArthur at Luzon. The invasion fleet consisted of six hundred ships, an impressive armada. Hoffmann wrote, "Truly a magnificent sight which one will never forget, ships from horizon to horizon." The troops hit the beach on the morning of October 20, 1944, after an all-night shelling. Deep trenches hindered the movement of equipment on the beach until bulldozers could get in and fill the holes. Hoffmann wrote, "Hades could never present a worse bedlam," but added:

> Troops did make progress and, unbelievably, equipment moved off the beach. Fortunately only two or three enemy aircraft attempted interference, but were driven off by MILLIONS of rounds from naval craft.... Our contingent (the main body of HQRS SIXTH ARMY) landed during one of the enemy attacks, but we were all too busy trying to hang onto our equipment as we disembarked via the landing net—a tricky proposition.... We got ashore but not off the beach as advancing troops were meeting strong resistance, all of which required the re-employment of Naval gun fire over our heads into the hills ahead of us. And the entire afternoon and night we spent under this blanket of fire, undoubtedly the most nerve-wracking experience of my entire career.

General MacArthur landed at noon that first day.

William Hoffmann survived many harrowing experiences on Leyte, including a burning enemy plane just clearing him and crashing nearby, and repeated machine-gun strafings of his Jeep. A direct hit from an aerial bomb sank the LST on which he was supervising the unloading, throwing him into the sea and forcing him to swim a distance after which he was "more dead than alive." Navy fireboats put out the fires and pushed the hulk to a floating dock. Hoffmann's commanding officer ordered him to continue to supervise the unloading, the first order of business being to remove the dead bodies and body parts of some forty men wedged under and into machinery.

Hoffmann and the rest of Sixth Army witnessed the Battle of Leyte Gulf four days after their landing. The Japanese navy committed essentially its entire fleet in the Pacific in an attempt to drive off the U.S. fleet and bottle up the Sixth Army on Leyte. Hoffmann wrote, "We had complete information on the maneuver and among other safeguards taken we were issued additional weapons, ammunition and rations with the prospect of having to take to the hills." The men on shore could hear the continuous thunder and see black smoke on the horizon. The Americans emerged with a major victory after a fierce three-day engagement.

Hoffmann moved on with the Sixth Army to the landing on Luzon in early 1945. He wrote that the entire voyage was plagued by Japanese kamikaze planes. The landings on Luzon met with much heavier resistance. "I recall seeing much cannon fire and, of course, the continuous RRRRRumph RRRRRumph—the diving planes—fires—and a very messy looking beach which was downright inhospitable," he wrote. Once ashore, he met an old friend from his days at Fort Snelling, a Major Volkman, who had escaped from the Bataan Death March and been in hiding for almost four years. Hoffmann proudly wrote of the rescue of hundreds of prisoners at Santo Tomas University in Manila by the advance units of Sixth Army. He wrote of the retaking of Corregidor: "The ordeal of retaking the rock lasted 12 days with many, many casualties on our side and, of course, the slaughter of most of the enemy as surrender was not in their vocabulary." The Sixth Army prepared for the invasion of Japan, their role being a massive landing on Kyushu targeted for November 1, 1945.

The end of the fighting did not mean the end of the duties for the Sixth Army, as they were ordered to proceed to Japan as part of the Army of Occupation. Hoffmann wrote of being greeted by Japanese civilians in top hats, formal wear, and striped pants. Nonetheless, he wrote, "we, of course, were heavily armed as no one knew for sure what to expect—and it must be remembered we fought these people for almost three years. But all went well."

Colonel William Carl Hoffmann later served in Korea. He retired from military service in 1955 after thirty years of duty. He offered his services to the U.S. Army in 1980 at the age of seventy-four, making reference to an army program to recall regular army retirees. The Department of the Army graciously declined. Hoffmann passed away on August 28, 2002, at the age of ninety-six. He is buried in section D, grave site 354, at Fort Snelling National Cemetery.

Theodore Frederick Spreigl

Ted Spreigl was the youngest of four brothers from St. Paul who served in World War II. His brothers—Clarence, Herbert, and George ("Sonny")—served in the U.S. Army in the European theater. Ted enlisted in the navy in April 1944 and shipped out to the Pacific theater after basic training. He was serving aboard the light aircraft carrier USS *Princeton* by July 1944. The *Princeton* was one of nine Cleveland-class cruisers under construction that the navy had converted to light carriers after Pearl Harbor. They became known as Independence-class light carriers. The quarters and facilities on these modified ships were very cramped. The carriers had a unique profile, with four funnels and a smaller bridge island than the larger Essex-class carriers.

The main thrust of the U.S. military effort in the Pacific in October 1944 was the invasion of the island of Leyte in the Philippines. The Japanese Imperial Navy was determined to stop the Americans in this crucial stage of the war in the Pacific and committed everything it had. The Seventh Fleet, consisting of older battleships and eighteen escort carriers, was to cover the landing of the U.S. Sixth Army at Leyte. Admiral "Bull" Halsey's Third Fleet, which consisted of the most powerful ships in the U.S. Navy, was to protect the landing force by engaging the Japanese fleet. Halsey's command included Vice Admiral Mark Mitscher's Task Force 38. Task Force 38 was divided into four powerful task groups. Task Group 38.3 was made up of two fleet carriers, the *Lexington* and the *Essex,* and two light carriers, the *Langley* and the *Princeton,* in addition to two modern, fast battleships, four light cruisers, and fifteen destroyers.

The Battle of Leyte Gulf consisted of a series of naval actions between October 23 and 26, 1944. The Japanese command hoped to lure away Halsey's Third Fleet with their aircraft carriers and in this way allow their battleships and cruisers to destroy the Seventh Fleet and the exposed landing force. This plan, if successful, would have delivered a crushing blow to American interests in the Pacific theater.

The *Princeton* was in the Sibuyan Sea, one of the larger bodies of water in the Philippine archipelago, on the second day of the fighting. Japanese Vice Admiral Onishi Takijiro launched a powerful force of eighty dive-bombers against American Task Group 38.3. American fighters intercepted and devastated the attacking air force. However, a single D4Y Judy dive-bomber somehow escaped notice and followed the fighters back to the American carriers. The Japanese pilot dropped down over the *Princeton* and released two five-hundred-pound bombs onto the flight deck. Fires that ignited below deck raced through the interior. The aft magazines ignited and the ship rocked with a tremendous explosion. The blast killed 229 men and wounded another 420. The carrier began to sink with the stern blown away. Those seamen who could jumped into the sea. One hundred and six drowned before rescue. Seaman Ted Spreigl managed to survive, although his family spent anxious days awaiting word of his rescue when they learned of the loss of the *Princeton*.

The U.S. Navy lost ten ships during the four days of fighting around Leyte, the most important of these being the *Princeton*. The Japanese Imperial Navy, in contrast, lost thirty-five warships, including four aircraft carriers and three battleships. The

Aircraft carrier USS *Princeton* (CVL-23), on fire and sinking after being hit by a bomb in the Philippine Sea, October 24, 1944. Photograph courtesy of the National Archives (80-G-287970).

American victory was decisive. The Battle of Leyte Gulf was the last major engagement of the Japanese Imperial Navy. The victory ended any further threat of Japanese naval power to the landings at Leyte and elsewhere in the Philippines and to the supply of those ground forces in the coming months. Further, the eclipse of Japanese naval power left hundreds of thousands of Japanese soldiers isolated in the Philippines for the remainder of the war. The largest naval action in history became one of the most decisive battles of World War II.

Seaman Spreigl returned to the States, where the navy placed him in gunnery school. A letter from a friend, dated December 24, 1944, reads, "Hi Ted, Is that so that you was on a aircraft carrier and the Japs sunk it? It must be hell over there." After graduation in April 1945, the navy assigned Spreigl to the main battery of a newly launched

Survivors from the sinking *Princeton*. Photograph courtesy of the National Archives (80-G-281662-6).

cruiser, the USS *Columbus*. The cruiser was commissioned just before the war's end and deployed into the Pacific in early 1946. Ted Spreigl served in the occupation of Japan before leaving the service in 1947. He passed away on March 31, 1987, and is buried in section V, grave site 5267, at Fort Snelling National Cemetery. He shares the cemetery with brothers Clarence and Herbert, both army veterans.

Everett A. Forslin

Everett Forslin was born and raised in Isanti Township, Minnesota, not far north of the Twin Cities. His parents were born in Sweden. Everett, as the oldest son, took care of the family after his father died in 1938. He entered the service in June 1942 at the age of twenty-six. Corporal Forslin was assigned to the 317th Troop Carrier

Group, which shipped overseas in December of that year. The 317th transported people and supplies into the combat zones of the Pacific theater. The group first operated out of Australia, but then moved north toward Japan as Americans took the offensive.

The U.S. Sixth Army landed on the island of Leyte in the Philippines on October 20, 1944. In the aftermath of the decisive naval victory of the Battle of the Gulf of Leyte, the Americans built up their forces on Leyte. The Japanese knew they had to resort to desperate measures, and launched their last airborne assault of the war on Leyte on December 6, 1944. Japanese paratroops were to have coordinated with their ground forces, but the plan was poorly executed as one ground element attacked a day before the drop. An attack on the American airfield at Buri "caught some AAF service group personnel and a portion of a troop carrier squadron by surprise." Corporal Everett Forslin was among those Americans killed in action. The next day, the Japanese airborne offensive led to fighting across the island at key air bases. The Allies secured the area by December 11, and the way lay open for the real prize in the Philippines: Luzon.

Everett Forslin is buried in section C, grave site 7657, at Fort Snelling National Cemetery.

Louis Testa

Louis Testa was a nineteen-year-old living in St. Paul when the Japanese struck Pearl Harbor. He joined the army and became a private in the First Cavalry Division. The division shipped out to Brisbane, Australia, arriving there in late July 1943. Six months of intensive combat jungle warfare training followed.

Their training and discipline paid off. The "First Cav" fought in the Admiralty Islands campaign from March through May 1944, having made an amphibious landing under fire and engaged in fierce jungle combat against suicidal Japanese soldiers. The First Cavalry landed on Leyte Island in the Philippines in October 1944. Leyte was covered by dense vegetation and dominated by a rugged volcanic range, which allowed for a multitude of positions for enemy guns. Operations went well for the Americans on the east half of the island. However, the Japanese managed to land an additional thirty thousand fighting men and substantial weaponry and ammunition onto the beaches on the west side of the island. The Ormoc Valley on the west side remained a Japanese stronghold. The Americans met determined resistance from seasoned Japanese troops. Advances were measured in yards and lives lost, including those to disease. Louis Testa contracted cholera in early December, but survived and immediately returned to the front.

The First Cavalry Division received orders on December 18 to complete the drive south through the Ormoc Valley. Private First Class Louis Testa was awarded the Silver Star for gallantry in action at Balucanad on December 20. His citation reads:

> At dusk a large enemy force attempting to take a ridge line on which one section of 81mm mortars was emplaced, laid in an extremely heavy mortar and automatic weapons barrage. The section sergeant in command was wounded and left lying in an exposed position. The need for rifle support was imperative and Private Testa voluntarily and with complete disregard for his own safety left his cover and under intense enemy fire worked his way to an adjoining rifle troop requesting support. Two rifle squads were assigned to return with him to the location of the besieged mortar section. Private Testa retracing his former route led the two squads successfully through the enemy fire to his original position. After orienting the squad leaders as to the position of the enemy, effective rifle fire was brought to bear upon the Japanese. This sudden burst of fire momentarily stunned the enemy troops, causing a break in the attack and permitted the mortar section to withdraw from their exposed position. Private Testa took this opportunity to crawl forward to the mortar position and evacuate the wounded section sergeant to the safety of nearby cover. He made a second trip to the gun positions and dragged the two 81mm mortars from their exposed emplacements, thus preventing possible capture by the enemy. The outstanding initiative and great courage displayed by Private Testa were contributing factors to the ultimate success of the operation.

The Ormoc Valley operation ended on December 21 with the closing of the pincer movement in the valley. The Leyte campaign cost 15,584 American casualties, including 3,504 killed in action. The Japanese lost an estimated fifty thousand troops.

The Imperial Japanese Army still had a quarter of a million fighting men on the island of Luzon. The First Cavalry made the landing on Luzon and engaged in fierce fighting on that island until the war ended. The division went on to Japan with the distinction of being the first U.S. division to enter Tokyo.

Louis Testa ended the war with a chest full of decorations. These included the Distinguished Service Cross, the Silver Star, the Bronze Star, and the Purple Heart. He died in 1984 at the age of sixty-two. His remains are buried on the main avenue of Fort Snelling National Cemetery in section DS, alongside others honored with the Medal of Honor, Distinguished Service Cross, or Navy Cross. The grave site is 71-S.

Fred Hauer Otto

Fred Otto was a Mankato, Minnesota, milkman working for Marigold Dairies at the time of the Japanese attack on Pearl Harbor. The talk along his route the next morning was all about the terrible devastation. Fred was thirty-two years old and married to wife Elizabeth. He was an active sportsman who had played in the city softball leagues since the age of fifteen. The war engulfed the nation and Otto entered the U.S. Navy in September 1943. He went through boot camp at Farragut, Idaho, and shopkeepers school at Toledo, Ohio, before being transferred to San Diego. The navy assigned Seaman Otto to the light carrier USS *Belleau Wood,* which was undergoing overhaul at Pearl Harbor. He shipped out to Pearl Harbor on June 1 to report for duty. The *Belleau Wood* was one of nine Cleveland-class cruisers converted to light carriers for the war. Otto issued supplies from the storeroom when the ship was not in action, "everything from stationery to window cleaner."

The *Belleau Wood* rejoined the fleet in the summer of 1944 in time to take part in the reoccupation of Guam. It was Fred Otto's first combat experience. The light carrier became part of Task Force Thirty-eight, one of sixteen carriers. Warplanes from the task force pounded Palau and Peleliu in support of American forces landing on the beaches. The group steamed into the Philippine Sea, from where the carrier planes hit Okinawa and Formosa (modern-day Taiwan), as well as Japanese positions in the Philippines. When the ship's fighter and torpedo bomber planes flew missions, Shopkeeper Fred Otto was arming and rearming the aircraft with shells and torpedoes. This duty was not without its hazards. The *Belleau Wood* withstood forty-seven Japanese air attacks on the night of October 12–13, 1944, while its planes participated in raids on Formosa and the Nasei Shoto. The ship headed south to Luzon, where planes from the *Belleau Wood* attacked the Japanese air base at Manila and Japanese ships in Manila Bay on October 14–15. This was only a prelude to the major battle, which took place on October 23–26. The crew and pilots of the *Belleau Wood* endured four exhausting days during the Battle of Leyte Gulf, from which the United States emerged victorious.

The *Belleau Wood* was cruising ninety miles off Leyte Gulf on patrol duty with Task Group Thirty-eight A just four days later, on October 30, 1944. Japanese planes were reported around noon and all hands rushed to battle stations. *Belleau Wood* managed to launch six fighter planes before the enemy arrived. A kamikaze slammed into the USS *Franklin,* setting her flight deck ablaze. A second enemy plane began what appeared to be a kamikaze dive toward the *Franklin.* The dive-bomber dropped a large bomb near the *Franklin,* then suddenly changed its course and crashed into the *Belleau*

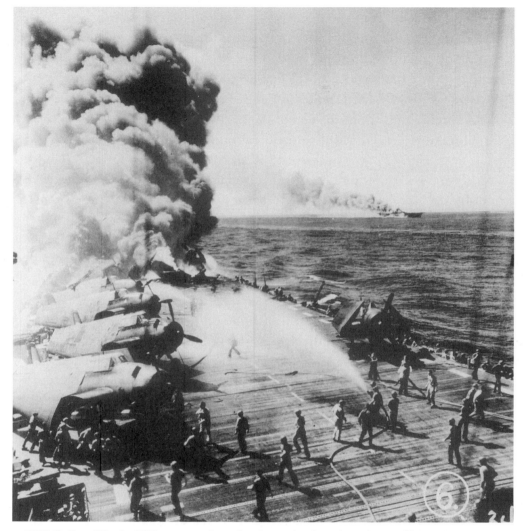

USS *Belleau Wood* 9CVL-240 on fire after being hit by a kamikaze off the Philippines on October 30, 1944. The USS *Franklin,* in the background, has also been hit by a kamikaze. Photograph courtesy of the National Archives (80-G-342020).

Wood. There was a tremendous explosion on the aft portion of the flight deck. The crew rushed to control the spreading flames, but were unable to prevent ammunition and depth charges from catching fire and exploding. The battle to contain the fire lasted for hours. The carrier suffered heavy damage, as well as the loss of ninety-two men. The *Belleau Wood* and the *Franklin,* escorted by destroyers, limped home to San Francisco for repair.

The crew received leave to go home while their ship was being repaired. Fred Otto returned to Mankato for ten days' leave. His appearance, fresh from the action off Leyte, made the hometown boy's return a big event. The *Mankato Free Press* placed Otto's story on the front page of its December 7, 1944, edition. He told the reporter that "the road to Tokyo is hard and bloody and long." The paper added, "The seaman is making no predictions about the end of the war."

Otto returned to San Francisco to rejoin his crew on the *Belleau Wood.* The carrier steamed to Pearl Harbor and proceeded on January 29 to rendezvous with the fleet. *Belleau Wood* from this point onward was involved in raiding Japan. The *Mankato Free Press* published in October 1945 a long letter that Otto wrote to his wife, Elizabeth. The letter described the carrier's activities of the last month of the war up to the Japanese surrender, during which "we had freely ranged over the entire empire's home islands." Otto described the initial emphasis on airfields and airfield installations "that left us in complete control of the air over the empire by the time the cruise ended." Later attacks hit railroad yards, locomotives, and factories. Planes from the *Belleau Wood* battered beyond use the *Nagato,* the last modern battleship in the Imperial Japanese Navy, on July 18. They devastated the islands of Shikoku and Honshu. A dogfight between a *Belleau Wood* squadron and "fifteen of the Japs' fast new fighters" ended with seven Japanese planes fleeing the area. News of Japan's surrender on August 15 resulted in everyone breathing a sigh of relief, yet the pilots had to scramble for their planes at word of enemy approaching. The American pilots shot down at least twelve planes that day before the situation calmed down. Fred Otto wrote, "We haven't seen anymore of them since that afternoon and we hope that those were the last we'll see unless we find one on a visit to Japan or take our grandchildren down to a local museum some day and show them what grandpappy did in the big war."

Fred Otto died in 1995. He is buried in section 15, grave site 639, at Fort Snelling National Cemetery.

Patrick E. Ward

The U.S. Coast Guard is one of the nation's five armed services. The commander of the U.S. Armed Forces ordered the Coast Guard to operate as part of the navy on November 4, 1941, the month before the Japanese attack on Pearl Harbor. Coast Guard personnel manned a wide range of ships and amphibious craft, from large troop transports to small attack craft, during the four years of war. They landed infantrymen and Marines in every important invasion landing in Europe, North Africa, and the

Seaman First Class Patrick Ward of the U.S. Coast Guard manning a gun on an invasion transport. Ward took part in the landings in the Marshalls, Guam, at Peleliu and Leyte, and at Luzon. The transport on which he served was among the first ships to hit the beach at Luzon. Photograph courtesy of the Minneapolis Public Library, Minneapolis Collection.

Pacific. The navy decorated nearly two thousand Coast Guard personnel with several awards, including one Medal of Honor, six Navy Crosses, and one Distinguished Service Cross.

Patrick Ward of south Minneapolis entered the Coast Guard in April 1943 when he was not quite eighteen years old. Ward completed training and shipped out to the Pacific theater. His first taste of action came on January 31, 1944, when American forces, including nearly three hundred ships, commenced Operation Flintlock, the assault on the Marshall Islands in the Central Pacific. Seaman First Class Ward handled a gun aboard a Coast Guard–manned invasion transport. The Marshall Islands group consists of five islands and twenty-nine atolls. Only after numerous landings was the

American occupation completed in late April 1944. The navy allowed the fleet little time to rest after securing the Marshall Islands. Patrick Ward and the many others who made up the heart of the fleet participated next in the retaking of Guam during July and August.

The landing at Leyte in the Philippines, code-named "King-Two," commenced October 20, 1944. Thirty-five Coast Guard vessels took part, including five large transports, two attack cargo vessels, ten frigates, and twelve landing ship transports. Additional Coast Guard personnel were scattered on other navy ships. Patrick Ward was again aboard his invasion transport. Coast Guardsmen from the USS *Aquarius,* which put LCVPs over the side for an advanced beach party, were among the initial wave at Leyte. The LCVP, or Landing Craft, Vehicle and Personnel, was perhaps the most famous of the Higgins boats. This tough, highly maneuverable craft could land a platoon of thirty-six men and their equipment and extract itself to return to the mother ship for more troops. Japanese kamikazes posed a continual threat to navy and Coast Guard personnel throughout the landings and the movement of supplies to the infantry on shore.

Ward later took part in the Luzon landing, again facing coastal artillery and gunfire and the ever-present threat of kamikazes descending from the sky. Dr. Robert M. Browning Jr., Coast Guard historian, wrote:

> Coast Guard boat crews faced this particular danger repeatedly while Marine passengers faced it only once. During all the major landings in the Pacific, Coast Guardsmen steered their boats onto the rugged coral beaches, unloaded their cargoes, backed off, steered back through the gunfire, and reloaded their craft time and time again. Having done this for months against enemy fire, tough beaches and heavy seas . . . won an almost legendary reputation with the fleet.

Patrick Ward served three years with the Coast Guard. He left the service in 1946 at the age of twenty years. He died in 1994 at the age of sixty-nine and is buried in section 8, grave site 361, at Fort Snelling National Cemetery.

Chapter 6

Pressing into Germany

Osmund C. Skarning

All who joined the Ninety-ninth Battalion spoke Norwegian and many were from the Norwegian-populated areas of Minnesota. Yet only a few of the men had visited the land of their parents and grandparents. The original purpose in forming the Ninety-ninth was to conduct commando raids and sabotage within German-occupied Norway, but most of the men never made it there. The battalion insignia was a shield with a Viking ship in the Norwegian national colors of red, blue, and white. The Ninety-ninth left Fort Snelling on December 17, 1942, and arrived at Camp Hale, Colorado, for mountain training after a two-day train ride, followed by a long march to the camp. Osmund Skarning was among them.

The U.S. Army sent the Ninety-ninth to Europe, where they arrived on the beaches at Normandy on June 21, 1944. The battalion advanced across France in July and August 1944 while attached to the Second Armored Division of General George S. Patton's Third Army. They drove into Belgium, reaching the Albert Canal on September 8 and attacking across the canal on September 13. The fighting was fierce, and the dikes along the canals allowed for good defensive cover for the German soldiers.

Company A of the Ninety-ninth was attached to Combat Command A of the Second Armored Division early on the morning of September 14. Company C of the Ninety-ninth moved with the Second Battalion of the Sixty-sixth Armored Regiment on September 16 to attack east of the Zuid Willems Vaart Canal and secure Reckheim.

Sergeant Osmund Skarning of the Ninety-ninth Infantry Battalion, training in Colorado before shipping overseas. Photograph from the official Ninety-ninth Infantry Battalion Web site.

Companies A, B, and D moved to support Company C's attack. The offensive would continue through September 18 before the objective was secured.

It was during this engagement that Company A's advance was halted at a canal with a destroyed bridge. Yngvar Stensby of Company A wrote:

We were greeted by occasional bursts from Nazi Burp guns, as well as harassed by snipers hidden in trees on the other side of the canal. "Volunteers" from various squads in the 99th soon lined the canal bank, intent on locating the snipers and putting them out of action. Among the riflemen was Sgt. Skarning. He had a pleasant, reassuring air of confidence about him, and his ever-present smile was balm for the harried soul. At his urging, we spread out along the bank so as not to provide a group target to the snipers. His eyes narrowed to slits as he surveyed the trees on the east side of the canal; then, without a word, he emptied several clips of ammunition at what he surmised was a suspicious-looking treetop. Riflemen to his left and right joined in until it was obvious at least one of the snipers had been dispatched.

Stensby wrote that several tanks arrived the next morning. The date was September 15. Riflemen climbed onto the rear decks of the tanks and rode on combat patrol along the Zuid Willems Vaart Canal. Skarning and Stensby rode on the same tank, Skarning sitting behind Stensby. Stensby later wrote, "One moment he was there; the next moment he was missing." At first it was assumed that Skarning simply had slipped off the lurching tank as it traversed the terrain. Since a stationary tank was a target for an antitank gun, it did not stop for missing riflemen. But a lieutenant soon approached and reported, "Sergeant Skarning is dead!" A sniper had killed him. Stensby wrote, "In a seething rage I checked my rifle and headed for the canal again. I was joined by every rifleman in the area." He recalled one rifleman cursing, "Some damn sniper got him!" and another responding, "Some damn sniper is going to get his just reward!" They fired volley after volley of rifle fire across the canal.

"The 99ers had suffered many deaths before, but none struck me as numbingly as the knowledge that our beloved Sgt. Skarning had been killed," Stensby added. "Sgt. Skarning's smile still lingers in my memory. And never do I listen to the plaintive notes of the bugler's Taps but what I feel his presence, and hear again his reassuring assessment in a tense situation." Osmund Skarning grew up in Minneapolis, the son of a Norwegian immigrant. He left behind an older brother. His body was returned to Minnesota after the war, and his remains were reinterred on May 18, 1949, at Fort Snelling National Cemetery. He is buried in section C-3, grave site 7859.

Gerald Galarneau

Operation Marketgarden. The name conjures up controversy and debate to this day. The plan was a daring gamble that failed and cost many lives. The Allies were pushing back the German armies in the low countries in September 1944. Allied planners were concerned about securing key bridges across the Rhine, the wide river at Germany's western edge. They conceived a bold plan to drop massive numbers of paratroopers into Holland to seize several key bridges. The plan called for fast-moving armor to penetrate through German lines and cross the secured bridges into Germany.

The main assault was made on September 17, 1944. The First British Airborne was dropped near Arnhem and Oosterbeek, the U.S. Eighty-second Airborne near Nijmegen, and the U.S. 101st Airborne near Son and Veghel. British paratroopers occupied the north end of the bridge at Arnhem on that first day, but Allied intelligence had failed to discover that two of Germany's crack panzer divisions were in the area. The surprised Germans acted quickly to reclaim the bridges, and Allied armor never would break through.

Gerald Galarneau was born in Minneapolis and enlisted in 1941 after graduation from the University of Minnesota. He volunteered for service as a glider pilot, a unique breed of fearless fliers. The gliders were unforgiving and required careful piloting from trained professionals. The towplane controlled when the gliders would be released to land, regardless of the intensity of ground fire. The towplane brought the gliders in low to the ground, making them easy targets as they neared the landing zone. The speed of the gliders dropped off considerably after release, increasing their vulnerability and reducing the possibility of a safe landing. Furthermore, as the glider was made of little more than wood and canvas, the pilot was the first to go if the glider hit a tree or a German antiglider barrier.

Only six thousand American glider pilots flew in World War II. They were invaluable because of their specialized training, so headquarters made every effort to control the number of men lost on each mission. Consequently, the men's orders upon landing were clear: get back to Allied lines. They were not to risk their lives in combat. In reality, these orders were difficult to follow. Gliders by definition landed behind enemy lines, and there was generally no easy way back until the fighting was done. They were not about to tell the glider troops they carried in that they would not fight alongside them until they contacted the main units.

Galarneau underwent advanced glider pilot training at Victorville, California. During training, he and his copilot managed to survive a glider crash when their plane went into a tight, uncontrollable spiral. The near-death incident was a turning point for the young man, who wrote: "I looked death in the eye and it backed down; and then something beyond death looked me in the eye and I backed down.... At that moment, everything changed and my life has never been the same."

Galarneau graduated from advanced training on February 8, 1943, and was appointed a flight officer. Soon thereafter he was assigned to the 316th Troop Carrier Group, whose motto was "Valor without Arms." He participated in several landings in the Mediterranean theater, but missed the D-Day-minus-one landing. The Americans loaned some of their best pilots, including Galarneau, to the British. The American glider units did so well that the British gliders never went in. Galarneau felt bad that he had missed being with his comrades in the colossal D-Day expedition.

Second Lieutenant Gerald Galarneau flew his glider with its cargo of six Eighty-second Airborne paratroopers and a Jeep into the landing zone behind German lines in Holland during Operation Marketgarden. Photograph courtesy of Lillian Galarneau.

Galarneau's load for Operation Marketgarden was six men from the Eighty-second Airborne Division and a Jeep. His targeted landing zone, sixty miles behind German lines, was near the town of Nijmegen, Holland. The paratroopers were to hold a key bridge over the Waal River and prevent the Germans from destroying it. Galarneau's orders after delivering the men and equipment to the target were to disengage with the airborne and make his way back to the Allied lines. Unfortunately, German panzer divisions stood in his way. He happened to run into his good friend and fellow glider pilot Bob McQuillan.

> We became engaged in the process of bringing order out of the chaotic conditions around us. In other words, we began looking for a safe place to wait until the British Army arrived. This was not going to be easy, but we did stumble onto the airborne command post set up by General Gavin who was the commanding general of the 82nd Airborne. His command post was hidden in a pine forest and we reasoned that if anyone would survive this mess, it would be the general.

German artillery exploding in the treetops and showering the area with shrapnel soon prompted the two pilots to abandon their half-finished foxholes and move on.

Galarneau and McQuillan came across twenty paratroopers of the Eighty-second. The commanding officer requested their support in stopping German tanks reportedly coming into the area. Galarneau later wrote, "With nothing better to do and with little choice, we volunteered." The two pilots marched down the road with their new comrades for about half an hour. The officer ordered his men to dig in, then instructed Galarneau and McQuillan to follow him. Galarneau wrote:

> The three of us then continued down the road for about another mile. Here the terrain narrowed and any approaching tank would move down on the road in order to advance. At this place, he handed us his bazooka and a couple of rockets and told us to dig in. Our duty was to stop any tank or tanks from getting beyond this point. It was becoming dark and he left us with the chilling words, we would be relieved in the morning. At that moment, we knew that if any tanks came down this road we would never see the morning. We possibly could get off one shot or maybe two and alert the officer and his men, but tanks do not come alone, but usually in groups and their infantry follows close behind. Lucky for us there were no tanks that night and in the morning we were relieved by the officer.

Galarneau and his buddy made it to Allied lines three days later with the help of the Dutch Resistance. Operation Marketgarden was a disaster, with some twelve thousand Allied casualties. It was the last great glider raid against the Germans.

Gerald Galarneau returned home to Minneapolis a second lieutenant. He married and raised a large family around which he built a good life. He died on February 11, 2004, at the age of eighty-five. He is buried in section 20-A, grave site 838, at Fort Snelling National Cemetery.

Warner Squires

Private Warner Squires served in Operation Marketgarden with Company F of the 325th Glider Infantry Regiment of the Eighty-second Airborne Division. The glider regiment was mobilized on September 19, but grounded by limited visibility until September 23, when the weather finally cleared. By this time, the situation in Holland was desperate. The British were holding out at the Arnhem Bridge, but at great loss.

The 325th flew in fifteen-man squads, each group flying in on a CG-4A glider. The aircraft, consisting essentially of canvas stretched over balsa wood, was towed to the battle site and released. It then glided into the landing zone through flak bursts. Landing casualties could be significant if impact was not in an open field. The advantage was that glider infantrymen did not require the extensive ground training necessary for paratroops. They also landed as a squad, rather than individually and scattered as so often happened with paratroopers, and were ready to go into action immediately as a unit. Wayne Pierce, historian of the 325th Glider Infantry Regiment, estimates that about two hundred of the regiment's 258 gliders landed in the target zone.

The 325th relieved the 505th paratroopers of the Eighty-second, who were defending a line south of Groesbeek facing the Reichswald Forest. Their objective was to maintain the open corridor so that supplies and armor support could move north to secure the Arnhem Bridge, which the British paratroopers were so bravely holding. The 325th was engaged in heavy fighting in this position in the Kiekberg Woods September 24–27. The Germans attacked in force on September 26 but were repulsed. The Second Battalion mounted an attack into the Kiekberg Woods on September 27 to clear the position of Germans. Company F, Private Squires's unit, and Company G attacked from the north while Company E advanced from the finger ridge. The advance met heavy resistance, running into two German battalions preparing to drive into Nijmegen. The fighting was fierce in the thickly forested hills and ravines. It was during this fighting that paratrooper Warner Squires lost his life.

On September 25 the remnants of the First British Airborne withdrew from Arnhem. The British lost nearly eight thousand of ten thousand paratroops who participated, one of their greatest losses of the war. The Eighty-second Division lost fifteen hundred men, and the 101st slightly more than two thousand. The Dutch have never forgotten the sacrifice of the British and Americans on their behalf. Neither should future generations of British and Americans.

Warner Squires entered the service in Racine County, Wisconsin. His remains lie in section C-6, grave site 8365, at Fort Snelling National Cemetery.

Ragnar Abrahamson

Ragnar Abrahamson was among the rugged Minnesotans who volunteered for the Ninety-ninth Battalion. He was made acting section sergeant. His machine gunner was Olaf Ellefsen, a man "as old as my father," who would have been excused from service by virtue of his age. But when Ellefsen learned he could not return to his job at the sawmill back home, he decided to remain with Abrahamson. Sergeant Abrahamson wrote: "The Army couldn't send you overseas until you were a citizen. So then, in the weeks before we were going to leave Camp Hale, they proceeded to take us into Leadville [Colorado] and swear us in to make us citizens." The Ninety-ninth was sent to Europe and landed at Normandy on June 21, 1944. The battalion was engaged in heavy combat at Elbeuf at the end of August. The Ninety-ninth entered the town through heavy artillery fire. The fighting was "from street to street, from house to house and door to door" for two days. The battalion accounted for knocking at least four Nazi tanks out of commission before the tank destroyers arrived. Lieutenant Colonel Turner, the battalion commanding officer, was among the numerous wounded and killed in the fight for Elbeuf. Major Harold Hansen assumed command.

The Ninety-ninth moved across northern France and Belgium into Germany. The battalion became engaged in the Battle of Aachen, also called the Battle of Wurzeln, on October 16, 1944. The battalion history called it "nine days' continuous nightmare." The Thirtieth and First Divisions closed in around Wurzeln. The Germans remained in a well-entrenched pocket at Aachen. Their only way out was up a narrow highway to the north, which the Ninety-ninth held "in the face of a continual and accurate concentration of artillery, mortar and point-blank tank fire." Each time the enemy dislodged the Ninety-ninth, the battalion retook the position with counterattack. The accurate enemy fire made it nearly impossible for food and water to be delivered to the front. The Ninety-ninth went without food and water, sleeping on cold, wet ground until relieved on October 24. As Ragnar Abrahamson wrote, "I don't believe we had any water for 24 hours. That's worse than going without food, but we didn't care. We

American soldiers march a long line of German prisoners out of Aachen, the first German city to fall. Thirty-five hundred German troops surrendered on October 21, 1944. Photograph courtesy of the National Archives (260-MGG-1061-1).

just kept struggling on." All of the battalion's officers had been killed or wounded. Ragnar's closest call came when a grenade explosion threw him into the air, but somehow didn't wound him seriously. "For me," he wrote, "this was the worst time during the war. We were more or less getting annihilated."

The Ninety-ninth later became involved in the Battle of the Bulge in December 1944. German infiltrators, of which there were many, were disarmed and arrested by American soldiers, especially the Minnesotans whose heavy European accents fooled the enemy. The Ninety-ninth Battalion was sent to Oslo, Norway, at the end of the war. They served as part of the honor guard for King Haakon VII of Norway on June 7, when he returned from five years of exile in England. Abrahamson, who was born in Norway, wrote: "I was so happy about going to Norway... because my whole family lived in Norway." He met his father's brother for the first time.

Ragnar Abrahamson, known as "Rung" to his friends, lived for many years in Bloomington. He was a long-standing member of the Norwegian Glee Club, an organization active in the Twin Cities since 1909. Abrahamson died in November 1993. He is buried in section Y, grave site 1950, at Fort Snelling National Cemetery.

Robert D. Farmer

Robert Farmer won the welterweight boxing championship at the University of Minnesota while attending school there in 1928 and 1929. He returned home to Mankato and worked for a weather-stripping company while serving as a boxing instructor at the Mankato YMCA. He enlisted in the army in June 1942. Farmer went overseas in October 1943, assigned to the Sixteenth Infantry Regiment of "the Big Red One," the famed First Infantry Division. Farmer and his comrades became involved in amphibious training in Britain in preparation for the D-Day landings at Normandy. The First Division, while having made combat landings in North Africa and Sicily, included many replacement soldiers without combat experience. The Allied command anticipated heavy casualties.

The First Division was in the first wave to go ashore on Omaha Beach the morning of June 6, 1944, and the Sixteenth Regiment spearheaded the assault. The Sixteenth landed alongside the Second Ranger Battalion and, consequently, were mistaken by reporters for Rangers. The Sixteenth have been known as "Rangers" ever since and are the only non-Ranger unit in the army to carry this distinction. The survivors of the initial landing were pinned by enemy fire when Regimental Commander Colonel George Taylor, commanding the Sixteenth, jumped to his feet and shouted his now famous cry, "The only men who remain on this beach are the dead and those about to die! Let's get moving!" The regiment rushed forward and pushed its way off the beach to its objective, Colleville-sur-Mer. Robert Farmer and the rest of the Sixteenth earned the Presidential Unit Citation and the praise of General Eisenhower, who told the regiment on July 2, "You are the finest regiment in our army... a sort of Praetorian Guard."

The fighting on Omaha Beach cost the lives of hundreds of men. Farmer narrowly escaped death with a bullet hole through his helmet. Those who survived the horror of Omaha Beach faced months more of fierce fighting as the Allies pressed into Germany to force the end of the war. Farmer was a staff sergeant as he advanced with the Sixteenth Regiment through France and entered Belgium in September 1944. He was thirty-seven, considerably older than many enlisted men. On October 16, 1944, his regiment had the honor of helping capture Aachen, Charlemagne's ancient capital and the first German city to be taken by the Allies. The regiment then advanced into the Huertgen Forest. The battle in the thick woods lasted several months. Nine U.S. combat divisions were involved and casualties numbered twenty-four thousand in what some called the worst fighting of the war. The forest claimed more lives, yard for yard, than any other objective in the war.

The Germans were entrenched in well-camouflaged permanent positions in the Huertgen Forest. Elaborate bunker systems protected their guns from Allied air and artillery attack. Extensive fields of barbed wire and booby traps made advance treacherous. Artillery shell bursts in the treetops covered large areas with shrapnel from which there was little protection, even in foxholes. The dense vegetation made American air and artillery support useless. Without such protection, infantry worked their way forward through the thickets against well-mined machine-gun positions, suffering much higher casualties than usual.

The Sixteenth Regiment's initial objective in the Huertgen was the village of Hamich. The weather was particularly bad and the attack did not commence until November 16. Fog, rain, and snow further reduced what little visibility there was in the dense forest. Concealed enemy positions poured deadly fire on advancing troops. Individual pockets of Americans held out while German counterattacks overran adjacent positions. Troops fought German tanks with hand grenades. Survivors reported that the smell of cordite from the explosives was constant. The regiment made ground, then dug in to repel seven counterattacks the Germans hurled at them that day. The fighting through the next several days was just as fierce, and it was not until November 19 and after much loss of life that the Sixteenth Regiment took Hamich.

Staff Sergeant Robert Farmer distinguished himself in the advance to Hamich. He was awarded the Distinguished Service Cross for extraordinary heroism in action against the enemy on November 18, 1944. The citation reads:

> Although severely wounded during an enemy attack, Sergeant Farmer drove the foe back from his position with rifle fire, and crawled to a machine gun emplacement. Opening fire, he forced the enemy to disperse and seek cover. When his ammunition was exhausted, he crawled through heavy hostile fire to a second machine gun. Despite artillery and mortar fire falling upon his position, he held his ground in the face of a second enemy assault and poured withering fire into the hostile ranks. His

machine gun ammunition again expended, he once more fired his rifle until his position was overrun and he himself was killed by enemy fire.

Captain Edwin Elder Jr., commanding Company H of the Sixteenth Infantry, wrote Farmer's parents in Mankato:

> December 7, 1944. Condolences of the officers and men of Company H, 16th Infantry on the death of your son. . . . Robert, at all times, was a good soldier and was well liked by both officers and men. He continually displayed the habits and bearing of a soldier and a gentleman, and had a real respect and friendship of all who knew him. He died, as he lived, courageously; in the performance of a difficult mission.

The family's next-youngest son, Matthew, was serving with the army in the Philippines at the time.

The army buried Staff Sergeant Robert Farmer in an American military cemetery in Belgium. His remains were returned home to Minnesota in 1947. He was buried with full military honors in the DS section, grave site 62-S, at Fort Snelling National Cemetery on December 5, 1947, by virtue of the Distinguished Service Cross that he earned and his two Purple Hearts. The Reverend Kirby Webster, Farmer's pastor before he himself went off to war, presided over the service. Reverend Webster served in the war as a chaplain and had been just a few miles from Farmer when he died. The Mankato YMCA flew its flag at half-mast on the day of Farmer's final interment.

The victory in the Huertgen Forest cost the Allies twenty-four thousand in killed, wounded, captured, or missing. The U.S. First Army was left in shambles, with entire divisions in need of replacement. The loss of officers and noncommissioned officers made command control difficult. The Allies were ill prepared when the German army began its major counteroffensive that became the Battle of the Bulge in December.

Norman E. Dow

Norman Dow was a resident of Morton, Minnesota, when he entered the service in May 1943. He was nineteen years old. He went overseas in December of that year as a private in the Fifty-first Armored Infantry Battalion in the Fourth Armored Division. The Fourth was part of General George Patton's Third Army, for which General Eisenhower had big plans. Patton's Third Army led the breakout from Normandy in the summer of 1944 and swept across France toward Germany. The German army fought tenaciously to defend their fatherland and casualties were high. The hard-

American GIs advancing. Every town across France and Germany presented another obstacle and cost additional American lives to the end of the war. Photograph courtesy of the National Archives (111-SC-205298).

fought Lorraine Campaign, which took place between September and December 1944, left Patton's victorious army on the verge of thrusting into Germany. However, there were serious casualties on both sides. Private Norman Dow was among them.

Lieutenant Colonel Dan Alanis, commanding the Fifty-first Battalion, found the time during a lull in the action to write Norman's mother:

> The War Department has no doubt notified you of the death of your son . . . who was killed in action in our advance near Sarre Union, France on December 1, 1944. Norman has served with us for several months here and in losing him we have lost an excellent soldier and man, but also a friend who can never be replaced. Norman was buried in an Army cemetery in eastern France. As Norman's Battalion Commander, I want you to know that his comrades in this battalion feel his loss most keenly.

Norman Dow's remains lie at rest in section A-22, grave site 5459, at Fort Snelling National Cemetery.

Gaylord Winmill

Gaylord Winmill was twenty years old, from Stanton, North Dakota, when he enlisted in the U.S. Army at Fort Snelling on November 18, 1942. He worked as a cement finisher before enlisting. Those who came to know Winmill during the war remember him as a genuine character. He had a reputation for enjoying beer and a good fight, as evidenced by a nose that was noticeably broken sometime in the past. He was the kind of tough guy who would volunteer for the paratroopers, and he did. After finishing jump school, Winmill was assigned to Company F, 501st Parachute Infantry Regiment, and became a member of Major General Maxwell Taylor's 101st Airborne Division. Brigadier General William Lee commented on August 16, 1942, "The 101st . . . has no history, but it has a rendezvous with destiny." The 101st would end the war having earned the legendary name "Screaming Eagles."

Nick Schmidt remembers Winmill well, saying, "He was probably my best buddy." Schmidt recalled that Winmill "goofed up in some way after we came over" and was demoted from a rank of T-5 to T-4 and then to private by August 1944. Winmill's military record confirms this. But Schmidt is quick to add of his friend, "He was a good soldier. He did what he was told to do." Schmidt said that he often thinks of Winmill, who was tall and lanky and walked with a lope. He was "a cross between Damon Runyon and Ichabod Crane." Schmidt laughs in recollecting that "he was a funny guy and a fun guy to be with."

The 101st Airborne shipped to England at the beginning of 1944 for final training and preparations for the invasion of Hitler's Fortress Europe. The plan was for thirteen thousand paratroops of the 101st and Eighty-second Airborne to drop behind Utah Beach the night before the scheduled landings. It required eight hundred planes to make the drop. The paratroopers were to secure the inland crossroads and causeways to prevent German reserves from moving up and reinforcing the units defending the beach and, perhaps, ultimately pushing the American soldiers into the sea. This was the first combat jump for the 101st Airborne; the Eighty-second had already made two such jumps. The Normandy assault would be the first night paratrooper attack in history—a bold tactic, but perhaps a necessary one. In any case, military planners expected huge losses on the beaches and in the paratroop zones behind German lines.

The C-47s carrying the paratroopers across the English Channel to Normandy met heavy antiaircraft flak as soon as they passed into French airspace. Many planes were hit, and in the confusion pilots broke formation to be less of a target and then took evasive action. Without a lead plane to follow, careful plans for prescribed altitudes and flying speeds fell apart and pinpointing the correct target zones became impossible. The paratroopers on the planes felt the same terror as the pilots as shells exploded around them. To make matters worse, the paratroopers jumped into high winds, which scattered them across the area, sometimes into trees. Many of the paratroopers found themselves alone and in unknown coordinates once they were on the ground. The airborne units spent most of the first day dodging German units and hooking up with other paratroopers. The scattered jump into Normandy confused the Germans just as much as the Americans. The Germans did not know where to fight the Americans as there were no real front lines. Fighting consisted of small unit actions. The Germans found American paratroopers seemingly everywhere, ambushing and seizing strategic positions. Private First Class Gaylord Winmill was awarded the Purple Heart for wounds suffered on June 6, 1944, D-Day.

A little humor was greatly appreciated by the small groups of men, anxious about their precarious position behind German lines, and Winmill was a funny guy, whose country-boy humor could make nearly anyone laugh. He was a free spirit with his own way of expressing himself. When he was late returning to camp and questioned as to where he had been, he might say, "Slapping sore-ass ducks with towels." If he felt he had told someone off, he would say, "I showed what the bear shit in the buckwheat." If matters appeared to be heading toward a fight, Winmill had been heard more than once to say, "I'm gonna kick your ass 'til you bark like a fox."

The infantry landings, while costly in terms of lives, secured the beaches by the end of the first day and the infantry and airborne were linked. The Allies had a foothold in France. The 101st gathered on D-Day-plus-two to regroup and receive supplies by gliders. The division then moved toward its objectives and secured four key causeways over the Cotentin lowlands in the next two days of heavy fighting. The 101st took part in the heavy fighting for the strategic city of Carentan, which they took and held for two days against German counterattacks. Gaylord Winmill was a seasoned fighter by the end of the Normandy campaign.

Winmill and his comrades made their second combat jump in September 1944 as part of Operation Marketgarden. The objective was to seize the major bridges across the Rhine River into Germany. While this jump was less chaotic than D-Day, intelligence was poor and the Allied paratroopers faced two ace panzer divisions in the immediate area. Operation Marketgarden was a disaster, but Winmill gained more experience.

The 101st Airborne Division was in reserve when the Germans began their major offensive through the Ardennes Forest in December 1944. The Battle of the Bulge took its name from the broad penetration of the Germans. Allied command rushed the 101st in to seize the critical crossroads town of Bastogne and hold it at all costs. Bastogne was at the center of the road network that traversed the thick Ardennes. Nick Schmidt and Gaylord Winmill served together with the 501st in the defense of Bastogne. Winmill's sarcastic sense of humor was again important in providing his comrades a good laugh now and then amid the carnage and danger of combat.

The 501st led the 101st into Bastogne. The regiment's commanding officer previously had visited the area while on leave to see a nurse based there. He had become familiar with the terrain, never imagining this knowledge would prove valuable. Southbound traffic, fleeing the German advance, blocked the roads into Bastogne. The advance to contact and destroy the enemy turned into a desperate defensive operation. The days of December 20–22 consisted of holding out against fierce assaults by German infantry and armor. A military history of the battle noted that Winmill's company, Company F of the 501st, was involved in the biggest action of the day on December 20, repelling a heavy enemy attack. The German tanks and men should have overrun the 501st, but the paratroopers were tough and well trained. They chose good ground and were dug in. Airborne were conditioned for such situations, holding out against superior numbers while concealing their exact strength and intentions.

Nick Schmidt was wounded during one of these actions and was pulled off the line. There was no way to evacuate the wounded, but the men of the 501st did not know they were surrounded until December 24. Schmidt remembers how throughout the war he and Winmill and others used to rhetorically ask one another, "What's the big picture?" Never was that question more present in their minds than at Bastogne. The Germans surrounded the town and cut off all roads. The 101st had no chance of receiving much-needed supplies. The 101st had deployed so rapidly that there was no time to obtain winter uniforms and other gear. That the winter of 1944–1945 was the coldest and snowiest in memory made what was already a distinct hardship even worse.

Brigadier General Tony McAuliffe, acting commander of the 101st, delivered his famous response "Nuts!" to the German demand to immediately surrender or face total annihilation on December 22 after five days of German attacks with supplies dwindling. The 101st held out for three more days of intense bombardment and fighting until the clouds lifted and supplies and reinforcements began to arrive by plane. The 101st denied the Germans the strategic crossroads town of Bastogne and played a major role in stopping the last German offensive of the war. Nazi Germany lost large numbers of irreplaceable men, tanks, aircraft, and materials. Hitler's risky gamble failed because of the determination of the American citizen-soldier to follow orders at all costs in whatever conditions. Approximately nineteen thousand American soldiers gave their lives in this monthlong battle involving more than one million men.

Gaylord Winmill and his comrades were awarded the Bronze Star for their conspicuous gallantry. The 101st Airborne was elevated to the pantheon of elite military units by virtue of their fabled defense of Bastogne. Schmidt never saw his good friend, Gaylord Winmill, after the war. While he showed few visible physical wounds, the combat veteran carried other wounds perhaps not so apparent to others. He settled in Minnesota after the war, but was hospitalized and died of a cerebral hemorrhage on August 11, 1953. Gaylord Winmill, a true American hero, was laid to rest in Fort Snelling National Cemetery on August 13, 1953. He was thirty-one years old. The grave site is 11026 in section C-15.

It was some time before Winmill's comrades learned of his passing while tracking down "lost" men of the 501st PIR when the reunions began as the men got up in age. Nick Schmidt remarks of his old war buddy, "I'm glad he was with us. He's been gone a long time, but I think about him often."

Henry George Lemke Jr.

Hank Lemke grew up on St. Paul's East Side with his brothers, Erv and Carl. Hank Lemke entered the service in November 1942 and was assigned to the newly formed Seventh Armored Division. This was to become part of General George Patton's Third Army. Lemke and his comrades spent a year in training before being shipped overseas. The twelve thousand men of the Seventh Armored crammed aboard the *Queen Mary* and made the Atlantic crossing. The division crossed the English Channel just one week later, landing on the Normandy beaches August 10.

Patton's Third Army moved into action in August 1944 with Operation Cobra and the breakout from Normandy. Lemke served in a recon platoon with the Headquarters Company of the Fortieth Tank Battalion of the Seventh Armored Division. Several young men from St. Paul were in the Fortieth. The Seventh Armored Division entered combat on August 13 and saw action in the hedgerow fighting in Normandy. The division and other armored units in Patton's Third Army played a key role in the breakout, moving through German resistance and racing across France to cut off German units left behind. The Seventh was the first Allied unit to cross the Seine River, doing so on August 24. The Allies liberated Paris on August 25, 1944, but the war was far from over.

Patton's Third Army pressed forward, not allowing the veteran German army, which had not collapsed despite its huge losses, to regroup. The Seventh Armored

Private Henry (Hank) Lemke Jr. soon before joining the U.S. Army to serve in Europe. Lemke was killed in action in France on August 28, 1944. Photograph courtesy of the Lemke family.

Division moved out of Paris toward the east. Three days later, Private Henry Lemke was riding over hilly terrain in a half-track, probing for resistance ahead of the battalion column. It was midday and the weather was clear. The morning report of Headquarters Company of the Fortieth Tank Battalion for August 28, 1944, reads:

Company left old bivouac area NE of La Ferte Gaucher and contacted the enemy at approximately 1225, resistance strong and reconnaissance half track knocked out. The assault platoon knocked out one German truck and captured 15 of the enemy. Company arrived in new bivouac area 2 miles north of Reims. Weather fair, morale good.

A direct hit from German artillery had stalled the half-track Private Lemke was traveling on, and the burning vehicle blocked the road. The Germans pounded the motionless half-track and the supporting vehicles moving forward. The Americans secured the position, but could not save the crew in the half-track. Private Lemke died just eighteen days after landing on French shores. He, no doubt, was involved in heavy fighting throughout that period. He was twenty-two years old when he gave his life in the defense of freedom. The U.S. Army buried him at the U.S. Military Cemetery at Villeneuve-sur-Auvers, France. His remains were returned home to Minnesota in 1948 and reinterred at Fort Snelling National Cemetery in section C-3, grave site 7797.

The Seventh Armored Division took Verdun on August 31.

Erwin Edward Lemke

Erwin (Erv) Lemke joined the service in January 1943, just two months after his older brother Hank enlisted. Erv Lemke trained at Camp Roberts in California and was assigned as a replacement soldier with the Sixth Armored Division. It is not clear when he joined the Sixth Armored Division in Europe. Patton's Third Army was racing across France. Brother Hank's unit, the Seventh Armored Division, was also with Patton.

The Sixth Armored Division penetrated the Maginot Line in late November 1944 and was on the Saar River in early December. The Sixth turned for Metz when the Germans launched their surprise Ardennes offensive in December. The division arrived in Metz on Christmas Day and proceeded north to relieve the Tenth Armored near Mersch, Luxembourg. The Sixth Armored attacked German forces east of Bastogne on New Year's Eve. The American reinforcements were part of the first major counteroffensive to drive back the Germans from Bastogne. The Sixth met stiff German resistance for the next several days, while fighting in the bitter cold. At one point the Sixth faced six German divisions. The Americans consolidated their position on January 3, and for the next week faced wave after wave of determined German counterattacks, but managed to hold on.

Erv Lemke fought with the Ninth Armored Infantry Battalion in Combat Team (CT) Nine within Combat Command A of the Sixth Armored Division. The combat record of the Ninth Armored Infantry Battalion reads as follows:

Lemke brothers and friends. From left: Private Erwin Lemke (killed in action in Belgium), Private Henry Lemke Jr. (killed in action in France), Erwin Young (killed in action in Okinawa), and Vincent Schettner (died of a heart attack at age thirty-nine). Photograph courtesy of the Lemke family.

3 January 1945—After three days of bitter fighting and constant enemy counterattacks in deep snow and near-zero weather, the Division halted temporarily to consolidate its positions and secure some much needed rest.

4 January 1945—During the latter part of the period, while he maintained continuous pressure on the Division's left flank, the enemy launched a major counterattack against the right flank. At the time [Sixth Armored] front line units were displacing to newly assigned positions.

The Germans concentrated 150-millimeter artillery and Nebelwerfer (mobile six-barrel rocket launcher) fire on the boundary between CT 9 and CT 44 for twenty minutes before launching a major counterattack at 5:00 p.m. A force of SS troops advanced into the woods behind CT 9's position. The combat report stated:

This day marked the only withdrawal of any consequence by the Division under enemy pressure during the war, and even this would not have been forced had the line not been over-extended.

The men of the Sixth Armored Division managed to recover and drive back the SS troops after dark. Both sides suffered serious losses in the bitter fighting.

Private Erv Lemke was among the courageous Americans who paid the price of freedom with their lives that day. One of Erv's sisters married a veteran from St. Paul after the war. He told her of his brother being around Bastogne around the time of Erv's death. His unit was moving positions and passing another unit. Soldiers always traded information in such situations. The brother mentioned that he was from St. Paul. One of the soldiers from the other unit told him that they had just lost a soldier from St. Paul, Erwin Lemke. The brother had known Erv from the neighborhood. They paid their respects to Erv's memory and moved on.

The German attacks continued for several more days, but the Americans held their position around Bastogne. The Germans finally exhausted their manpower. The Sixth Armored went back on the offensive. The Ardennes fight was over by the end of January 1945 and the Allies pressed on into Germany.

Erwin Lemke, just twenty-one years old, was buried at U.S. Military Cemetery 1 at Foy, Belgium, on February 10, 1945. It is not known if he knew that he had lost his older brother, Hank, in action just four months earlier. When younger brother Carl went to Germany as part of the occupation force after the war, he recalled his mother breaking down as he boarded the train. The army assigned the young man duty as a guard at an ammunition depot in Berlin. He traveled on leave to photograph the graves of his two older brothers for the family.

Erv Lemke's remains were returned to Minnesota, where they were reinterred on April 8, 1949, at Fort Snelling National Cemetery, section B-1, grave site 438-S. The grave of his older brother, Henry, lies not far away. Their nephew, John Lemke, faithfully tends to the graves of his uncles, the Lemke boys, American heroes.

Mabel Johnson

The Robots are certainly deadly things, aren't they? Whoever invented them must have a diabolical mind. . . . If this thing would only end. We are a bit on edge and that's to be understood.

So wrote First Lieutenant Mabel Johnson of Eveleth, Minnesota, on January 2, 1945, from her station in Liège, Belgium, with the Twenty-eighth General Hospital. Johnson was referring to the world's first guided ballistic missiles, which the Germans were raining upon Allied-liberated Europe. The Nazi propaganda ministry named the missile the *Vergeltungswaffe* ("retaliation weapon") 2, which was more commonly known as the V-2. Upon launch the V-2 rose fifty miles into the stratosphere and then raced down to its target. Its range was 250 miles. A sonic boom, resulting from the 3,600-miles-per-hour speed of the rocket, preceded the impact of its one-ton warhead. There was no warning, no opportunity to take cover.

The first V-2s targeted England on September 8, 1944. The Germans launched as many as eight a day. They later began to target cities in Belgium. A V-2 hit Liège on November 29, 1944. Hundreds rained down thereafter, subjecting Johnson and her colleagues to "severe nervous tensions." She noted that patients from the front lines commented that it was safer at the front, and that the proximity of the rocket strikes was of far more concern than their numbers. A V-2 that hit a cinema in Antwerp on December 16 took the lives of 567 people, including nearly three hundred Allied servicemen.

Lieutenant Johnson wrote, "Robots, Bombs, Ack-Ack, and even a threatened evacuation of the entire unit did not stop the festive holiday spirit." A V-2 hit the Twenty-eighth Hospital on December 26. A second V-2 hit on January 9. Johnson wrote later in January: "Things are a little more quiet now, thank goodness. They have been tough." A week later she enclosed a poem about the V-2s in a letter, commenting that the poem "is a bit morbid but it is really descriptive. They are awful."

More than fifty thousand women served as U.S. Army nurses in the Second World War. They tended to wounded and dying soldiers at more than four hundred hospitals in the United States and in more than six hundred hospitals overseas. Army nurses also served on the beachhead and in the battlefield in close support of the front line. More than two hundred army nurses died during the war, sixteen in combat as the result of enemy fire. More than sixteen hundred were decorated for service and bravery.

Mabel Johnson was forty years old when she entered the Army Nurses Corps in July 1943. She was with the Twenty-eighth General Hospital in Wimborne Minister, England, from March through July 1944. Wimborne was on the English Channel, and the Twenty-eighth acted as a transit hospital during the Normandy invasion. Johnson wrote: "There we realized the hope we all had of giving service to our country . . . we saw a good share of the casualties." The Twenty-eighth crossed the channel to France on August 13, 1944, and then moved near the front at Liège, Belgium, in September. The nurses endured shortages, much of their diet consisting of K rations and C rations.

First Lieutenant Mabel Johnson served with the Twenty-eighth General Hospital in Belgium. Photograph courtesy of the Minnesota Historical Society.

Johnson wrote a friend, "Just wish you could experience K rations for a week plus." But she was very clear: "The only thing I need is letters and more letters."

Christmas was a difficult time for all men and women in service overseas. Johnson lamented, "No lutefisk!" But far more upsetting was the German counteroffensive that became known as the Battle of the Bulge, causing her to write, "The war news is terribly disappointing." The Twenty-eighth Hospital was hit by enemy fire on the day after Christmas during the fighting. Johnson wrote, "We were plenty busy that night and things were a bit out of commission for a while but all is OK now." She described the hospital in a March 1945 letter: "Things which can wait are done farther back. We are functioning more as an evacuation hospital although we still are a general. They call us a holding hospital." She added, "We are rejoicing at the First Army's advance across the Rhine. That really is big news." An opportunity to travel into occupied Germany was eye-opening. She wrote home of "the terrific destruction...Julich in particular... simply pulverized," and noted that the Germans "act very detached." She expressed concern for "several pale youngsters—what they must have endured through all this!"

As the Allies pressed into Germany, Lieutenant Johnson wrote of the hospital admitting American soldiers who had been captured during the Battle of the Bulge and recently liberated:

> I haven't seen them all (80) but have checked all for Danny and Biederman. Of course, there are many hospitals for them to go to so my not seeing them doesn't mean they are still missing. I feel sorry for these kids—they're emaciated and were lousy, tired and skinny. But we'll have them OK to send home soon. We are busy again. Must close.

Johnson wrote again just days later as to how "pathetic" other liberated American POWs were, having lost an average of forty pounds since their capture only five months earlier and suffering from disease.

The Twenty-eighth Hospital received mattresses for the nurses in May 1945. Johnson and her colleagues had gone ten months without. More important, she noted in her letter of May 6, "Peace is near at hand." She was eager to get home by the end of May. Travel leaves that allowed her to see Paris, the Riviera, and Switzerland helped ease her homesickness. She finally returned home and was discharged at Fort Des Moines, Iowa, on January 14, 1946.

The 1956 reunion news for the Twenty-eighth General Hospital noted that Mabel "Black Label" Johnson was nursing director at a large clinic in St. Paul. Johnson retired and was approaching her eighty-seventh birthday when she passed away in December

First Lieutenant Mabel Johnson and her fellow army nurses in Europe.
Photograph courtesy of the Minnesota Historical Society.

1992. She is buried in section 15, grave site 2487, at Fort Snelling National Cemetery.
A few lines from her narrative might suffice as an epitaph:

> Our hours were long but never tedious because each and every one of us felt that we
> were helping those boys who were offering their best to help hasten peace and vic-
> tory. The courage and bravery of them all stimulated us to work uncomplainingly.

George Spreigl

George Spreigl, known to family and friends as "Sonny," enlisted in the army in June
1942. His older brothers Clarence and Herb were already in the army. He underwent
surgery in late 1942, and when he recovered George Spreigl proceeded to desert training in California in March 1943. He was hospitalized in May 1943 for arthritis and was
offered a medical discharge, which he declined. He married Kay Welters in St. Paul in
September 1943 while home on furlough. He went to Fort Benning, Georgia, for jump
school in November and was assigned to the parachute infantry. Spreigl shipped overseas to England in August 1944 and was one of the rookie soldiers thrown into the
Battle of the Bulge who survived. He was wounded, however, and treated for shell

188 .... Pressing into Germany

shock as well. Yet Spreigl was determined to return to action and rejoined his unit in February 1945. He wrote home to his mother:

> *February 14, 1945.* It is far from being over here. Fight for a week and only gain maybe a hundred yards. The trouble over here is the newspapers. They always gloat over our victories...never mention how many boys and equipment we lost....If you could see the hospitals over here. Halls and rooms crowded with the poor boys with arms and legs missing and the fellows lying around on the fields who will never move again!

The U.S. Army was back on the move by March, as reflected in the following letter from Spreigl:

> *March 16, 1945.* I am sorry I didn't get around to write sooner. But we are busy as heck over here. Chasing the Jerries up and down hills through rivers and forests.

Spreigl wrote again in April:

> *April 2, 1945.* The other day as we were traveling in Germany I seen Clare's [brother Clarence's] outfit [Third Infantry Division]. I wish I could have gotten off and looked him up. It is too late now for we are quite a ways from there.

The letter was to be his last. George "Sonny" Spreigl was killed in action in Germany on April 16, 1945. He was buried in a military cemetery in Europe.

Herbert Spreigl

George "Sonny" Spreigl's older brother, Herb, fought through France in early fall 1944 and in Luxembourg, and fought in the Ardennes during the Battle of the Bulge as well. He was involved in the fierce fighting in Germany as the war neared its end. Like so many thousands of soldiers, Herb Spreigl had seen enough fighting in only a few months and began to focus on getting home safely. He wrote home:

> *May 3, 1945.* Germany. Sweating out the end of the war, of which I hope will finish almost any day now. Can't understand how these people still keep fighting and haven't anything left to fight for.

> *May 13, 1945.* So don't believe everything you read in the papers, they just make it sound good.

Bad news reached the family that something had happened to Sonny Spreigl. His brother was in disbelief:

Corporal Herbert Spreigl (left) and comrade in the forests of Germany in early 1945. Photograph from the Minnesota Historical Society.

June 12, 1945. Frankfurt. You know, Mom, I don't believe Son is dead yet. It seems so funny that you haven't received a notice.

Unfortunately, the rumor of Sonny's death was substantiated. Herb Spreigl wrote his mother:

June 20, 1945. Received your letter several days ago. It made me feel pretty bad, as I hadn't seen Son for almost four years. I believe he would have been in the Army three years this month. Anyway it's done only too bad he couldn't have held out for another two weeks. I'm trying to find just where he is buried here in Germany.

July 1, 1945. Southern Germany. As I write this letter I am actually crying. Ma I feel so bad. I got some of the last letters I wrote Sonny back today marked "deceased." I have up until now been living in hope that it was all a great error. But now I know it's true. I've only been kidding myself all this time. . . . So now in closing I'll just say take it easy and keep the coffee warm. I might drop in one of these days yet. One never knows what's going to happen from one day to another.

Corporal Herbert Spreigl survived the closing days of the war and returned home to his mother, other brothers, and sisters. He died in 1976 and is buried in section T, grave site 2446, at Fort Snelling National Cemetery.

Gideon Frederick Pond Jr.

Fred Pond Jr., as he was known to his friends, grew up on the family farm near Shakopee, Minnesota. The family has a long, proud legacy in Minnesota. Fred's great-great-grandfather, Gideon Pond, was among the first white men in the Minnesota River Valley. Gideon Pond and his brother arrived at Fort Snelling in 1843 as Christian missionaries to the Dakota people. He and his wife Cornelia raised sixteen children in the two-story brick house he built in 1848 in what is now Bloomington. Gideon Pond served as the first pastor for Oak Grove Presbyterian Church, which remains an active community in Bloomington to this day.

Fred Jr.'s dad served in the army in World War I and Fred was determined to do his part, as well, when totalitarian forces threatened American democracy twenty years later. Fred volunteered to go in the army in June 1942 at Fort Snelling. The army processed the nineteen-year-old farm boy and sent him to Camp Roberts, California, for field artillery training. He volunteered for a tank destroyer pioneer platoon and was sent to Camp Hood, Texas. Fred wrote, "We then found out the Pioneer Platoon were the 'Little Engineers.' We did a lot of grunt work, including building a log bridge for our 32-ton TDers [tanks]." The reorganized 631st Tank Destroyer Battalion did not have a pioneer platoon, and Fred became part of the reconnaissance platoon. "So instead of being in a Grunt platoon, we acted as the gun company's eyes." The unit consisted of half-tracks, Jeeps, and motorcycles. The unit moved from Camp Hood to Camp Claibourne, Louisiana, to Camp Shelby, Mississippi. Fred made note of the fact that Hood and Shelby were noted Confederate generals. Fred Pond was ready for war and concerned when his unit remained at Camp Shelby for some time. He and some other men went to a captain, commanding another unit, to request transfer, but nothing came of that. Pond wrote:

> I was afraid the war would end before I could get overseas. I heard from my cousin Wilson St. Martin. He was in the 8th Air Force and in England—drove me wild. I thought I could get overseas if I joined the paratroopers (and I'm scared to death of heights!), so I memorized the eye chart and got all the papers from the 631st to try for the airborne troops. The next day word came out to turn in everything but one's duffle bag—we were going overseas!

The 631st Tank Destroyer Battalion boarded a navy transport and crossed the Atlantic in a small convoy. They landed in Scotland and trained in Wales while they awaited orders. Pond wrote, "We got hung up in Wales for a while because the USA forces got stuck in the hedgerows around St. Lo, France." Orders finally came to go to Liverpool, where the men boarded an LST, which Pond noted "had a hole where an 88 armor-piercing shell went in one side and out the other." They landed at Utah Beach and "caught up to Third Army as Patton's herd ran out of gas." The 631st was assigned to protect key bridges necessary to keep the flow of troops and supplies moving north toward Germany. One 75-millimeter gun was assigned to each bridge. Pond was quite clear as to the capabilities and limitations of the artillery piece, which he towed around behind his half-track:

> The German Tiger tanks with their 75mm had a longer tube [and higher muzzle velocity] than our towed mounts. One did not want to get into a slugging match with German Tiger tanks. Tiger Royal tanks carried 88mm. Tank destroyers are supposed to find a defilade [protected] position, fire a couple of rounds and move to a new location.

One afternoon, while on the move, Pond drove his Jeep around a corner to find two Sherman tanks, each carrying two 88-millimeter armor-piercing shells "dead-on in front." The Sherman's twelve inches of armor was insufficient to stop the 88s. There were many such reminders to American tankers and tank destroyers that it was

Fred Pond of the 631st Tank Destroyer Battalion. Photograph courtesy of
Inez M. Pond.

suicidal to go head-to-head with German tanks. There was other evidence of the
formidable German weaponry. The 631st guarded General Patton's headquarters for
several days. During this time, Pond saw "a small flame like a blowtorch going over us.
Found out later it was a Messerschmitt 262, Germany's new jet." Fortunately, it was
too little too late for Germany.

Pond's platoon was assigned duty as military police (MPs) while stationed in Nancy,
France. It was a difficult position and he later wrote, "I felt differently towards MPs
after being in their shoes." They were sent into the red-light district, where all the
trouble took place, including several clashes and even shootings between black and
white soldiers. Pond wrote of meeting African American tankers and tank destroyers.
He was surprised, knowing that the segregated army allowed very few African Americans in frontline units. Pond was familiar with the African American soldiers who
drove the six-by-six supply trucks with the red ball painted on their doors. He noted,
"The Red Ball Express supplied all of the US Armies in Northern Europe."

Sergeant Fred Pond (leaning on the half-track) and comrades of the 631st Tank Destroyer Battalion. Photograph courtesy of Inez M. Pond.

The 631st crossed the Rhine River into Germany at Worms across a pontoon bridge. The battalion's half-tracks, each pulling an antitank gun, weighed six to seven tons each and weighed down each section of the pontoon bridge, which popped back up as the trucks passed. The 631st passed through the city of Weimar. Wrote Pond: "There was a concentration camp nearby. In the ditches on both sides of the road lay inmates in striped clothing. It appeared that they were trying to escape when they were shot."

They wound up in Bavaria at war's end. Two small German girls began to come around the hotel where the GIs were staying. A closet in the hotel turned out to be full of bags of sugar, and Pond gave a ten-pound bag of sugar to the girls. They returned the next day with a cake. A friendship grew between the GIs and the family. Pond corresponded with the family for some time and sent them care packages over the years. The war was over and Europe could begin the long path of reconciliation and healing.

Fred Pond returned home. He married in 1947 and he and Inez raised four children in Bloomington. He died June 30, 2003. The memorial service was held at Oak Grove

Presbyterian Church. His remains lie in section 20-B, grave site 760, at Fort Snelling National Cemetery.

❧

The Germans fought ferociously to defend their fatherland and extracted a terrible cost in the lives of Allied soldiers long after the outcome of the war was clear. Germany surrendered on May 8, 1945—Victory in Europe Day, or VE Day. Imperial Japan remained committed to fighting in the Pacific.

Chapter 7

Closing In on Japan

Bernard L. Meister

Submariners were known as the "Silent Service." Stealth was their method for approaching the enemy and achieving their objective of sinking enemy surface ships. Success was often spectacular, but usually followed by hours of terror as depth charges exploded around their hull. Even a near miss could result in a watery grave for the entire crew. Their numbers were small, representing only 2 to 3 percent of U.S. Navy personnel, but they accounted for 55 to 60 percent of tonnage sunk during the war.

Bernie Meister grew up in northeast Minneapolis, graduating from Edison High School. He was the youngest of six boys. His five older brothers were all in the service when Bernie convinced his father in December 1942 to sign for him so he could enlist in the navy at the age of seventeen. He subsequently volunteered for the navy's elite Submarine Service. Meister became part of the crew for the newly christened USS *Guavina* (SS-362) in early 1944. *Guavina* was one of twenty-eight submarines launched by the Manitowoc Shipbuilding Company of Manitowoc, Wisconsin. The new warship arrived at Pearl Harbor on April 5 and left the following day for its first war patrol. The *Guavina* got two big kills on April 26, torpedoing two large merchant ships, which exploded and sank upon impact. The crew's first encounter with Japanese depth charges followed. The sub witnessed another sensational explosion on its second patrol in June–July when it torpedoed a single merchant ship accompanied by four escort vessels. This time the depth charges continued for three hours. The *Guavina* also rescued twelve B-25 pilots on this cruise. Her third patrol in August–September

Submariner Bernie Meister of Minneapolis in uniform.

The USS *Guavina* (SS-362) earned five battle stars in the Pacific during World War II. Seaman Second Class Bernard Meister and his fellow submariners survived a harrowing four and a half hours of depth charges in February 1945. Photograph courtesy of the Naval Historical Foundation.

1944 off Mindanao resulted in the sinking of a large Japanese transport ship. She sank three tankers on the fourth patrol.

Guavina shipped out for her fifth patrol on January 23, 1945, as part of a team of attack subs working the South China Sea. Her first kill was a seven-thousand-ton tanker on February 6. The submarine escaped depth charging by lying on the bottom near the stern of the tanker that she had just sunk. Meister would remember well the day later that month when the *Guavina* torpedoed an even larger tanker, which was protected by three destroyer escorts. There was no room to run silent and deep. The skipper laid the sub down on the ocean floor in a depth of only 130 to 150 feet. In a *Grand Forks Herald* newspaper interview in 2003, Meister pointed out:

> The sub from the bottom to the top of the periscope was 90 feet, so we did not have much water above us. The destroyers started to drop depth charges. The three would crisscross, laying a pattern of depth charges. Then they would stop dead in the water, trying to pick up a sound from our boat. We were at silent running, which

means everything is shut down. Everyone had to be as quiet as possible. . . . It gets to be kind of scary when you can't fight back.

The three Japanese destroyer escorts dropped a total of ninety-eight depth charges from 7:30 in the morning until noon. Meister reflected, "How we made it out I'll never know. God was on our side." The Japanese were still probing and searching for the American sub that night. *Guavina*'s oxygen supply was nearly depleted when the sub finally hit the surface after being underwater all day.

Meister, like many veterans, could share a funny twist on a serious story. Submarines carried provisions for eighty days and the men ate well. As ship's cook, he had put four turkeys in the oven for that evening's supper just before the alarm was sounded that morning. He turned off the ovens as he raced to his battle station. The raw turkeys spoiled in the course of the long day. "As we came up, the boat really smelled until we got fresh air coming in," he recalled. The odor was nothing compared to the near-death experience of the crew. The crew repaired extensive damage on station before they were able to take their battered sub back to base. An American warplane mistook *Guavina* for the enemy as she cruised on the surface, en route to base. Aerial bombs fortunately missed as the *Guavina* dove for safety.

Meister "transferred into the relief crew to catch another boat. After a time, I was supposed to go aboard the USS *Bullhead,* but a friend wanted out of Subic and he had a higher rank and friends to help him get me bumped off. So he took my place. The *Bullhead* was the last submarine lost with all hands a couple of days before the war ended."

Bernie Meister survived the war, as did four of his five brothers. He returned to Minneapolis and in 1946 met Rose, who would become his wife. They raised seven children, of whom two sons served in the navy and a third in the army. Bernie and Rose were married for fifty-five years. He passed away near the end of 2003, just one month after his last interview. He is buried in section 20-A, grave site 328, at Fort Snelling National Cemetery.

The Submarine Service of the U.S. Navy suffered the highest percentage of losses of any branch of the American armed forces, with almost one in five vessels failing to return. The service lost 52 of 263 submarines in the course of the war. Over 3,500 of some 16,000 submariners lost their lives. Their contribution to the war effort was significant. They accounted for the sinking of 1,178 enemy merchant ships and over 200 enemy warships, including four large aircraft carriers and a battleship. Over

16,000 Japanese merchant seamen lost their lives in attacks by U.S. submarines. The Submarine Service effectively isolated the homeland of Japan and prevented the resupply of the Japanese Imperial Army across the Pacific. Submarines scouted each Pacific invasion landing, landed scout and raiding parties, and rescued many downed American pilots. The submarine veterans of World War II have much to be proud of.

Donaciano J. Martinez

To anyone familiar with the U.S. Army and World War II, the Philippine island of Corregidor is known as "the Rock." This island in Manila Bay was the key to the defense of Manila. Despite the warning of Pearl Harbor, however, the Philippines fell easily to Japan. Corregidor, on the other hand, served as the defiant symbol of American and Filipino resistance, holding out against the enemy into May 1942. The Japanese recognized the island for the impregnable fortress that it was. They expanded the existing fortifications and positioned massive artillery, capable of devastating enemy warships and transports, into the cliffs of the island. The Americans returned to Manila Bay in early 1945, and the Japanese were ready for them. General Douglas MacArthur knew his military strategy needed to be bold to minimize the American blood that would be shed in the assault on Corregidor. His plan centered on his shock troops, the 503rd Parachute Infantry Regiment (PIR).

The 503rd PIR was the first of a number of such regiments formed by the army in World War II. While other PIRs earned accolades for heroism in Europe, the army sent the 503rd to the Pacific theater. The 503rd served more than three years in the Pacific and played an important role in five major combat operations before the end of the war.

Donaciano Martinez was born in Cisco, Texas, in 1918. His father and mother, natives of Mexico, moved to Minnesota to work in the beet fields when Donaciano was a boy. His father, Salvador, seeking better employment and stability for the family, secured a job with the railroad in Minneapolis. There, Donaciano Martinez—or "Marty," as he came to be known—graduated from Minneapolis's North High School in 1938. He was a popular young man who had participated in sports and studied hard.

Martinez entered the military service at Fort Snelling in June 1941, ready to serve his nation. His wife, Paula, recalls that her patriotic husband felt it was everyone's duty to fight for their country. Martinez completed basic training at Camp Roberts, California. He and a number of friends he knew from Fort Snelling volunteered

Private Donaciano Martinez (center) with friends J. V. Melander (right) and Herbert Abernathy of the 503rd Parachute Infantry Regiment. Photograph courtesy of the Donaciano Martinez family.

together for jump school and became a part of Company B of the 503rd Parachute Infantry Regiment. The regiment began jump school at Fort Benning, Georgia, in March 1942. Six hundred paratroopers showed off their skills for Winston Churchill at Fort Jackson, South Carolina, on June 24, 1942, jumping from transport planes at an altitude of no more than eight hundred feet and in a high wind. Churchill remarked afterward that he was "enormously impressed by the thoroughness and precision." This was the beginning of an illustrious period for the 503rd.

The regiment traveled by railroad from Fort Benning to Alta, Utah, where they became the only PIR regiment to train as alpine skiers. Dick Durrance, arguably the best downhill skier the United States had ever seen up to that time, was owner of the Alta Lodge, a resort in the fledgling ski industry. Durrance had lived in Bavaria for five years in his youth and was the 1932 German junior champion in alpine skiing. His family returned to the United States upon Hitler's rise to power, and Durrance led Dartmouth College to four national ski titles before graduating in 1939. The 1940 U.S. Olympic team never competed, but Durrance was on his way toward nine U.S. championships. He had moved to Alta just prior to the outbreak of war. Durrance and a team led the men of the 503rd through rigorous training. Marty Martinez and one of his buddies were among those who suffered broken ankles, injuries they had not incurred in numerous parachute jumps. In any case, the men of the 503rd never used their alpine training. Orders came for the regiment to go to San Francisco, where they boarded a transport ship to Australia. They trained in Queensland before shipping out to Port Moresby, New Guinea, in August 1943.

The 503rd's first combat jump took place in the Markham Valley of New Guinea on September 5, 1943. The strategic valley lay over the rugged Owen Stanley Mountains from Port Moresby. Kunai grass standing six to ten feet high with razorlike edges covered much of the valley, including the drop zone. The grass not only presented a hazard to paratroopers coming down, but also could impede efforts by the soldiers to organize and prepare for counterattacks. Nevertheless, the 503rd made a low-altitude jump into this enemy region, seized control of the Nadzab airfield, and held the valley against Japanese counterattacks for seventeen days. A note by Martinez mentions that he went on patrol on September 10 and encountered the enemy. One of his friends, Sergeant Edward T. Wojewodzic of his company, was awarded the Silver Star for his gallantry at Nadzab. The 503rd, in seizing the airfield and blocking the evacuation route of a major Japanese force, forced the enemy to take an alternative route, which led to their elimination as an effective fighting force.

Donaciano Martinez was as religious as he was patriotic. He wrote on December 25, 1943, in a journal:

> Although Christmas of 1943 was spent far from home and the ones we hold dear, it was for us at this battle station one of the most enjoyable experienced; for we discovered that peace with God is more conducive to happiness than any of those tinsel gifts which some people consider to be a necessary part of the festive season. We likened ourselves to the shepherds on that first Christmas night, nearly 2000 years ago. A bright star shining from a cloudless sky seemed like a beacon lighting our path to Mass to pay homage to our Creator, who thought so much of his people that he took a body and soul like ours in order to redeem and save us. Many of us were fortunate in being able to follow that star and attend Midnight Mass, thus beginning Christmas Day in true Catholic spirit. . . . We had no fine church . . . it made one feel proud to be associated with such men. . . . We sang the Great Alleluia and as the breeze wafted the music back to us, we stood with lumps in our throats and pride in our hearts for belonging to the church, which embraces all colors and classes of men. As Mass ended, each turned to his companions and as each shook hands and wished each other Merry Christmas, one could detect sincerity in their clasps and joy and happiness in their faces. As we winded through the trees, with shoulders squared and heads held high, we were convinced that were we to fall in battle on the Morrow, we would die in Grace.

Private Donaciano Martinez of the 503rd Parachute Infantry Regiment preparing to make a jump. Photograph courtesy of the Donaciano Martinez family.

The whereabouts of the 503rd were confidential for much of the war because of their use as an advance force. Martinez's wife, Paula, whom he married in 1941 before going to war, could follow the unit only as reports appeared in the press weeks later. She also met with various wives with whom she shared and pieced together pieces of information as to the regiment's location. Paula Martinez preserved the clippings in a family scrapbook, which she retains to this day.

The 503rd jumped onto the island of Noemfoor off the coast of New Guinea in July 1944, dropping directly onto their primary objective: a coral bed runway. They made an amphibious landing on the Philippine island of Mindoro in December of the same year. The American seizure of these islands in both cases led to the installation of Army Air Corps bases, which helped support the Allied advance across the Pacific. Private Donaciano Martinez was awarded the Bronze Star "for exemplary conduct in ground combat against the armed enemy during the New Guinea Campaign." The men of the 503rd were combat-hardened veterans by the time of the assault on Corregidor in February 1945.

The 503rd's jump on Corregidor in the Philippines was one of the boldest moves of the war. The Presidential Unit Citation later given to the regiment referred to the assault on the Rock as "one of the most difficult missions of the Pacific War." It was their most vicious fight and their riskiest jump of the war. Their drop zone was so small that only six men jumped on each pass. Sheer cliffs that bordered the drop zone on the west side of the island caused variable wind currents and turbulence for the paratroopers as they landed. Heavy bombardment from air and sea had destroyed the trees across the top of the island, turning the sharp, jagged stumps into a serious hazard for landing paratroopers. Finally, the enemy outnumbered the Allies three to one. The 503rd landed on the top of the island at 8:30 a.m. and secured the objective by nightfall. The next day there followed a bloody, systematic annihilation of the enemy forces dug into the island. A major counterattack nearly caught the 503rd off guard when the Japanese blew up the regiment's ammo dump within the cave system and the explosion shook the entire island. Japanese infantrymen swarmed from various caves and penetrated to the battalion command post during the melee. They overran and mauled one company of the 503rd, but the veteran American paratroopers held on and finally repelled the attack, ending the enemy's last major effort to hold Corregidor.

Private Martinez suffered a wound when he took a piece of shrapnel in his neck during the fighting on Corregidor. He was later awarded the Purple Heart. Sergeant Robert Heyer, Martinez's good friend from the 503rd and a buddy from their days at Fort Snelling, died of wounds and was posthumously awarded the Silver Star. Corregidor was the 503rd's finest hour. The Presidential Unit Citation closes with the statement, "Their magnificent courage, tenacity and gallantry avenged the victims of Corregidor of 1942."

When Martinez returned home, he told his wife, Paula, "Don't you ever feed me Spam. That's all we got to eat." He kept in close contact with several of his comrades for the rest of his life. His daughter Ginger remembers the men being treated as uncles within their family. She recalls "such genuine happiness and tears at seeing each other—tears for those who didn't make it home and lots and lots of laughter with the retelling of some of their stories." Donaciano Martinez was well known and respected in St. Paul's Hispanic community until his death on March 22, 2000. Paula flies the American flag daily in front of her house and treasures the memories of her husband. "We miss him. He was such a good man." Donaciano Martinez, the first generation of his family to be born in the United States, remains an American hero. He is buried in section 6-C, grave site 316, at Fort Snelling National Cemetery.

John Riley Brown

MacArthur's return to the Philippines and the retaking of Manila, Corregidor, and Bataan were important psychological and strategic accomplishments in the Pacific theater. However, much fighting remained before the Philippines would be secured. General Tomoyuki Yamashita, the notorious "Tiger of Malaya," had a powerful force of more than 150,000 veteran troops in the nearly impenetrable mountains of Luzon, and was prepared to kill as many Americans as possible. The fierce fighting in this rugged terrain indeed cost many lives.

John Brown was born in Florence, Montana. He worked on several ranches around Stevensville, Montana, before taking a job in the smelter for Anaconda. He married Hazel McCune of Victor, Montana, in 1941. The U.S. Army drafted Brown in 1944 and sent him to Camp Roberts, California, for training. Hazel and their two-year-old daughter, Janet, rode the train to California to attend his graduation. Private Brown was home from December 29, 1944, until January 11, 1945, when he departed for war. The troop transport ship did not arrive in the Philippines until near the end of February. Brown went overseas as a replacement soldier and was assigned to the veteran Twelfth Cavalry Regiment of the First Cavalry Division. The regiment had made its first assault one year earlier and later was involved in heavy fighting in the Layette-Samar campaign. The First Cavalry Division landed on Luzon on January 26, 1945. A column of the Twelfth became the "First in Manila" on February 3, 1945, fighting through fierce resistance from the Japanese defenders. MacArthur made a much-heralded return to Corregidor on March 2.

The "First Cav" was among the units positioned east of Manila in late February. Their objective was to gain control of the water supply for Manila. The Japanese were well entrenched in the mountainous terrain and advance was slow and costly. Japanese soldiers slipped back through the lines to kill from ambush. The First Cav lost its

Private John Riley Brown (with guitar) and comrades in training before shipping overseas. Photograph courtesy of Hazel Brown Burch and Nancy Brown Johnson.

commander, Major General Verne D. Mudge, on March 4 when he was wounded by a grenade while inspecting newly secured ground. It was not until March 8 that the Americans engulfed some of the Japanese defensive positions and began advancing. The next day, as the Americans pressed forward, Private John Riley Brown was killed in action. Brown, like so many American replacement soldiers in the war, had had little time to learn the tricks of survival. American troops captured Ipo Dam intact on May 17, 1945. Yamashita withdrew deeper into Luzon and continued his fight until the war's end in August. He came out of the jungle leading fifty thousand well-armed men.

Hazel McCune Brown received a yellow telegram from the U.S. War Department on April 3, 1945, reporting the death of her husband. She was three months pregnant with their second child, Nancy.

Nancy Brown Johnson is active in the American World War II Orphans Network (www.awon.org), an organization of support and information for those who lost fathers in the war. Through AWON, Johnson met Glenn Kennedy, who served with John Brown. Kennedy recalled for her how happy her father was upon learning that his wife had become pregnant with Nancy while he had been home on leave.

John Riley Brown is buried in section C-24, grave site 13695, at Fort Snelling National Cemetery. His wife and daughters, as well as four grandchildren and six great-grandchildren, all proudly honor his memory and service to his nation.

Herman Hansen Jr.

Reconnaissance and photographic reconnaissance flights in the midst of enemy fighters require nerves of steel and more than a standard dose of courage. Assistant Wing Photographic Officer Herman Hansen Jr. arrived on Guadalcanal in November 1942 in the midst of intense fighting. Hansen had enlisted in the Marine Corps in 1939 after graduating from the Junior College of Kansas City, Missouri, with an associate degree in geology. The Marine Corps Reserve commissioned him a second lieutenant in September 1940. He served with Marine Scout-Bomber Squadron 232 at Hawaii in 1941, departing just two weeks before Pearl Harbor. Hansen completed the naval school of photography at Pensacola in April 1942 and left for the South Pacific in September 1942 with the rank of captain in the regular Marine Corps.

Captain Hansen served with the First and Second Marine Air Wings at Guadalcanal from November 10, 1942, to February 6, 1943. During this time, he flew eighty reconnaissance and photography flights over Guadalcanal and the neighboring islands in an unarmed, unarmored plane "with complete disregard for his own personal safety." He frequently was under fire from Japanese antiaircraft batteries, being shot down into the sea on one mission, "but, displaying valiant courage and unswerving devotion to duty, he voluntarily returned to his tasks the next day." Hansen was awarded the Distinguished Flying Cross for his brave deeds and promoted to major in May 1943. He shot down a Japanese Zero over Rendova Island in June 1943 and was awarded an Air Medal, after which he returned to the States to assume command of Marine Fighter Squadron 112.

Major Hansen returned to the war in December 1944 as commander of a carrier-based squadron on the USS *Bennington*. The *Bennington* was part of Task Force Fifty-eight, consisting of 122 ships, including eleven Essex carriers. The mission was to mount fighter sweeps and strikes against airfields and industrial targets in and around Tokyo. Hansen led VMF-112 with eleven Corsairs on the first sweep on February 16, 1945. The squadron caught the Japanese off guard at O Shima, Mobara, and Katori airfields, destroying twenty planes on the ground in the first major engagement over Japan. Hansen and his squadron returned to Tokyo on the morning of February 17,

Major Herman Hansen Jr., a Marine Corps aviator shown in the cockpit of his
F-441 Corsair fighter, distinguished himself in action in the Pacific theater.
Photograph courtesy of the U.S. Marine Corps.

during which he was credited with shooting down an Oscar fighter that was attacking
the formation.

The *Bennington* was off Okinawa in mid-March 1945 in preparation for the landings
when Japanese kamikaze attacks ensued with terrible effect. Major Hansen and his
squadron managed to take off from the *Bennington* at 5:45 a.m. on March 18 during a
brief respite from the attacks. Their objective was the Kanoya airfield. The squadron
encountered a Japanese formation en route and a dogfight ensued. VMF-112 destroyed
nine enemy aircraft and damaged six others with no losses of its own. Hansen earned
credit for one-half destroyed and one damaged. The squadron proceeded to Kanoya
and wreaked considerable damage.

Hansen's most significant achievement took place on April 12, 1945, his twenty-
fifth birthday. The kamikazes were thick that day. His Navy Cross citation reads:

Marine Corps pilots running to their Corsair fighters. Photograph courtesy of the National Archives (80-G-54301).

Leading a flight of twelve carrier-based fighter planes against a numerically superior force of hostile aircraft, Major Hansen skillfully shot down three enemy fighters and aided his squadron in destroying or seriously damaging the entire formation. On returning to base, he again led his flight in destroying a formation of enemy dive bombers which were attempting to make suicide attacks on our surface forces. A superb leader and airman, Major Hansen contributed to the destruction of twenty aircraft and to the infliction of crippling damage on six others, returning his entire flight to base, intact and undamaged.

Between February 21 and May 17, 1945, Major Herman Hansen earned his second, third, and fourth Air Medals, his first and second Silver Stars, and the Navy Cross.

He went on to serve his nation in Korea and Vietnam. A position on the staff of the commander in chief of U.S. Naval Forces in the Eastern Atlantic and Mediterranean was among his assignments. He also served as the commanding officer of Marine Aircraft Group 32, Second Marine Aircraft Wing. Herman Hansen Jr. retired in 1967 with the rank of colonel. He died November 4, 1993, and is buried in section DS, grave site 81-N, at Fort Snelling National Cemetery.

Kenneth Rolla Thompson

Minnesotan Ken Thompson was a Spam salesman in St. Paul before enlisting in the U.S. Marines. One of his comrades wrote, "We never stopped kidding him about Spam, which had become part of our regular diet." Thompson served with the Ninth Marine Regiment, the Third Marine Division, and proved himself a leader early in the Pacific campaign. He received a field commission to second lieutenant for his performance as a noncommissioned officer in the fighting on Bougainville in November–December 1943 and Guam in July–August 1944.

Iwo Jima, only 750 miles from Tokyo, became the focus of the Pacific theater in early 1945. The Marines landed on the shores of the strategic island shortly after 9:00 a.m. on February 19, 1945. The defending soldiers of Imperial Japan, entrenched in fortified underground positions, had survived seventy-four days of aerial attack and the pounding by U.S. Navy warships before the landing. They were ready, even determined, to die to protect their threatened homeland.

The Marines controlled one-third of the island by the end of the second day, but the price in human lives was horrific. Lieutenant Patrick Caruso of Company K, Third Battalion, Ninth Marine Regiment, later wrote, "Of the original seven officers in our company, [Ken] Thompson and I were the only two left at the end of the second day of fighting." The fighting continued as the Marines slowly gained ground against the Japanese soldiers.

Thompson's unit was pulled out of the line a day or two later to reinforce a threatened sector. Caruso recalled a meeting near the north end of Motoyama Airfield 2 on the island of Iwo Jima, in which he and Thompson were receiving orders from Lieutenant Colonel Harold C. "Bing" Boehm, commanding the Third Battalion, Ninth Marines. The conversation turned to the huge losses that had been incurred. "We were tired, dismayed, confused," Caruso recalled. He never forgot a statement that Thompson made to him:

> It's only a matter of which lasts longer, Marines or Japanese ammunitions, and it looks as though they have plenty to go.

U.S. Marines going ashore at Iwo Jima. Photograph from Heritage Photographs.

Thompson confided to Caruso that his biggest regret was that he did not marry the girl he left back home, saying, "Once I get back home to Minnesota and I marry my girl, I'll never leave." The official history of the Battle of Iwo Jima states that the Third Marine Division encountered the most heavily fortified section of the island in their move to take Airfield 2.

A Marine major who knew Thompson passed by the two lieutenants and told Thompson that he heard he had been killed. Thompson smiled and told the major that he was sorry to disappoint him. The assault commenced the next day. Caruso wrote: "Later, during a Japanese counterattack, Thompson was shot through the head. The major's ill-timed remark preyed on my mind." The fight for Iwo would continue for many more days, claiming the lives of thousands of fine young men such as Ken Thompson, before the strategic island was secured. Ken Thompson died in action on March 2, 1945, the twelfth day of the fighting on Iwo Jima. American losses at the end

Marines inching forward against fierce Japanese opposition on Iwo Jima.
Photograph courtesy of the National Archives (127-N-110249).

of the thirty-six days of combat totaled over 24,000, including 6,140 dead. Approximately one in three Marine or navy corpsmen who landed on Iwo became a casualty.

The U.S. government returned Ken Thompson's remains to Minnesota in 1949. He is buried in section C-22, grave site 12748, at Fort Snelling National Cemetery.

James Dennis La Belle

"Iwo was hell."

James La Belle was born in Columbia Heights, Minnesota, in 1925. He enlisted in the U.S. Marine Corps the week he turned eighteen. He was small, wiry, and intensely competitive, having starred in athletics in high school. He was assigned to the Twenty-seventh Marine Regiment, which was formed in January 1944 at Camp Pendleton,

Eighteen-year-old Private James La Belle survived weeks of fierce fighting on Iwo Jima only to willingly give his life to save two fellow Marines and hold the line against a Japanese night attack. The Marine Corps awarded him the Medal of Honor posthumously. Photograph courtesy of the U.S. Marine Corps.

California, as part of the Fifth Marine Division. The regiment shipped out to Hawaii in August 1944, and their first combat assignment was the invasion of Iwo Jima. The U.S. military delivered the longest, most intensive bombing and shelling of any island in the Pacific on Iwo Jima before landing. However, the Japanese were huddled within an elaborate network of man-made tunnels and natural caves. The Twenty-seventh Marines stormed ashore at 9:00 a.m. on February 19 onto Beaches Red 1 and Red 2. The regiment's initial assignment was to isolate Mount Suribachi from the rest of the island. The Twenty-seventh Marines moved north once Mount Suribachi was isolated to join with the other units in continuing the attack on the main enemy defenses set within the rugged terrain. The combat was often at close quarters.

Combat often consists of a large number of small, intense fights, any one of which may prove to be the critical element of the offensive breakthrough or defensive stop. Private James La Belle and his comrades became veteran Marines as the fighting on Iwo continued through February and into March. While the fighting may be characterized by small unit clashes, the integrity of the line was important to prevent breakthroughs, which could be costly and even devastating. La Belle moved with two fellow Marines to fill a gap in the line. They dug in and waited. The Japanese would do all they could to exploit such gaps if the Marines did not close them. The basic approach of the Japanese was to attempt to blast their way through with grenades and hope to fill the gap with bayonet-wielding infantrymen. La Belle maintained a vigilant watch throughout the night. When a grenade landed in the foxhole beyond his reach, La Belle quickly shouted a warning and threw his body onto the grenade, absorbing the explosion to protect the lives of his comrades. Private James La Belle was awarded the Medal of Honor posthumously for his heroism. His citation closes with the following:

> His dauntless courage, cool decision and valiant spirit of self-sacrifice in the face of certain death reflect the highest credit upon Pfc. La Belle and upon the U.S. Naval Service. He gallantly gave his life in the service of his country.

Twenty-seven Medals of Honor were awarded to Marine and navy servicemen for their bravery on Iwo Jima—more than for any other single battle in U.S. Navy history. Admiral Chester Nimitz told the nation, "Among the Americans who served on Iwo Island, uncommon valor was a common virtue."

Marines reached the top of Mount Suribachi on February 23 and raised the U.S. flag. The capture of Suribachi and the airfields on Iwo made American victory certain. Yet the Japanese fought on. Their vast complex of interlocking caves and pillboxes proved to be formidable and cost many courageous Americans their lives. Iwo Jima was not declared secure until March 26. The thirty-six-day assault cost the lives of nearly seven thousand Americans and more than twenty-six thousand American casualties. Just over one thousand of the twenty thousand Japanese defenders remained alive at the end of this heroic Marine victory.

James La Belle's remains lie at rest in section B-1 of Fort Snelling National Cemetery, just off of Mallon Avenue. The grave site is 422-S.

The tenacious Marines rightfully claimed credit for the important victory won on Iwo Jima. The navy provided support, not only with gunfire, but also through courageous actions, time and again, to supply the Marines and provide medical care in the field.

Eugene R. Olson

Eugene Olson was born in Minneapolis in 1924. He joined the navy right out of high school in June 1943 and became a medical corpsman. Olson spent his first six months working in navy hospitals before being assigned to the Fifth Marine Division at Camp Pendleton, California. He was headed for the Pacific theater. Pharmacist's Mate Third Class Olson landed on the beach at Iwo Jima with the Second Battalion, Twenty-sixth Marines, Fifth Marine Division.

An American surgeon from the war wrote, "The first angel of mercy that the wounded soldier sees is the medic, and I think the greatest heroes during any war are the medics, 'cause they will go to the aid of a soldier regardless of what the circumstances are." Eugene Olson lived up to that praise. He exposed himself to enemy fire repeatedly to aid wounded Marines and help carry them to safety. The U.S. Navy later awarded him the Navy Cross for his numerous acts of heroism on Iwo. War correspondent Ray Coll Jr. later asked Olson how many men he thought he had saved. His reply was simply, "I lost count." Coll wrote that Olson was "exceptionally modest and didn't like to talk about his experiences." He told Coll, "That was my job. There wasn't anyone else there to look out for those wounded. Somebody had to get them out so I did."

Olson's citation for extraordinary heroism in action reads:

On March 3 1945 Pharmacist's Mate Third Class Olson voluntarily left a protected position to assist an adjoining company that was experiencing heavy casualties. Completing this work, he returned to his company and a few minutes later he went out beyond his own front line to attend to a wounded man, who was lying in the line of fire. Bullets pierced his first aid pouch and canteen. With complete disregard for

Pharmacist's Mate Third Class Eugene Olson receiving the Navy Cross from Major General Thomas Bourke, commanding the Fifth Marine Division, for Olson's heroism as a corpsman on Iwo Jima. Photograph courtesy of the Olson family.

his own safety, he brought the wounded man back behind the lines and administered first aid. Again on March 5 he went into a known fire lane and, in the face of grenades thrown from a cliff, removed and treated a wounded Marine. A few minutes later, when his whole platoon was pinned down by machine gun fire, he moved out ahead of the front lines and treated a wounded Marine. Throughout the entire operation, PhM3/c Olson's repeated acts of courage were an example to his company and an inspiration in perilous situations. His conduct was at all times in keeping with the highest traditions of the United States Naval Service.

Eugene Olson survived Iwo Jima. He told Coll that the time he was most scared took place when a Marine general pinned the Navy Cross on his chest. Major Amedeo Rea, Olson's commanding officer, wrote a letter of reference for Olson as Olson left the service. The letter, dated October 15, 1945, reads in part: "Olson impressed me as an outstanding man. . . . I have no idea what Olson intends to do in the future for this letter was unsolicited. Whatever he chooses to do, I sincerely feel he will do well."

Olson answered the call to duty to return to serve his nation in Korea before settling down and living a long and fruitful life in the Twin Cities. He died in 1991 and is buried in grave site DS 81-S on the Avenue of Honor in Fort Snelling National Cemetery.

The Marine victory on Iwo Jima prepared the way for the battle for Okinawa and, ultimately, the invasion of Japan.

Albin Glavan

Albin Glavan of Kinney, Minnesota, was one of eight children. His parents emigrated from Slovenia to Minnesota's Iron Range in the early 1900s, married in 1914, and had seven sons and a daughter. Six sons served in the U.S. Army during World War II, the seventh being only sixteen when the war ended. Four of the brothers fought in Europe and two in the Pacific. The family was fortunate in that none were injured during the first years of the war. A case in point was Louis, the second youngest. He was a sergeant with the First Infantry Division, which saw considerable action in North Africa and Sicily, went ashore in the second wave at Omaha Beach, fought his way across France, and survived heavy fighting in the Huertgen Forest and the Battle of the Bulge.

The Glavan family's good fortune changed in 1945. Fred, the youngest of the brothers in the service, was killed in action in Belgium, just west of Bastogne, in early January 1945. The nineteen-year-old, serving with the Seventeenth Airborne Division in his first combat operation, was walking point on a reconnaissance patrol when a sniper killed him. Fred's older brother Albin wrote home from the Philippines after receiving the news of Fred's death, "I never will be the same man, for there will always be a vacant space in my heart for him. . . . Why did it have to be him? He was so young. He hardly knew what life was."

Sergeant Albin Glavan, whom his crew called "Chief," commanded a tank in Company C of the 706th Tank Battalion, 307th Regiment of the Seventy-seventh Division. Glavan and his comrades had their initial combat experience alongside the Marines in the retaking of Guam in July 1944. They later took part in the fierce fighting in the Leyte campaign in the Philippines. Pacific command assigned the Seventy-seventh Division to take Ie Shima in April 1945. Ie Shima, a small island two miles off the northwestern coast of Okinawa, offered an ideal base for air support of operations already escalating on Okinawa and later for attacks on the Japanese homeland. The Iegusugu Pinnacle, rising nearly six hundred feet above sea level on the east side of

Albin Glavan on the streets of Los Angeles before shipping out to the war in the Pacific. Photograph from Tony Glavan's personal collection.

Ie Shima, dominates the island, which is only five miles long by two miles wide. The limestone pinnacle is honeycombed with connected caves, which the Japanese augmented with extensive fortifications.

The American landings began on the morning of April 16, 1945, when the 305th Regiment of the Seventy-seventh Division hit the beaches of Ie Shima. Division headquarters committed the 307th to land on April 17 after the 305th met increasing resistance throughout April 16. The beaches had to be secured so that heavy construction equipment could be landed to build an air base. The plan to take the airfield on Ie Shima the first day put even more pressure on the ground forces. The equipment necessary to repair damage done by the Japanese was backing up on the beaches. Time was also of the essence because the 307th Regiment was scheduled to make a demonstration off the beaches at the southern end of Okinawa on April 19. Assistant division commander Brigadier General Edwin H. Randle secured permission to retain the 307th Regimental Combat Team on Ie Shima to help clear the beaches. The plan for April 18 called for continuation of the attack by the 307th Regiment, supported by the 305th, against the defense established by the enemy south of the Iegusugu Pinnacle.

As the Japanese held the high ground on the island, they poured accurate fire down on the attackers. The rugged terrain, narrow roads, and extensive use of mines made matters worse. The fighting consisted of a series of bloody skirmishes, often marked by hand-to-hand combat, for each position up the ridge toward the Iegusugu Pinnacle. The American advance was costly, and the high ground became known as "Bloody Ridge." Sergeant Albin Glavan was pressing his tank forward on April 19 when he saw a Japanese soldier rise from a concealed position and toss a satchel charge under the lead tank commanded by Lieutenant William Siegel. The blast disabled Siegel's tank, pinning the crew inside. The Japanese aimed a murderous fire at Siegel's tank from their position on a nearby ridge. Siegel radioed for the next tank to move forward and rescue him and his crew. Glavan moved his tank forward while his close friend, Sergeant Ben Yanich, followed in his tank. A Japanese soldier appeared with another satchel charge. Yanich, protecting Glavan's right flank, fired a burst that killed the Japanese soldier, but not before he tossed the satchel charge under Glavan's tank.

The explosion momentarily lifted Glavan's tank, disabling it and injuring Glavan and Private First Class Ray Belcher, while shaking up everyone else inside. The crew, knowing that they were an easy target for an antitank gun, scrambled to get out. Japanese machine-gun fire swept the tank as Glavan and his men exited. In the confusion of the moment, Corporal Kenneth Rogers ran toward the Japanese line and machine-gun fire cut him to pieces. Glavan moved as quickly as he could with a smashed right

Sergeant Albin Glavan of the 706th Tank Battalion (holding shell) with his tank crew. Photograph from Tony Glavan's personal collection.

heel and dove into a shell hole. Moments later, a Japanese mortar shell scored a direct hit on him. He lived only because the shell did not explode, but the impact mangled his right hand and he lost a finger. Medics removed Glavan from the field and evacuated him to a hospital ship.

Albin Glavan ultimately ended up at Barnes General Hospital in Vancouver, Washington, where his mail finally caught up with him. The first letter he received was from his family, informing him that his twenty-three-year-old brother Louis had been killed in action in Germany on March 30, 1945. The family had frantically tried to get word by letter to Glavan's company commander. War Department Circular Number 24, dated January 19, 1945, stated that on the death of two service sons in a family, the surviving sons in service were to be placed into noncombatant roles or to be discharged. Albin already had survived heavy fighting and the Glavan family knew he was headed into more in the Pacific theater as the front moved closer to Japan. They enlisted the aid of the Red Cross to speed delivery of their letter, which reached Glavan's commanding officer two days after Glavan had been wounded in action.

Other letters arrived for Sergeant Glavan, including one from Lieutenant Siegel. He explained that had he recognized the proximity of the enemy, he never would have allowed Glavan's tank to move forward to cover his. He closed his letter, saying, "Your efforts on behalf of the crew and myself will not soon be forgotten." Sergeant Yanich wrote to express his guilt that Glavan's tank had been hit instead of his: "That was supposed to be me. I followed Siegel. In turn, you told me you were going. My tank was turned to the extreme right and I had to back up. This must have been evident in your mind. You pulled up ahead of me and you know the rest."

The assault on the Iegususgu Pinnacle itself began on April 20 and continued for nearly a week. The cost to take Ie Shima was well over one thousand American casualties, including 218 dead. Famed war correspondent Ernie Pyle died while reporting on the fighting on Ie Shima. His memorial reads: "At this spot, the 77th Infantry Division lost a Buddy, Ernie Pyle, 18 April 1945." The Seabees went to work repairing Ie Shima's three landing strips even before the fighting was over. One fighter group was based on Ie Shima by May 10. Three fighter groups and one night fighter squadron operated from the island by June 14. Ie Shima played an important role in the fierce battle for Okinawa. Both Okinawa and Ie Shima became key air bases that brought Japan to its knees to end the war.

Lieutenant Siegel recommended Sergeant Albin Glavan for the Bronze Star. The citation reads:

> For meritorious service in connection with military operations against the enemy on Ie Shima. . . . Throughout the entire operation, by his skill, initiative, and coordination with the infantry he contributed materially to the success of the operation. He unhesitatingly pushed forward in the face of intense enemy mortar fire to aid in the infantry's advance. He negotiated his tank over hazardous terrain to seek out and destroy the enemy in caves and pillboxes. Upon reaching the ridge overlooking Iegusuku-Yama, he tenaciously held the ground until the gain could be consolidated by the infantry troops. When his platoon commander's tank was knocked out of action, Sergeant GLAVAN was seriously wounded. Sergeant GLAVAN's initiative and aggressiveness were a source of inspiration to the men of his platoon.

Albin Glavan spent months recuperating at Barnes General Hospital. He was discharged from the army in November 1945, in time to return home to Kinney, Minnesota, and reunite with his family for Thanksgiving. His parents lived long lives and saw their family multiply. Glavan lived a long and full life. He remained close to his three surviving brothers and their families. He suffered in his later years from rheumatoid arthritis and other health issues related to his wartime service. He died unexpectedly of a stroke in 1995 at the age of seventy-nine. Albin Glavan is buried in section 14, grave site 3076, at Fort Snelling National Cemetery.

Millard Charles Boie

Millard Boie was twenty-six years old, married, and living in Plainview, Minnesota, at the time of the Japanese attack on Pearl Harbor. He became a Marine and was assigned to Company G, Second Battalion, Twenty-second Marine Regiment, Sixth Marine Division. It was Boie's destiny to take part in one of the most important and bloodiest campaigns of the war. The invasion of the Japanese island of Okinawa involved the greatest naval armada in American military history. The assault force, consisting of three Marine divisions and four army infantry divisions, totaled more than 180,000 men. The American fighting men went ashore on the morning of April 1, 1945. It was Easter Sunday. Their grim work was to last eighty-two days.

The Battle of Okinawa was not going well as the fighting moved into May. Japanese kamikaze planes were taking a heavy toll of American ships off Okinawa. American land forces had suffered horrific losses and fell short of claiming the objective targets set by military planners. A coordinated Tenth Army attack was scheduled for May 11 on the formidable defenses around Shuri Castle. The Japanese commander anticipated this, and committed his reserves to bolster the strength around Shuri.

The Twenty-second Marines crossed the Asa estuary early on the morning of May 10 on a small footbridge completed during the night. They secured the town of Asa such that engineers of the Sixth Marine Division were able to build a modular Bailey bridge across the estuary that night in preparation for the assault on the morning of May 11. The Japanese subjected the Marines in the town to continual artillery fire from their excellent positions on the Shuri heights, and the Marines incurred severe losses.

The massive, coordinated assault that commenced on May 11 soon slowed into a series of fierce contests for a multitude of pillboxes and bunkers.

The Marines, before contending with formidable Shuri Castle, had to take two low ridges, Sugar Loaf and Horseshoe, into which the Japanese had built several gun positions. Millard Boie's unit, Company G, Twenty-second Marines, was involved in the initial engagement with Japanese troops on Sugar Loaf. Accompanied by tanks, Company G advanced against heavy resistance and reached the crest of Sugar Loaf on May 12. The company commander frantically radioed for reinforcements, received none, and was ordered to withdraw due to heavy casualties. Company G suffered additional heavy casualties in falling back. The battle for Sugar Loaf continued for several days. Boie was killed in action on May 13.

Marines in action on Okinawa. Photograph courtesy of the National Archives (27-N-123170).

Millard Boie's remains were returned to Minnesota in 1949 and laid to rest in section C-6, grave site 8155, at Fort Snelling National Cemetery.

The Japanese fought fiercely to defend Okinawa, which they considered their home soil. American forces did not secure Okinawa until July 2. Well over one hundred thousand Japanese soldiers lost their lives, and there was a high price paid in American lives. Total American battle casualties were nearly fifty thousand, including over twelve thousand dead. The Americans demonstrated their resolve to defeat the Japanese at any cost. But the cost of Okinawa made planners reassess the estimates of the loss of life that would occur with the invasion of the Japanese mainland.

William S. Acheson

The end of the war did not seem imminent, even as American ships cruised along the coast of Japan and American planes bombed the Japanese homeland. The determination of Japanese soldiers to fight to the death gave every indication that the war could

Lieutenant William Acheson distinguished himself in combat on the island of Luzon in the Philippines. Photograph courtesy of the Acheson family.

drag on. Military planners prepared for the invasion of Japan, even as they dreaded the magnitude of the casualties anticipated. Meanwhile, the fierce fighting in the Philippines continued.

William Acheson was born in Fargo, North Dakota, in 1916. He married and settled down to raise a family in Moorhead, Minnesota. The war upended those plans. Acheson entered the military service in June 1942. He trained at Camp Roberts in California and received his officer's commission at Fort Benning, Georgia, in February 1943. First Lieutenant Acheson was assigned to the 151st Infantry Regiment of the Thirty-eighth Division with responsibilities as a company executive officer. His older brother, Bob, wrote to him before his departure overseas:

When you do go, I feel confident that you will conduct yourself and lead your men as an officer should. I want you to know that I personally feel that you will do all that can be done, but remember kid, that as an officer your primary duty is to your men. You not only have to lead them, but you also have to be father, mother and father-confessor to them. . . . They are good men, Bill, but that is not enough, it is only by the example that you will set for them that they will finally achieve the best that is in them. I have seen a lot of units fall by the wayside because of a lack of junior officer leadership. Train them to fight at night, hard and viciously, the enemy has little stomach for either night fighting or cold steel in the guts, and if you kill them you don't have to take them prisoners. . . . I could write reams about what you could do in the way of training, but most particularly are the basic things you have already learned. A thorough knowledge of them and a skillful application of the same are the most vital things that are needed; night fighting, scouting and patrol, bayonet and hand grenade and DISCIPLINE. . . . Best wishes of one soldier to another.

Bill Acheson shipped overseas in December 1943 with these words of wisdom. His wife, Ginny, delivered a boy, William Kirby, on December 23, 1943, just after her husband went off to war.

The Thirty-eighth "Cyclone" Infantry Division gathered in Hawaii in January 1944 and departed for New Guinea, where it trained in jungle warfare until the end of November. The Thirty-eighth landed at Leyte in the Philippines on December 6, remaining there for a month. One veteran of the Thirty-eighth later wrote, "Then we shipped out again, back on a troop carrier in a large convoy of ships. . . . We knew we were in for something big, but we didn't know what, until we arrived off the coast of Luzon Island in the Philippines at Subic Bay." American forces had just taken Manila, but the Japanese remained entrenched on Bataan and Corregidor. The Thirty-eighth Division was given the assignment of retaking Bataan. American troops landed northwest of the Bataan Peninsula on January 29. The Japanese were well entrenched in the rugged mountains of Bataan, and the ensuing encounter, which came to be known as the Battle of Zig-Zag Pass, lasted two weeks. All three infantry regiments of the Thirty-eighth took part in this battle. A veteran of the division wrote: "We started our push into Zig-Zag pass. The Japs didn't push very easily, they were dug into the ground, with tunnels and bunkers, so concealed you could step over them, or fall into them. It was really slow advancing. We were pinned down with sniper, or machine gun fire so much of the time."

The reinforced 151st Infantry Regiment then made an amphibious landing on the south end of Bataan at Mariveles on February 15. The Japanese hurled a major counterattack at the Americans that night, but were repulsed. Lieutenant William Acheson earned the Purple Heart that night from wounds he sustained. American forces were once again in control of Bataan Peninsula on February 21. General MacArthur nicknamed the Thirty-eighth Division "the Avengers of Bataan." A copy of lyrics by an unknown author found in Acheson's personal papers reads:

Westward, southward, still we fought them
Til we rid them from the land
That is how we won the title
The Avengers of Bataan

The stanzas went on and on.

The 151st Regiment made combat landings to seize the islands of Caballo and El Fraile on March 28 and Carabao on April 16. The entire division was deployed in the rugged Sierra Madre northeast of Manila in May 1945 to crack the Japanese Shimbu line. The men of the Thirty-eighth outlasted determined Japanese resistance in a series of fierce engagements, ultimately seizing control of the Marakina watershed and the Wawa Dam. Effective Japanese resistance in the more mountainous regions of Luzon continued for months. Lieutenant Acheson was awarded the Bronze Star "for heroic service in connection with military operations against the enemy in Rizal Province, Luzon, during the period 11 June to 20 June 1945 as company executive officer."

William Acheson earned the respect of his men by leading combat patrols. He took any risk he expected his men to take in getting the job done. Acheson was credited with saving the lives of three of his men on June 19, 1945. The men lay wounded at the mouth of a large cave, which they had been checking out when Japanese opened fire. Acheson rushed to the cave and pinned the occupants within by delivering a withering fire while others evacuated the three wounded men. Acheson's patrol captured the cave, killed many of the enemy, and took a large number of prisoners, as well as seizing a large cache of weapons and ammunition. He made a personal reconnaissance on the following day over a killing ground well covered by Japanese sniper and machine-gun positions. The result was the capture of the enemy position with minimal casualties.

Acheson and his men remained engaged in combat in Rizal Province up to and even after the official Japanese surrender on September 2, 1945. General Yamashita led more than fifty thousand well-armed soldiers down from the mountains of Luzon at the close of the war to hand over their weapons and disband. The Allies tried Yamashita for war crimes and executed him. William Acheson and his comrades returned home

Lieutenant William Acheson (center) and comrades with a war trophy, a Japanese flag. Photograph courtesy of the Acheson family.

after months of fighting in the bamboo-covered mountainous terrain and living in trenches often filled with several inches of water.

William Acheson moved to the Twin Cities in 1957 and lived for many years in St. Louis Park. His wife, Ginny, recalled, "He never really talked much about the war," and, like so many veterans, "he never really got over the war." Acheson passed away on January 20, 2004, and was buried in Fort Snelling National Cemetery, section 20-A, grave site 208.

Lillian Conkey Henke

"All who knew her loved and respected her, such sincere dedication she exhibited." So wrote a friend of Lillian Henke, born Lillian Conkey in 1919 in Little Falls, Minnesota. Henke moved to Minneapolis after high school graduation and became a beautician. She met and married a man home on leave after boot camp in October 1942. He soon shipped out to North Africa. The war did not go well for a time, and the nation was desperate for additional military personnel. Lillian Conkey McKnight Henke stepped up to serve. She enlisted in August 1943 and became part of the Women's Army Corps, the WACs. She did not tell her husband or her family until she had done so. Her husband strenuously objected via mail, but he could do nothing about her decision. "It

Sergeant Lillian Conkey Henke earned her wings and served as a radio operator on C-47 transport planes flying across the nation during the war. Photograph courtesy of Judy Borgeson.

made me nervous not to be doing something worthwhile," Lillian later wrote, adding, "Women going into the Army [then] was a never, never. We were the first."

Lillian went first to Des Moines, Iowa, for basic training, then to Kansas City for training as a radio operator. The army assigned Lillian and several other women to the headquarters of the Second Air Force Colorado Springs. One of her fellow WACs later wrote that the women "formed a strong bond as we worked in a ground radio station. . . . It was a big step at that time for women to venture into men's territory." The army soon gave the women flying status and transferred them to nearby Peterson Field to serve with the headquarters of the 204th Army Air Force Base Unit (204 AAF BU).

The army activated the 204 AAF BU in late 1944 to administer the Second Air Force Inter-Station Transport Service, which would serve the forty installations of the Second Air Force spread out across the midwestern and western United States. The Second Air Force was training B-29 Superfortress crews for the air war against the Japanese homeland. Major Superfortress bases included Walker Field near Salinas, Kansas, Biggs Field in El Paso, Texas, and Wendover Field in Wendover, Utah. Pilots and B-29s from the 509th Composite Group, based out of Wendover Field, would drop the atomic bombs on Hiroshima and Nagasaki, Japan, in August 1945. The 204 AAF BU was an "air line within an air force," according to an army press release, "its workhorse fleet of C-47s a mighty adjunct to the sleek Superfortress." The press release reported:

> A group of "WACs with wings" serve as radio operators on all the transport planes. They are graduates of an AAF radio school, who are then placed through a special course of instruction at Peterson Field.

An official commendation, issued after the war's end by Brigadier General Harold McGinnes, stated:

> It was essential, because of the nature of the service to be provided, that a radio operator accompany each flight. The then existing shortage of enlisted men radio operators was critical to the point where none were available for assignment to this transport service. There was available at that time a number of highly trained WAC radio operators. Accordingly, the Second Air Force Inter-Station Transport Service was manned entirely by WAC radio operators. From the beginning of this transport service, the efficiency of the WAC operators has been outstanding.

Henke's first uniform was a man's military overcoat. The coat was so large that the weighted bottom bruised her ankles. When WACs later received their own olive drab uniform, all agreed "they were horrible." Enlisted men chanted "WAC, WAC, quack, quack, quack" as they passed. But none of this deterred Lillian, who recalled, "I was happy as a lark. I loved the Army and everything about it."

She had always wanted to fly, but felt sure that she would never have the chance. However, the demands of the war were straining the nation. The Eighth Army Air

Sergeant Lillian Conkey Henke and her six fellow WACs, who earned their wings and proudly served. Photograph courtesy of Judy Borgeson.

Force alone consisted of more than two hundred thousand personnel at the peak of the daily bombing missions over Germany. Twenty-six thousand Eighth AAF men died and another twenty-one thousand were shot down and imprisoned over the course of the war.

The air war over Japan required a new weapon, the largest and most modern plane in the U.S. arsenal. The B-29 Superfortress had an effective range of over three thousand miles. The United States had only seventy-three qualified pilots and sixteen combat-ready B-29s at the beginning of 1944. The U.S. strategy in the Pacific theater focused on securing air bases in the Marianas Islands for B-29 bases from which to destroy Japan's ability to wage war. The distance to Tokyo was twelve hundred miles, well within the range of the B-29. U.S. forces took Saipan on July 9, 1944, which set up the landings at Guam and Tinian later that month. Guam and Tinian were secured on August 9, 1944. The construction of B-29 airfields on these islands, so proximal to the Japanese homeland, began immediately. The first B-29 arrived at Saipan on October 12, and there were over one hundred based on the island by November 22. The first American bombing raid against Japan took place two days later. The mission, although largely unsuccessful, was the first against Tokyo (since Doolittle's daring raid off of aircraft carriers) in over two years. Forty B-29s were lost in the first eleven bombing missions.

The 204 AAF BU was activated in late 1944 as the B-29 bombing effort against Japan built up. Over three hundred B-29s using incendiary bombs destroyed sixteen square miles in the center of Tokyo on the night of March 9–10, 1945. Fourteen B-29s went down. The United States systematically devastated Japan, accepting heavy B-29 losses. The Second Air Force in the United States was responsible for the training and supply of B-29 bombers and crews to maintain the pressure on Japan. The Army Air Force accepted nearly four thousand B-29s before the war ended. More than one thousand B-29s conducted twenty-eight thousand combat sorties against Japan in 1944–1945 with a loss of 371 of the heavy bombers. The effort was staggering.

Henke and her fellow radio operators were delighted to become one of the four-person crews on the C-47s, which traversed the routes between the forty installations under Second Army Air Force control. They were charged with rushing priority airplane parts or emergency mechanics to wherever needed. Official-duty passengers sometimes rode the C-47s to visit other bases. The transport service manifested more than two thousand passengers in one month. Henke later recalled, "I'd do it over again. It was a great experience and I made great friends." An Army Air Force press commendation noted:

> Radio receiving stations throughout this Air Force have often referred to the exceptionally high quality of their radio sending and receiving technique. As integral members of the flight crews, they have accepted and carried out each flight mission in a manner superior to that of any other group of radio operators that I have ever known. They have reflected great credit upon the WAC organization. They have clearly proved that the field of flight radio operation should be open to women.

The WACs continued in the charge of this duty for two years before being returned to civilian life. Lillian and her fellow "WACs with wings" gathered periodically for reunions and remained close for the rest of their lives.

Lillian McKnight was reunited with her husband after the war. They lived in St. Paul and had three children, a girl and two boys. The marriage ended in divorce in 1959, and Lillian struggled as a single parent to raise her children during a time when her status was socially unacceptable to many. She supported the family as a beauty operator. Lillian married Winston "Bud" Henke in 1970, and the couple moved to Bella Vista, Arkansas, in 1984 after retiring. Lillian, with her husband Bud Henke, spent the rest of her life active in nonprofit ministry, serving those in need through the Shoebox Ministry.

The "WACs with wings" kept in close touch over the years and all gathered in Colorado Springs in 1983 for an emotional reunion. Lillian Henke became a charter member of the Women in Military Service for America Memorial Foundation in 1990 and traveled to Washington, DC, to attend the dedication of the memorial in Arlington National Cemetery on October 18, 1997. Women had made large strides in career opportunities by the time of her death on September 24, 2001. She had every right to be proud of the role she had played. Sergeant Lillian Henke was buried with full military honors at Fort Snelling National Cemetery on October 26, 2001. The location is section 6-D, grave site 167.

George Orrben

George Orrben served aboard the USS *Murray* (DD-576), a Fletcher-class destroyer, during the Pacific campaign. He wrote home on December 18, 1944:

> It's a very lucky ship, having been through 13 battles and had never had a serious hit scored on it. I hope its luck hold.

The *Murray*'s luck was not to continue. She was too much in the thick of the action. She sank a Japanese picket ship about two hundred miles off the coast of Japan on February 26, 1945. A Japanese bomb struck the *Murray* on March 27 during the pre-invasion bombardment of Okinawa. She withdrew to Pearl Harbor for repairs.

Orrben wrote home from Pearl on May 6, 1945:

> We were one of the first surface units to see the Jap homeland. We came into about 18 miles from the coast. We've been under air attacks several times and have shot down two planes.

The *Murray* returned to action by midsummer 1945. She participated in one of the war's most daring raids when her squadron penetrated deep into Suruga Gulf on Honshu to bombard the Japanese city of Shimusu. The *Murray* accepted the surrender of the Japanese submarine *I-14* on August 27, 1945, east of northern Honshu. It was a fitting end to the service of the *Murray*'s crew when the boarding party from the *Murray* accepted the swords relinquished by the Japanese sub's officers. The *Murray* was present in Tokyo Bay for the formal Japanese surrender on September 2, 1945. Minnesotan George Orrben was proud to be present.

Orrben returned to Minnesota after the war. He died in 1965 and was buried in section I, grave site 4653, at Fort Snelling National Cemetery.

Robert J. Stone

The 333rd Fighter Squadron was part of the 318th Fighter Group formed in October 1942. The squadron's P-47s were launched by catapult off of "Jeep carriers" during

The USS *Murray* saw considerable action in the Pacific theater and was present in Tokyo Bay for the formal Japanese surrender. Photograph courtesy of the Naval Historical Foundation.

the battles of Saipan in June–July 1944 and Tinian in July 1944. The fighter group provided air defense after the taking of these islands in the Marianas. The 318th Fighter Group moved to Iwo Jima after the Marines captured it in March 1945. Iwo Jima was located halfway between the Marianas and Japan, just 750 miles from Tokyo. Iwo Jima made an excellent base from which American fighter planes could command the skies over Okinawa and also escort B-29s on their raids over Japan. The squadrons of the 318th Fighter Group were reequipped in early 1945 with P-47Ns, new long-range planes for attack missions deep into Japan, and assigned to Ie Shima for the Okinawa campaign.

Robert J. Stone was born in Tracy, Minnesota, in 1921. He entered the service in October 1942. He was an aviation cadet through most of 1943 and into 1944. Stone received his officer's commission on March 12, 1944, and joined the 333rd Fighter

Squadron, 318th Fighter Group. Eight P-47s from Ie Shima strafed Japanese air force seaplane ramps at Amami-O-Shima on May 31, 1945. Lieutenant Stone registered his first kill on that mission. One week later, thirty-six P-47s from Ie Shima attacked the southern part of Kyushu on the Japanese mainland. They took out numerous targets with rockets and machine-gun fire. They also claimed nine Japanese fighters sent to stop them. Stone received his second official kill on that mission. Four days later on June 10, the Ie Shima–based P-47s again struck Kyushu. Japanese opposition was fierce but the Americans scored seventeen kills. Lieutenant Robert Stone became an ace that day by claiming five of the seventeen kills.

Stone finished the war with the Distinguished Flying Cross, the Air Medal, the Distinguished Service Cross, and numerous other awards. He retired from the service in 1979 as a colonel after having served in numerous responsible positions, including chief, Operations Division, Andrews Air Force Base, and also with NORAD. He died in August 1999 and is buried in section DS, grave site 82-S, at Fort Snelling National Cemetery.

James Roehl

James Roehl grew up in Hopkins, Minnesota, graduating from high school in 1939, and he went on to study electrical engineering at the University of Minnesota. He entered the service on July 3, 1942, at Fort Snelling, and completed his studies through the Reserve Officer Training Corps (ROTC) on campus and graduated in 1943. He received extensive radio training and qualified as a radio officer in late 1944. He met and married Laranetta Butts, an army nurse, before shipping overseas in January 1945. The army assigned First Lieutenant Roehl to the 3363rd Signal Service Battalion with the Fourteenth Army Air Force in China. Roehl's initial location was at Kunming, the capital of China's Yunnan Province and site of a major air base.

Roehl served as a radio operator for his first six months of service, after which time he was promoted to commanding officer of a signal equipment installation detachment. The highly specialized unit was responsible for setting up the communications array for airfields being established as the Japanese were pushed back. Roehl's detachment set up new installations at Nanning and Poseh in southern China and later at Lingling, not far north of Kweilin. Their final installation was at Enshih in Hubei Province, five hundred miles north of the initial installations. Signal Battalion Headquarters recognized the 3363rd with a Meritorious Service Unit Award for their

First Lieutenant James Roehl of the 3363rd Signal Service Battalion saw duty all over China with the Fourteenth Army Air Force. Photograph courtesy of James Roehl's daughters, Diane M. Blanchard and Debra A. Rasmussen.

accomplishments. The detachment returned to Kunming, the central air base for army operations in China, as the war came to an end.

The dropping of the first atomic bomb on Hiroshima on August 6, 1945, and of a second bomb three days later on Nagasaki, led to the unconditional surrender of Japan on August 14, 1945. Hostilities between Chiang Kai-shek's Nationalists and Mao Tse-tung's Communists were already under way. The United States ended co-operation with the Chinese Nationalists on August 22 for fear of becoming embroiled in a civil war. However, American personnel scattered throughout China remained exposed.

Chinese warlord Long Yun controlled Kunming through most of the war. His reign contrasted sharply with the harsh rule of Chiang Kai-shek across the part of southern

China that he controlled. Chiang tolerated no dissent or opposition. His Nationalist army moved into Kunming at the beginning of October, setting up considerable tension in the city.

Lieutenant Roehl wrote home from Kunming on October 3, 1945:

More riots etc. in town today and the Chinese have the air base surrounded and won't let anyone through. They have barricaded the roads and have set up machine guns etc. also mortars set up in the hills. Yep, the battle for Kunming is on again.

Conditions worsened. Nationalist soldiers fired into a massive protest rally at Kunming in November and subsequently looted the university campus, killing more in that rampage. The GIs waited for orders to leave. The withdrawal did not take place until January.

Roehl wrote his wife on January 24, 1946, from Shanghai, opening with, "I'm on the move again." He wrote of "the excitement of leaving China at last. I've been in a hustle and bustle and my head is in a whirl. It seems the last week has stretched out into a month judging by all I've done—but still it seems like only a few hours ago when I got that ole radiogram that said to go to Japan. . . . We should leave for Okinawa tomorrow. . . . From Okinawa we go to Fukuoka, Kyushu [Japan], where we go to work again. This place is near Nagasaki. I sure wish I was packing to go home and to you."

Roehl became an instructor of electrical engineering at the University of Minnesota Institute of Technology after the war. He joined Honeywell's aeronautical division as a design engineer in 1951 and worked there for thirty-nine years. He continued his service as a member of the Army Reserve, where he did research and development work. He had several active-duty stints at the Pentagon. Roehl retired as a lieutenant colonel after twenty-nine years. He was past post commander of George R. Wolff VFW Post 425 and served as part of the VFW Color Guard at the opening ceremonies of the Hubert H. Humphrey Metrodome in Minneapolis in 1982.

James Roehl died March 2, 2003. He is buried in section 6-C, grave site 256, at Fort Snelling National Cemetery.

⁓

While the war in the Pacific continued and the invasion of Japan seemed imminent, a top secret American weapon was about to be unleashed that would save the lives of hundreds of thousands of Americans and Japanese.

Catherine Filippi Piccolo

The war effort to save democracy called on many different kinds of people. Catherine Filippi, at first glance, might seem to some an unlikely war hero. She was born in 1916 and grew up in Keewatin on Minnesota's Iron Range. She went to Hibbing Junior College for a time and attended business college in St. Cloud. A summer vacation in Italy, the homeland of her parents, was the watershed of her life. It was the summer of 1939, and Europe was on the verge of war. Benito Mussolini had completed the transformation of Italy into a totalitarian state and appointed himself dictator. There was no freedom of speech and the people feared the Fascista. The Italians invaded Albania in April 1939 and Nazi Germany invaded Poland to officially begin the Second World War on September 1, 1939. Filippi managed to get home to America on the last ship out of Naples. An Italian American boy from St. Paul named Louis Piccolo, whom she had met, was not so fortunate. He was stranded in Italy for the duration of the war.

Filippi's experiences with totalitarianism and her desire to play a role in the defense of democracy led her to enlist in the Women's Auxiliary Army Corps, the predecessor of the WACs. Staff Sergeant Catherine Filippi was among two hundred WACs who reported to duty at 261 Fifth Avenue in Lower Manhattan in July 1943. Building security was tight in the Manhattan Engineer District. The WACs learned that the Manhattan Project involved the development of the atomic bomb. The headquarters for the Manhattan Project was soon transferred to Oak Ridge, Tennessee, where Filippi and others working on the project watched famous scientists, such as Dr. Enrico Fermi, routinely pass through the halls. Scientists at Oak Ridge separated nuclear fuel U-235 from U-239, natural uranium. The fuel was sent to Los Alamos, New Mexico, where a team assembled the bomb. Everything about the project was top secret and on a need-to-know basis. Filippi was promoted to lieutenant. She served as director of classified files throughout this period. She was also assistant public relations officer. Filippi told a reporter many years later, "My job was keeping news out of the papers instead of trying to get into the press."

The public relations office became a beehive of activity about six weeks before the atomic bomb was dropped on Hiroshima. They gathered information and prepared news releases categorized "hold for release" and awaited word from the White House. Filippi was told to monitor the telephone from Washington in the first week of August. On August 6, 1945, the phone rang and a voice said, "This is the White House. Release the stories. The confirmation will be coming over your Teletype." The bomb had been dropped on Hiroshima.

Captain Catherine Filippi Piccolo of the WACs worked on the top secret Manhattan Project during the war. Photograph from the Minnesota Historical Society.

A U.S. Army news release dated August 19, 1945, commended the "detachment of the Women's Army Corps which served in silence with the Manhattan Engineer District's atomic bomb project" and formally recognized the unit for "an outstanding contribution to the war effort." Lieutenant Catherine Filippi of Keewatin, Minnesota, was among those specifically mentioned. Four thousand women served on the Manhattan Project. Thousands and thousands of other American women served the nation across the globe during the war. While their contributions might not always be recognized, their service was essential to the war effort.

The bomb marked the beginning of the end of the Second World War. The Japanese capitulated and signed the surrender on the deck of the battleship USS *Missouri* on September 2, 1945.

Catherine Filippi remained with the U.S. Army through 1948, earning promotion to the rank of captain before departing. She returned to civilian life after helping to write the history of the Manhattan Project. She reconnected with Louis Piccolo, who had returned home at the end of the war. They married in 1949 and raised three children in St. Paul. She told a reporter on the thirtieth anniversary of the dropping of the bomb:

> It was only later when we realized how many had been killed that I had a sudden feeling of sadness. I wish it hadn't been like that.... If I didn't think the dropping of the bomb had saved thousands of American lives and also those of the Japanese by shortening the war... and that some day we are going to learn how to use atomic energy properly and peacefully... then, I don't know.

Catherine Filippi Piccolo died in September 2001. She is buried in section S, grave site 2732, at Fort Snelling National Cemetery.

George Tadashi Tani

The Japanese attack on the American forces at Pearl Harbor was a disaster in more than one way for George Tadashi Tani. The twenty-six-year-old California native was an optometrist in Oakland in December 1941 when his ancestral homeland attacked the land of his birth. Federal agents began to pick up influential members of the Japanese American community almost immediately following the declaration of war. Tani worried about the fate of his parents, who were living in America but not as citizens. He also had two married sisters living in Japan. The Nisei (second-generation Japanese) American became depressed.

The first injustice imposed on the majority of Japanese Americans living on the West Coast was curfew. Eviction from their homes followed. President Franklin Roosevelt's Executive Order 9066, dated February 19, 1942, ordered more than one hundred thousand Japanese Americans, most of them U.S. citizens, to be removed from the West Coast. Tani wrote of his feelings at that time: "I was ticked off, knowing it wasn't right. I felt helpless." Government agents took the Tani family and their Japanese American neighbors and friends from the Bay Area to an assembly center at Tanforan Race Track in San Bruno, twelve miles south of San Francisco. The govern-

1946

Technical Sergeant George Tani served with the U.S. occupation force in Japan, where he was reunited with his two sisters and their families after Hiroshima was bombed. Photograph courtesy of the George Tani family.

ment housed some eight thousand evacuees in barracks on the racetrack infield, as well as in the stables.

The government later sent Tani to Minidoka Relocation Center in Hunt, Idaho, to serve as the optometrist in the camp hospital. There he met a young dietitian named Yoshiko Uchiyama. Tani remained at Minidoka until he received clearance for a job in Chicago. He entered the army in October 1944 and, after basic training, volunteered for Military Intelligence Service Language School (MISLS).

The U.S. Army opened the first Japanese language school in November 1941 at Fourth U.S. Army Headquarters at the Presidio in San Francisco. This was just one month prior to the Japanese attack on Pearl Harbor. That school ceased with Executive Order 9066, which forced the removal of Japanese Americans from the West Coast. The army sought to relocate the school to the Midwest, but several states declined. Governor Harold Stassen of Minnesota offered the former Civilian Conservation Corps camp at Savage, Minnesota, to the army as a site for the school. There was an increasing need for Japanese translators and interpreters, as well as men with an understanding of Japanese culture and psychology, as the war continued. The army relocated the school to larger facilities at Fort Snelling in August 1944, just prior to George Tani's arrival. MISLS graduated more than six thousand Nisei, who served the army as translators, interpreters, code breakers, and interrogators during the war.

George Tani discovered many of his Nisei friends from Oakland at Fort Snelling's language school. Yoshiko Uchiyama joined him there, and they married at the Fort Snelling chapel in February 1945. Technical Sergeant Tadashi Tani graduated from Military Intelligence Service Language School in the summer of 1945 and was in transit to the Pacific theater when the war ended. He joined U.S. occupation forces in Tokyo in October 1945, where he served as translator for the chief surgeon's office. He assisted in interviewing Japanese officers and recalled, in particular, one Japanese rear admiral admitting that American military personnel had better discipline in their ranks, as exemplified by their actions in the occupation of Japan.

Tani was assigned to the U.S. Typhus Commission in November 1945 and served in this capacity through June 1946. The commission was charged with preventing typhus outbreaks across Japan. In this capacity, he traveled widely across Japan to all the various ports into which repatriated soldiers were returning home.

Sergeant Tani, a graduate of the University of California at Berkeley, kept in close touch with his former German professor, Dr. Clair Hayden Bell. He wrote Bell on December 29, 1945:

> Went to Hiroshima. . . . I find it hard to forget Hiroshima. It is one place where every GI should go and see. In fact if all the leaders of the world and all the people's representatives went to this city they would come to the conclusion that wars are a thing of the past. It is hard to describe the devastation that took place. There is nothing which is left of any value—there is utter waste of land. All of these homes were burned and destroyed to the foundation. All the tiles seem to have been broken in hundreds of pieces. It seems as though a huge sledge hammer hit the whole city and flattened it to nothing. The only thing that remains standing are a few concrete frames of buildings in the center of the City where the bomb burst overhead.

Tani described a bridge about a mile from the bomb burst, which a medical officer showed him. "The heat and radiation of the atomic rays caused the asphalt of the bridge to turn black and the shadows of the people and carts were left white." He continued his description of the nightmarish landscape and added, "There can never be another war without the end of civilization."

Sergeant Tani had many profound experiences during his service in occupied Japan. He met victims of the bomb, malnourished children, homeless families, and defeated

Technical Sergeant George Tani saw firsthand the devastation wrought by the atomic bomb at Hiroshima. Photograph by George Tani and used courtesy of the George Tani family.

officers and soldiers. He was reunited with his two sisters, who had survived the bombings. He paid his respects to the sacred family cemetery, dating from the sixteenth century.

George Tani received his honorable discharge from the service on November 12, 1946. He graduated in 1950 from the medical school at the University of Minnesota. He completed his residency in ophthalmology as a Mayo Clinic fellow in Rochester, Minnesota, in 1955. He returned to the Twin Cities and was in private practice for years, while also serving on the clinical faculty of the University of Minnesota. He and his wife, Yoshi, raised three children and were blessed with seven granddaughters and a great-grandson. Dr. George Tani died in March 1999 at the age of eighty-three. His remains lie in section 6-C, grave 799, at Fort Snelling National Cemetery.

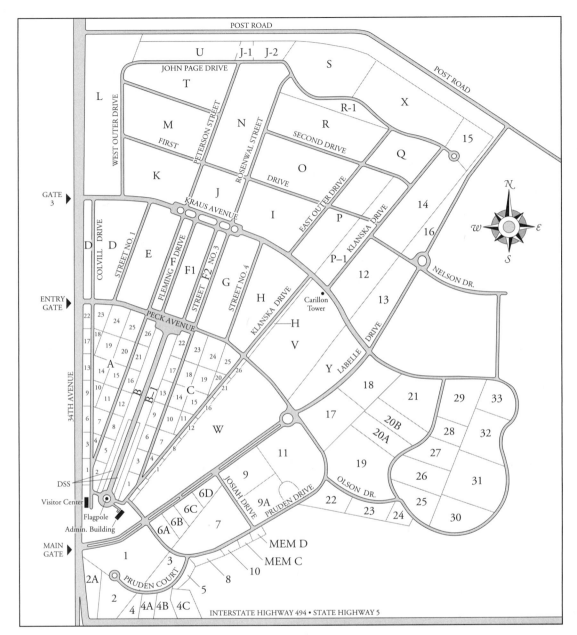

Fort Snelling National Cemetery

Guide to Grave Sites of Veterans
Profiled in the Book

Sources

Minnesota Historical Society State Archives Microfilm (SAM)

The Minnesota Historical Society is the repository of the World War II military records for Minnesota. Records of importance to this research are listed here.

SAM 232, 157 microfilm reels, which should be most useful to researchers.

They are arranged by bonus claim number and include the applicant's military service, proof of residence, and proof of honorable discharge (usually a copy of the discharge certificate). Unfortunately, these reels are generally illegible. There is a great deal of important information within these files, some of which may be decipherable. The files were microfilmed in the negative, rather than the positive, were often not focused, and have very small print; the researcher must use a number-three lens to have even a chance at guessing the words. It seems that the state disposed of the original documents after microfilming and before a reliable researcher could peruse the file to check the quality of the microfilming.

SAM 232-I, forty-eight microfilm reels that index the military records for Minnesota servicemen and women who survived the war and later applied for a postwar bonus.

The initial index for the SAM 232-I reels consists of forty-eight lines, advising the researcher as to which microfilm reel will have the basic information of the veteran: Reel 1 Aaberg–Anderson . . . Reel 47 Wigfield–Young, Reel 48 Young–Zywot.

The basic information consists of the name, address, military serial number, and the bonus claim number. While the military serial number provides access to other government military records, the bonus claim number provides access to the Minnesota Department of Veterans Affairs bonus records in SAM 232. The researcher begins with the T-to-Z volume of a series of black binders marked "State Agencies" (V for Veterans Affairs).

SAM 340, twenty-five reels of military records for those Minnesota servicemen and women who died in World War II.

The records must be accessed using the SAM 340-I index. This microfilm is quite legible and sometimes contains worthwhile information, such as copies of letters of condolence from commanding officers. These letters may or may not comment on the circumstances under which the individual died or what the officer's personal impressions of the soldier were.

SAM 340-I, two microfilm reels containing the index to the SAM 340 file.

The names of the deceased servicemen and women are listed alphabetically. There is a six-digit number associated with the name of each of the deceased. This number is taken to the T-to-Z volume of a series of black binders marked "State Agencies" (V for Veterans Affairs). There are a number of pages in this listing for SAM 340. The page in this volume that corresponds to the six-digit number indicates in which of the twenty-five reels in SAM 340 to locate the particular soldier's records.

General Resources for World War II

Anyone interested in studying World War II should consider reading at least three of Stephen Ambrose's books. *Citizen Soldier* (New York: Simon and Schuster, 1997) provides a wonderful overview of the various theaters and campaigns from a personal perspective. *D-Day, June 6, 1944: The Climactic Battle of World War II* (New York: Simon and Schuster, 1994) provides a similar personal perspective for the various units involved in the Normandy landings. *Band of Brothers: E Company, 506th Regiment, 101st Airborne; From Normandy to Hitler's Eagle's Nest* (New York: Simon and Schuster, 1992) follows one company through to the war's end.

A number of men featured in this book were Rangers and Airborne veterans. Patrick O'Donnell's *Beyond Valor: World War II's Ranger and Airborne Veterans Reveal the Heart of Combat* (New York: Free Press, 2001) offers firsthand accounts of these elite soldiers. The reader seeking a deeper perspective on a lesser-known but important theater of the war might wish to read Donovan Webster's *The Burma Road: The Epic Story of the China-Burma-India Theater in World War II* (New York: Farrar, Straus and Giroux, 2003).

The U.S. Army in World War II series, an amazing multivolume reference work, is available on the Internet through the U.S. Army Center of Military History at http://www.army.mil/cmh-pg/. Altus (Oklahoma) Air Force Base hosts a Web site, which includes the U.S. Army Air Force Chronology, day by day, from December 1941 through September 1945, at http://www.altus.af.mil/History/historycombat.htm. The Internet was the source of numerous important pieces of information, including "Chronology of the Attack from the Deck Logs of the Vessels Moored at Pearl Harbor on December 7, 1941: Compiled for the Pearl Harbor Court of Inquiry Hearings" at http://www.navsource.org/Naval/logs.htm.

Among the reference volumes worth perusing are *World War II Day by Day* (London: Dorling Kindersley, 2001) and Martin Gilbert's *Second World War: A Complete History* (New York: Henry Holt, 1991).

The History of Fort Snelling National Cemetery

The official Web site of the cemetery is maintained by the National Cemetery Administration of the Department of Veteran Affairs at http://www.cem.va.gov/nchp/ftsnelling.htm. A small pamphlet titled "Fort Snelling National Cemetery Informational Brochure" is available at the cemetery information office. A brief history of the fort can be found on the Web site of the Minnesota Historical Society at http://www.mnhs.org/places/sites/hfs/history.html. A list of Civil War veterans buried at Fort Snelling was compiled by the former cemetery director, William D. Napton, and can be found on the Web site of the U.S. Civil War Center at Louisiana State University at http://www.cwc.lsu.edu/cwc/projects/dbases/snelling.htm. Information regarding George H. Mallon, recipient of the World War I Medal of Honor, can be found on the Web site of the U.S. Army at www.army.mil/cmh-pg/mohwwi.htm.

1. Pearl Harbor through Guadalcanal

Gordon Prange's *At Dawn We Slept: The Untold Story of Pearl Harbor* (New York: Viking, 1991, 1981) remains an important source on the tragic attack that led the United States into World War II. An important line-item source as to the minute-by-minute events at Pearl Harbor that day is the "Chronology of the Attack from the Deck Logs of the Vessels Moored at Pearl Harbor on December 7, 1941: Compiled for the Pearl Harbor Court of Inquiry Hearings," at http://www.navsource.org/Naval/logs.htm. A comprehensive set of official Action Reports, filed by the commanding officers of each U.S. ship at Pearl that day, are posted on the Web site of the Navy Historical Center of the Department of the Navy at http://www.history.navy.mil/faqs/faq66-4.htm.

Karl Lasch and Ambrose Domagall's story came from Doug Bekke and Leland Smith at the Minnesota Military Museum at Camp Ripley.

Gordon Tengwall's story is from his son, Doug. Details on the USS *Louisville,* on which Gordon Tengwall later served, and its battle actions are included on a number of Web sites, including http://www.history.navy.mil/photos/sh-usn/usnsh-l/ca28.htm, http://www.multied.com/Navy/cruiser/Lousiville.html, and http://www.battleship.org/html/Articles/History/Leyte3.htm.

The Navy Historical Center of the Department of the Navy offers a brief memorial biography, "Captain Franklin Van Valkenburgh, USN," at http://www.history.navy.mil/photos/pers-us/uspers-v/f-vanvlk.htm.

Local newspaper articles regarding Ensign Ira Jeffrey included "1st Victim Wrote about Navy Care," *Minneapolis Star,* December 7, 1966, and "First City Man Killed in WWII to be Honored," *Minneapolis Star,* December 3, 1966. Both were sourced from the files of the Special Collection of the Minneapolis Public Library.

Byrl Carson's amazing story came from military records and other papers in the possession of his family. One document of particular interest was "Biography of Byrl Carson 1939 to 1943," a nine-page memoir he wrote and dated April 30, 1943. Minneapolis newspaper journalist Larry Batson featured Carson in a lengthy column, which appeared on page B2 of the *Minneapolis*

Tribune on December 7, 1976. Carson's obituary appeared on page B6 of the *Minneapolis Star Tribune* on February 25, 2004.

John Miller Jr.'s *Guadalcanal: The First Offensive* (Washington, DC: U.S. Army Center of Military History, 1995, 1947), available at http://www.army.mil/cmh-pg/books/wwii/guadc/gc-fm.htm, and Major John Zimmerman's *The Guadalcanal Campaign* (Washington, DC: U.S. Marine Corps, 1949), available at http://www.ibiblio.org/hyperwar/USMC/USMC-M-Guadalcanal.html, are important references. John Hersey's *Into the Valley: Marines at Guadalcanal* (Lincoln: University of Nebraska Press, 2002, 1943) and Richard Tregaskis's *Guadalcanal Diary* (New York: Random House, 1984, 1943), while not directly used in this book, remain among the classics of combat and are invaluable for a perspective of the personal experience of this most important campaign.

The reader is directed to http://www.higginsboat.org for more about Higgins boats. Dr. Robert Browning, historian for the U.S. Coast Guard, offers considerable insight into Coast Guard activities during World War II, including combat expeditions by small boat along the coast of Guadalcanal and inland up its rivers. Browning's article, "Douglas Munro at Guadalcanal," on the official Web site of the U.S. Coast Guard at http://www.uscg.mil/hq/g-cp/history/Munro.html, provides some detail in this regard.

Ernest Miller's story is from his autobiographical account, *Bataan Uncensored* (Little Falls, MN: Military History Society of Minnesota, 1991). Miller's citation from Headquarters Provisional Tank Group came from the Ernest Miller Collection at the Minnesota Military Museum, Camp Ripley. Stanley Falk's *Bataan: The March of Death* (New York: Norton, 1962) and Donald Knox's *Death March: The Survivors of Bataan* (New York: Harcourt Brace Jovanovich, 1981) are among many fine books on the Bataan Death March. Jennifer Bailey's *Philippine Islands: The U.S. Army Campaigns of World War II* (Washington, DC: U.S. Army Center of Military History, 1992), which offers an overview of the Japanese taking of the Philippine Islands, is available at http://www.ibiblio.org/hyperwar/USA/USA-C-Philippines/.

Richard Fleming's Medal of Honor citation is available at http://www.army.mil/cmh-pg/mohiia1.htm. Most books on the Battle of Midway refer to Fleming's heroism and the subsequent sinking of the cruiser *Mikuma*. Gordon Prange's *Miracle at Midway* (New York: McGraw Hill, 1982) is an important work on the decisive battle. The Web site of Fleming Field, South St. Paul's airport, honors its namesake with considerable coverage of this hero at http://www.visi.com/-sspairport/richardfleming1.html. The *St. Paul Pioneer Press* featured Fleming's mother with Admiral "Bull" Halsey upon his visit to the Twin Cities after the war in an article, "As St. Paul Gave Hero's Welcome to Halsey," that appeared November 14, 1945, on pages 1 and 11.

Thomas G. Miller's *The Cactus Air Force* (New York: Harper and Row, 1969) is an excellent source of information on the battle for air superiority over Guadalcanal. Other sources included Carl Hixon's *Guadalcanal: An American Story* (Annapolis: Naval Institute Press, 1999) and Eric Hammel's *Guadalcanal: The Carrier Battles; Carrier Operations in the Solomons, August to October 1942* (New York: Crown, 1987). Earle Rice Jr.'s *The Battle of Midway* offered technical specifics as to the various fighters involved. An excellent Web site also offers technical specifics on the F4F

Grumman Wildcat at http://www.acepilots.com/planes/f4f_wildcat.html. The remarks of Joe Foss are from his book *A Proud American: Joe Foss* (New York: Pocket Books, 1992).

Eugene Trowbridge's story originally came from Noel Allard's *Minnesota Aviation History 1857–1945* (Chaska, MN: MAHB Publications, 1993). His military service record is in State of Minnesota SAM 232, roll 133, record 235784. Noel Allard of the Minnesota Aviation Hall of Fame was most helpful in providing additional information about Trowbridge and introduced the author to Trowbridge's son, Gene. Trowbridge's unpublished "War Diary: Guadalcanal" was of particular interest. The Marine Corps Historical Center, Washington, DC, provided a news release on First Lieutenant Trowbridge and also a copy of a navy news release, "Seven Marine Officers, Five of Them Aces, Receive Decorations," dated November 29, 1943. Among his obituaries were "Eugene A. Trowbridge; band director was WWII hero" in the *Minneapolis Star Tribune,* May 17, 1994, and "Eugene Trowbridge dies; music teacher was World War II hero" in the *St. Paul Pioneer Press,* May 17, 1994.

2. North Africa and Italy

Gilmore J. P. Lundquist's story originally came from Noel Allard's *Minnesota Aviation History, 1857–1945* (Chaska, MN: MAHB Publications, 1993). Noel Allard of the Minnesota Aviation Hall of Fame was most helpful in providing additional information. Further information was obtained through Gilmore's son, Major Loren Lundquist, retired, USAF.

Edward Micka's story came from Wordell and Seiler's *Wildcats over Casablanca: U.S. Navy Fighters in Operation Torch* (Boston: Little, Brown, 1943). The Naval Historical Center of the Department of the Navy provided a memorial biography, "Lieutenant Edward Micka, USN," as well as the Action Report for Fighting Squadron 9 on November 8, 1942, and Lieutenant Micka's Navy Cross citation. The USS *Micka* is described in the *Dictionary of American Naval Fighting Ships* (1969), vol. 4, page 352. The *New York Times,* August 23, 1943, reported on the launching of the ship in an article, "They Sponsored a Fighting Ship"; clipping courtesy of Naval Aviation News, Department of the Navy. Two important books on the invasion of North Africa are Samuel Eliot Morison's *Operations in North African Waters: October 1942–June 1943* (Boston: Little, Brown, 1965) and Norman Gelb's *Desperate Venture: The Story of Operation Torch, the Allied Invasion of North Africa* (New York: William Morrow, 1992).

John Hougen's *The Story of the Famous Thirty-fourth Infantry Division* (Nashville, TN: Battery Press, 1979, 1949) was an important reference source for the Thirty-fourth "Red Bull" Division. Kenneth Davies's *To the Last Man: The Chronicle of the One Hundred Thirty-fifth Infantry Regiment of Minnesota* (St. Paul: Ramsey County Historical Society, 1982) focused on the regiment of that division in which both Albert Svoboda and Sylvester Hunter served with distinction. Additional information about the Thirty-fourth Division can be found in Lieutenant Colonel (Retired) Homer R. Ankrum's article "The 34th Infantry Division in World War II," at http://www.iowanationalguard.com. *To Bizerte with the II Corps* (Washington, DC: Center of Military History, U.S. Army, 1990, 1946) is an important reference for the campaign in North Africa. This is available at http://www.army.mil/cmh-pg/books/wwii/bizerte/bizerte-fm.htm. Matthew

Parker's *Monte Cassino: The Hardest-Fought Battle of World War II* (New York: Doubleday, 2003) is a recent contribution on that campaign. The Military Awards Branch of the Department of the Army in Alexandria, Virginia, provided the citations of Albert Svoboda's and Sylvester Hunter's Distinguished Service Crosses. Additional information about Svoboda was found in the 135th Infantry Historical Files, courtesy of Herb Schaper, New Ulm, Minnesota.

Leonard Vong's story began with an article, "St. Paul Soldier Awarded Star for Gallantry," in the *St. Paul Dispatch,* January 19, 1944. His citation was included in the article. *The History of the 30th Infantry, World War II* (Washington, DC: Infantry Journal Press, 1947) provided the setting for Vong's heroics on Sicily. A good history of the Third Division is available at http://www.grunts.net/army/3rdid2.html.

Arlo Olson's citation is available at http://army.mil/cmh-pg/mohiib1.htm. The best source for the bitter campaign along the Volturno River is *From the Volturno to the Winter Line, 6 October–15 November 1943,* first published 1945, and available on the U.S. Army's Center of Military History Web site at http://www.army.mil/cmh-pg/books/wwii/volturno/volturno-fm.htm.

Chester Moeglein's World War II service was featured in "Gen. Moeglein Is Man with Moving Spirit" on page 32 of the *Minneapolis Tribune,* February 20, 1961. Kenneth Davies's *To the Last Man: The Chronicle of the One Hundred Thirty-fifth Infantry Regiment of Minnesota* (St. Paul: Ramsey County Historical Society, 1982) and *Fifth Army at the Winter Line, 15 November 1943–15 January 1944* (Washington, DC: U.S. Army Center of Military History, 1945) at http://www.army.mil/cmh-pg/books/wwii/volturno/volturno-moving.htm provided background.

Harold Beasley's obituary came from the *Minneapolis Spokesman,* November 19, 1943.

Harold Gohman's story is from Wayne Dodds's *The Fabulous Fifty-seventh Fighter Group of World War II* (Marceline, MS: Walsworth Publishing, 1985). The introduction of P-47s is covered in "P-47 Thunderbolt: Aviation Darwinism," at http://www.cradleofaviation.org/history/aircraft/p-47/1.html. Wayne Dodds's *The Fabulous Fifty-seventh Fighter Group of World War II: Supplement* (Marceline, MS: Walsworth Publishing, 1985) covers the group's history and mentions Gohman in a number of places. Gohman's Bonus Beneficiary Files from the Minnesota Historical Society and Individual Deceased Personnel File from the U.S. Total Army Personnel Command, Department of the Army, also provided information.

Clarence Spreigl's story is in the Spreigl Family Papers, P2035, in the Manuscript Collection of the Minnesota Historical Society.

John Rice's story derived from SAM 340, roll 9, claim 804423 of the Minnesota Historical Society. Two excellent sources on the First Special Service Force are Joseph Springer's *The Black Devil Brigade* (Pacifica, CA: Pacifica Military History, 2001) and Robert Burhans's *The First Special Service Force* (Washington, DC: Infantry Journal Press, 1947). Burhans provided information on the circumstances surrounding Rice's death on page 186.

George Krasevac's Distinguished Service Cross citation is courtesy of the Military Awards Branch, Department of the Army. Sidney T. Mathews's "General Clark's Decision to Drive on Rome," at http://www.army.mil/cmh-pg/books/70-7_14.htm, provides the setting for the drive, which followed the Anzio breakout, including the fighting at Artena. Krasevac's sister, Virginia, and widow, Zorada, provided additional information.

William Brown's obituary was on the front page of the *Minneapolis Spokesman,* May 19, 1944.

Raymond Maxfield's story came from a feature article, "Missing Four Months, Lt. Maxfield Saw Plenty of Action behind Lines," in the *Mankato Free Press,* November 28, 1944. Additional details were forthcoming from Maxfield's sister, Mary Lou Ballman. His obituary appeared in the *Mankato Free Press,* April 27, 1991. The First Fighter Group's history is available at http://www.1stfighter.org/history/1944.html. Perspective on Maxfield's military experience in Alaska came from a Web site at http://209.165.152.119/units.html. Thanks also to Aaron Maxfield.

John Mork's story came from a lengthy Twelfth Air Force news release attached to his photo in the Minneapolis Public Library Special Collection.

Donald D. Johnson's story is from a wartime diary in the Donald D. Johnson Papers, P1963, in the Manuscript Collection of the Minnesota Historical Society. The history of the 351st Regiment is related in Campbell and Mulcahy's *History of the Three Hundred Fifty-first Infantry Regiment, World War II* (n.d.). Jami Bryan's article, "The 88th Infantry Division in Italy," from *On Point* and available at http://www.militaryhistoryonline.com/wwii/articles/88thinitaly.aspx, provides a broader context for the 351st at Vedriano.

3. Bombers over Europe

Gerald Astor's classic reference *The Mighty Eighth* (New York: Dell Books, 1998) offers background for the entire chapter.

The Ploesti bombing raid has been covered by many books. Robert Jackson's *Bomber! Famous Bomber Missions of World War II* (New York: St. Martin's Press, 1980) covers Ploesti, as does Martin Bowman's *Great American Air Battles of World War II* (New York: Barnes and Noble, 1994) and Robert Neillands's *The Bomber War: The Allied Air Offensive against Nazi Germany* (Woodstock, NY: Overlook Press, 2001). Rusty Bloxom, chief historian, The Mighty Eighth Air Force Heritage Museum, shared information pertaining to Robert Locky's capture, including excerpts from Carroll Stewart's *Ted's Travelling Circus: Ninety-third Bombardment Group* (Lincoln, NB: Sun/World Communications, 1996).

William "Andy" Anderson's story came from his pilot, Thomas Cushman Jr., of Brooklyn, Michigan. Statistics from that period of the bombing war are from "Table 2, Combat Groups Overseas," Army Air Forces Statistical Digest, World War II, at http://www.usaaf.net/digest/2b.htm. Raymond Butler's Ninety-first Bomb Group stories, at http://www.91stbombgroup.com, were useful, as were McFarland and Newton's *To Command the Sky: The Battle for Air Superiority over Germany, 1942–1944* (Washington, DC: Smithsonian Institution Press, 1991) and Robert Neillands's *The Bomber War.* Andrew J. Rooney describes James Howard's heroic actions as "possibly the best fighter pilot story of the war" in "Found: The Horatius at the Oscherslaben Bridge," *Stars and Stripes* 4, no. 66 (January 18, 1944), page 1. William Anderson's obituary appeared in the *St. Paul Pioneer Press,* June 5, 1952.

John Silvernale's story is from his own unpublished memoir, "Memoirs of John A. Silvernale," provided by his wife, Margery. She also shared the speech that he delivered to the Three Hundred Eighty-first Bomb Group Memorial Association at Ridgewell, England, on August 28,

1982. James Brown's *The Mighty Men of the 381st — Heroes All* (Salt Lake City: Publishers Press, 1986) made reference to Silvernale.

Herbert Bunde's story initially came from contact with World War II historian Dr. James Gerber, Bunde's nephew. Further detail came from Lieutenant Bunde's sisters, Elaine Gerber and Ruth Aker. Charles McBride, Bunde's pilot, told the story of the loss of their plane and their capture in his book, *Mission Failure and Survival* (Manhattan, KS: Sunflower University Press, 1989).

The original source of the story of George Radle's death over Germany is from State of Minnesota Records, SAM 340, roll 3, record 801241. Harold Jansen's *The History of the Four Hundred Forty-sixth Bomb Group* (Four Hundred Forty-sixth Bombardment Association, 1989) provided specifics as to the circumstances of the action.

Walter Shimshock's story is from the State of Minnesota World War II Bonus Beneficiary Files, SAM 340, roll 17, claim number 808517. The research department of the Three Hundred Ninetieth BG Memorial Museum, Tucson, Arizona, provided information on the crew members of *I'll Be Seeing You.* The best source for the mission on which Shimshock gave his life is Mark Conversino's *Fighting with the Soviets: The Failure of Operation Frantic, 1944–1945* (Lawrence: University Press of Kansas, 1997). He devotes all of chapter 5 to the Warsaw mission. The Web site of the American Chamber of Commerce in Poland provided information on President Bush and Vice President Al Gore's visits to the memorial of those killed in action, http://www.amcham.com.pl/glowna.phtml.

Eldon Personette's story began with his file in the State of Minnesota Military Records in SAM 340, roll 8, record 804059. Additional information, including crew information and old copies of *Wing Wash,* was obtained from Dick Gelvin of Mesa, Arizona, veteran and historian of the 445th Bomb Group.

4. Normandy Invasion

Denzil Carty's story is from the Denzil Carty Papers, P1725, of the Manuscript Collection of the Minnesota Historical Society. These papers, while quite extensive, only very briefly touch on the man's military service. An important reference work relating to the deployment of African Americans in the military service during the war is Ulysses Lee's *The Employment of Negro Troops,* chapter 20, "Service Units around the World" (Washington, DC: Center of Military History, U.S. Army, 1966). This is available at http://www.army.mil/cmh-pg/books/wwii/11-4/index.htm. *Liberators: Fighting on Two Fronts in World War II* (New York: Harcourt Brace Jovanovich, 1992), by Lou Potter et al., provides a more current perspective. Jennifer Delton's article, "Labor, Politics, and African American Identity in Minneapolis, 1939–1950," *Minnesota History* (Winter 2001–2002), includes mention of Reverend Carty. The excerpt from Reverend Carty's sermon is from http://rhet5662.class.umn.edu/heroes/carty.html.

Manford Christofferson's story is from the library of the Minnesota Historical Society. David Christofferson's six-page biographical booklet, *Manford Jerome Christofferson* (St. Paul: David Christofferson, 1992), relates the veteran's story. Leland Smith's article, "Ray Simeon

Miller, Founder of the Air National Guard," *Allies, Newsletter of the Military Historical Society of Minnesota* 11, no. 2 (Spring 2004), provides perspective on the history of the Minnesota Air National Guard.

Thomas McGovern's story is from a feature article, "St. Paul Pilot Completes 100 Fighter Missions," which appeared in the *St. Paul Sunday Pioneer Press,* October 29, 1944. Additional information was secured from McGovern's Military Record and Report of Separation, Certificate of Service, from U.S. Military Personnel Files in St. Louis. Richard Hallion's *U.S. Army Air Forces in World War II, D-Day 1944,* and *Air Power over the Normandy Beaches and Beyond,* available at http://www.aero-web.org/history/wwii/d-day/toc.htm, provided historical background.

George Ziemski's story is from his daughter, Marlene. The *Minneapolis Star Tribune* included Ziemski's story in a feature article, "D-Day Plus 50," on June 5, 1994. See also "Day of Destiny," *St. Paul Pioneer Press,* June 5, 1994, page 4.

Charles Parker's story is from Marcia Moen and Margo Heinen's *Reflections of Courage on D-Day and the Days That Followed: A Personal Account of Ranger "Ace" Parker* (Elk River, MN: DeForest Press, 1999). Henry Glassman's *Lead the Way* (1945), available at http://www.army.mil/cmh-pg/books/wwii/70-42/70-423.htm, and "Ranger Battalions of World War II," available at http://www.soc.mil/pao/factsht/Rangers/RWWIIBNs.htm, provided additional background.

Bernard Pepper's story began with his State of Minnesota Military Service records, SAM 232, roll 128, claim 227922. Victor Miller's "My Life with the Rangers," an account of the Fifth Ranger Battalion in Europe, available at http://www.geocities.com/oralbio/millervjbio.html, was an important resource, as was "The Fifth Ranger Battalion," World War II Army Rangers Web site, available at http://www.rangerfamily.org/Battalion%20Pages/fifth.htm.

Rex Kelsey's story began with his State of Minnesota Military Service records, SAM 340, roll 22, record 810511. Joseph Balkoski's *Beyond the Beachhead: The Twenty-ninth Infantry Division in Normandy* (Mechanicsburg, PA: Stackpole Books, 1999) provided valuable information. Personal communication with Joseph Balkoski and veteran Arnold Levin added additional insight. The quote by Dr. Joseph C. Flynn is from *The Surgeon's Story,* traveling exhibit presented by the American Academy of Orthopaedic Surgeons, 2004.

Donn Driver's story began with his wife, Wanda, and her self-published biographical piece, "A March through Donn R. Driver's Life." Driver's oldest son, Donn Jr., also was the source of much information. Walton R. Patrick's *From Texas to Teisnach with the 457 AAA AW Battalion* (U.S. Army, 457th Anti-Aircraft Artillery Battalion, 1945) included several references to Driver's heroics. The opening quote for the section on Donn Driver is from "Dr. Seymour M. Albert," *The Surgeon's Story,* traveling exhibit presented by the American Academy of Orthopaedic Surgeons, 2004. A later quote by Dr. Joseph C. Flynn is from the same exhibit.

Robert Hanson's story originally came from Noel Allard's *Minnesota Aviation History 1857–1945* (Chaska, MN: MAHB Publications, 1993). Noel Allard of the Minnesota Aviation Hall of Fame was most helpful in providing additional information about Hanson. The opening quote by Robert Hanson is from John Truman Steinko's *The Geyser Gang: The 428th Fighter Squadron in World War II* (Minneapolis: ROMA Associates, 1986). Hanson's obituary appeared on page 6B of the *Minneapolis Star and Tribune,* February 17, 1987.

5. Pacific Theater

John Millet's story is from his family. Biographies of most, if not all, of the original members of the Flying Tigers, including Millet, were compiled in Wayne Johnson's *Chennault's Flying Tigers: World War II Fiftieth Anniversary* (Paducah, KY: Turner Publishing, 1999). The official Web site of the Fourteenth Air Force presents its history and also the origins of the term *jing-bao* at http://www.vandenburg.af.mil/14af/14af_history/jing_bao.html. Harris B. Gibboney, one of Millet's comrades in the Flying Tigers/China Air Task Force, shared his insight on a number of different perspectives. Many consider Daniel Ford's *Flying Tigers: Claire Chennault and the American Volunteer Group* (Washington, DC: Smithsonian Books, 1991) to be the definitive work on this group of daring fliers.

Helen Roehler's story came from her family. The State of Minnesota SAM 340 military records offered additional information. *Guarding the United States and Its Outposts* by Conn, Engelman, and Fairchild (Washington, DC: Center of Military History, 2000, 1964) presents the backdrop of the U.S. defenses in the Aleutians before the Japanese invasion and occupation. This work is available at http://www.army.mil/cmh/books/wwii/Guard-US/.

James Carter's story is from the front page of the December 29, 1944, issue of the *Minneapolis Spokesman*. The statistics regarding African Americans in the military service are from Ulysses Lee's *The Employment of Negro Troops* (Washington, DC: Center of Military History, U.S. Army, 1966), available at http://www.army.mil/cmh-pg/books/wwii/11-4/. Much of this information comes from Harry Gailey's *Bougainville: The Forgotten Campaign* (Lexington: University Press of Kentucky, 1991), which addresses the role played by the Ninety-third Division in the context of the racism of the times. The medical quote concerning blood donations is from "Dr. John F. Hume," *The Surgeon's Story,* a traveling exhibit sponsored by the American Academy of Orthopaedic Surgeons, 2004.

Sheldon Gordinier's story came from his family. His commendation by Admiral Raymond Spruance for locating the Japanese fleet west of Saipan was reported in a 1944 newspaper clipping from the *Rock Island Argus* and in the *New York Sun,* June 29, 1944. Technical details on the Martin PBM Mariner are available on the "Aircraft of the Smithsonian" Web site, at http://www.nasm.si.edu/research/aero/aircraft/martin_pbm5a.htm. Samuel Eliot Morison's *New Guinea and the Marianas, March 1944–August 1944* (Boston: Little, Brown, 1953), vol. 8 of his History of U.S. Naval Operations in World War II series, provides much detail about the Battle of the Philippine Sea, June 19–20, 1944.

The original story of Lawrence Lundberg came from an article in the *Minneapolis Tribune,* October 13, 1956, "Airman Dies in Jet Crash South of Wold." Eventual contact with Larry Lundberg, son of the pilot, led to details regarding Captain Lundberg's military career and a considerable collection of letters written home during the war to his wife, Dorothy. James Rarick's *I'm in an Emergency: Minnesota's Cold War Military Aviation Disasters and Incidents, 1945–1960* (St. Paul, MN: Mindanao Printing, 2001) provided additional details regarding the tragic death of Captain Lundberg over the Twin Cities.

An article by Dave Scheuer, "The Birth of the Blues," at www.blueangels.org/History/Scheuer/Scheuer2.htm, tells the early history of the Blue Angels and includes the tragic story of Ross Robinson's death. A feature article, "First Strike at Manila," which appeared in *Life,* October 23, 1944, described the extraordinary success of Robinson's squadron and included a photo of him. One month later, when Robinson was home on leave, the front page of the *St. Paul Pioneer Press,* November 25, 1944, featured Robinson in an article, "St. Paulite Downs 4 Japs in Day in Philippines Battle; Visits Here."

Harry Hesslund's story began with the discovery of a wartime photo and accompanying news release in the Special Collection of the Minneapolis Public Library. Harry's son, Brad, later provided additional details and a copy of a book honoring Hesslund's Seabees unit, *Tradewinds: The Forty-eighth Construction Battalion* (U.S. Navy, 1945). Captain Larry DeVrie's article, "Navy Seabees on Guadalcanal," available at http://www.seabeecook.com/history/canal/cactus.htm, includes information on the formation of the Seabees and their overall contribution to the war in the Pacific.

A biography of Richard Kraus is included in "Who's Who in Marine Corps History" on the Web site of the U.S. Marine Corps History and Museums Division at http://hqinet001.hqmc.usmc.mil/HD/Historical/Whos_Who/Kraus_RE.htm. His Medal of Honor citation is at http://www.marinemedals.com/kraus.htm. Kraus's State of Minnesota military records are located in SAM 340, roll 17, record 808239. One important reference, which covers the Marine heroism on Peleliu, is Harry Gailey's *Peleliu 1944* (Annapolis, MD: Nautical and Aviation Publishing, 1983). There is a fine Web site at http://www.peleliu.net/ dedicated to this battle. U.S. Marine Corps statistics for World War II were obtained from http://www.usmc.mil/history.nsf/0/77F992B2ACB682EB852564D70059C642?OpenDocument.

Robert Meyer's story came from mention in his obituary of his role as a pilot with the Navy Black Cats. The family provided considerable information, including a copy of the Presidential Unit Citation for Meyer's squadron. The history of Patrol Bombing Squadron 33 (VPB-33) is available at http://www.daveswarbirds.com/blackcat/hist-33.htm. Technical specifications on the PBY Catalina planes and "The History of the Black Cats" are on the same Web site at http://www.daveswarbirds.com/blackcat/.

Lawrence R. Johnson's story is from an article in the *St. Paul Dispatch,* March 6, 1944. Additional information on his military career was obtained from the State of Minnesota military records, SAM 340, roll 7, record 803510, and from the Marine Corps Historical Center. Samuel Eliot Morison's *Aleutians, Gilberts, and Marshalls, June 1942–April 1944* (Boston: Little, Brown, 1962), vol. 7 in his series on World War II, provides details on the Tarawa landings. Online references include L. C. Kukral's "The Battle of Tarawa," from the Navy and Marine Corps World War II Commemorative Committee, at http://www.chinfo.navy.mil/navpalib/wwii/facts/tarawa.txt.

William Hoffmann's story came from his son, William Jr. Hoffmann's extensive unpublished memoirs were a primary source for this section. Walter Krueger's *From Down Under to Nippon: The Story of the Sixth Army in World War II* (Washington, DC: Zenger Publishing, 1979, 1953) provided additional background.

Ted Spreigl's story came from the Spreigl Family Papers, P2035 in the Manuscript Collection of the Minnesota Historical Society. Tim Lanzendofer describes the sinking of the USS *Princeton* in the context of the Battle of Leyte Gulf in "Glorious Death: The Battle of Leyte Gulf," at http://www.microworks.net/pacific/battles/leyte_gulf.htm.

Everett Forslin's story is from the State of Minnesota military service records, SAM 340, roll 11, record 805764. His death is described in Charles Young's *Into the Valley: The Untold Story of USAAF Troop Carrier in World War II* (Dallas: PrintComm, 1995), page 560.

Louis Testa's story began with the State of Minnesota military service records, SAM 232, roll 93, claim number 164026. The Military Awards Branch of the army provided Testa's citation. The Leyte campaign, including the action in which Testa distinguished himself, is covered in detail at the Web site for the U.S. Army's Center of Military History at http://www.army.mil/CMH-pg/brochures/leyte/leyte.htm. The overall WWII combat narrative of the First Cavalry Division is available at http://www.ibiblio.org/hyperwar/USA/OOB/1-Cavalry.html.

Fred Otto's story derived from two front-page articles in the *Mankato Free Press*: "Pacific Battle Veteran Never Thought, 3 Years Ago, That He'd Be in War," December 7, 1944; and "Task Force Saw Plenty of Action as Japs Quit," October 6, 1945. R. D. Fread's "History of the USS *Belleau Wood*," at http://members.aol.com/oldfungi/cv124his.html, provided background history on the carrier on which Otto served.

Patrick Ward's story came from a U.S. Coast Guard public relations photo in the Special Collection of the Minneapolis Public Library. The official Web site of the U.S. Coast Guard provided much information, including "U.S. Coast Guard: An Historical Overview," at http://www.uscg.mil/hq/g-cp/history/h_USCGhistory.html; Dr. Robert M. Browning's article, "Marshall Islands Invasion," at http://www.uscg.mil/hq/g-cp/history/MarshallIslands.html; and his article "The Coast Guard and the Philippine Landings," at http://www.uscg.mil/hq/g-cp/history/Leyte.html.

6. Pressing into Germany

Osmund Skarning's story came from the Web site of the Ninety-ninth Infantry Battalion (Separate), at http://www.99thinfbnsep.org. Yngvar Stensby, Skarning's comrade in arms, wrote of the day on which Skarning was killed in action in the Documents: Poetry, Art & Music section. Additional information on the Ninety-ninth Infantry Battalion is available in Howard Bergen's *History of the Ninety-ninth Infantry Battalion, U.S. Army* (Oslo: E. Moestue, 1956) and Gerd Nyquist's *The Ninety-ninth Battalion* (Oslo: H. Aschehoug, 1981). Another resource online is Bjorn Jervas's "Ninety-ninth Battalion (Separate), U.S. Army," available at http://www.nuav.net/usa.html.

Gerald Galarneau's story came originally from his obituary, which identified him as a glider pilot with the Army Air Corps. Contact with the family led to considerable information, including Galarneau's military records, personal papers, and reminiscences. Cornelius Ryan's *A Bridge Too Far* (New York: Simon and Schuster, 1974)—made into a movie in 1977—is the classic account of Operation Marketgarden. There is an extensive Web site devoted to this Allied disaster at http://www.marketgarden.com. The combat chronology of the 316th Troop Carrier Group is at http://www.usaaf.com/9thaf/Troop/316TC.htm.

Wayne Pierce's book, *Let's Go: The Story of the Men Who Served in the 325th Glider Infantry Regiment* (Chapel Hill, NC: Professional Press, 1997), provided much of the basis for Warner Squires's story. Cornelius Dwyer's "What Can We Do with Gliders?" a 1943 article reprinted in the *Glider Tow Line* (Spring 2002), the official newsletter of the 325th Glider Infantry Association, provided insight.

Much of Ragnar Abrahamson's story is from Gerd Nyquist's *The Ninety-ninth Battalion* (Oslo: H. Aschehoug, 1981), which made extensive use of the reminiscences of men of the Ninety-ninth Infantry Battalion, including Abrahamson.

Robert Farmer's story is from the State of Minnesota military service records, SAM 340, roll 1, claim 800293. The Military Awards Branch of the U.S. Army provided the citation for Farmer's Distinguished Service Cross. The Blue Earth County Historical Society provided several articles from the *Mankato Free Press* concerning Sergeant Farmer: notice of his being killed in action on November 18; a February 6, 1945, article stating that his Purple Heart was given to his parents; and a November 24, 1947, article declaring his reinterment in Fort Snelling National Cemetery. Gerald Astor's *The Bloody Forest: The Battle for the Huertgen* (San Francisco: Presidio, 2001) provides an excellent account of the battle in which Robert Farmer died. One account is Ernest Herr's "The Worst of the Worst: The Battle for the Huertgen Forest," at http://members.ols.net/~ernieh/HuertgenForest.html. The "History of the 1st Infantry Division" is at http://www.chgww2.com/1st/1st16th.htm; also see the Sixteenth Infantry Regiment Association Web site, the Historical Era: WWII section, at http://16thinfantry-regiment.org/sir/go/3338/Default.aspx.

Norman Dow's story is from the State of Minnesota military service records, SAM 340, roll 4, record 802032. *Combat History of the Fifty-first Armored Infantry Battalion* (1945) provided details on Dow's unit in action. The combat chronicle of the Fourth Armored Division is available at http://www.army.mil/cmh-pg/lineage/cc/004ad.htm.

Gaylord Winmill's story was compiled from his grave marker, the Veterans Graves Registration Report, his certificate of death, and his Military Service Record from the National Personnel Records Center in St. Louis, which included his Purple Heart decoration (Headquarters 101st Airborne Division, General Orders 128, Awards of Purple Heart, June 28, 1945). Communication with Nick Schmidt of Twinsburg, Ohio, Gaylord Winmill's old Army buddy, provided considerable insight. Gary F. Evans's *The 501st Parachute Infantry Regiment at Bastogne, Belgium, December 1944,* available at http://www.army.mil/cmh-pg/documents/wwii/501pirbulge.htm, gave perspective.

The stories of Henry and Erwin Lemke are from their nephew, John Lemke. George Hofmann's *Super Sixth: The History of the Sixth Armored Division in World War II* (Louisville, KY: Sixth Armored Division Association, 1975) and *The History of the Seventh Armored Division and the Seventh Armored Division Association* (Farmington Hills, MI: Seventh Armored Division Association, 1982) are good resources for more information. *Patton Unleashed: Patton's Third Army and the Breakout from Normandy, August–September 1944* (St. Paul: MBI, 2003) by Tim Ripley is a recent contribution on Patton's breakout. *The Ardennes: Battle of the Bulge* by Hugh Cole is one of the definitive books of that colossal battle. This book is available through the U.S. Army Center of Military History at http://www.army.mil/cmh-pg/books/wwii/7-8/7-8_cont.htm.

Mabel Johnson's story is from the Mabel L. Johnson Papers, P1946, of the Manuscript Collection of the Minnesota Historical Society. Included in this file is her "Narrative History of the Twenty-eighth General Hospital" and extensive correspondence. Information on the V-2 rocket that hit the Antwerp cinema is from an article, "V2 rocket kills 567 in Antwerp cinema," in *World War II Day by Day* (London: Dorling Kindersley, 2001). *The Army Nurse Corps: A Commemoration of World War II Service,* available at http://www.ibiblio.org/hyperwar/USA/ USA-Nurse/index.html, provided statistics on army nurses during the war. Technical specifics on the German V-2 rocket are available at the U.S. Air Force Web site at http://www.wpafb.af.mil/ museum/space_flight/sf9a.htm and also at http://www.accessweb.com/users/mconstab/v2.htm.

The stories of George and Herbert Spreigl are from the Spreigl Family Papers, P2035, in the Manuscript Collection of the Minnesota Historical Society.

Fred Pond's story is from his family. His unpublished memoirs were the source of much information in this section. The landing of the 631st on Utah Beach is documented on a Web site regarding LST 493 at http://www.wilmon.com/normandy.html.

7. Closing In on Japan

Bernie Meister's story is from a feature article on him, "How We Made It Out, I'll Never Know," in the *Grand Forks Herald,* November 11, 2003. Information on the submarine on which Meister served was obtained through "*Guavina* (SS-362)," at http://www.hazegray.org, originally from *Dictionary of American Fighting Ships,* vol. 3 (Washington, DC: Navy Department, Office of Chief of Naval Operations, Naval History Division, 1968). Additional information is from Rose Meister, Bernie's widow.

Donaciano Martinez's story is from his family. The story of Churchill is from a newspaper clipping in the scrapbook of Donaciano Martinez. The *St. Paul Pioneer Press,* April 10, 1945, mentioned Martinez in an article, "14 St. Paul Area Men on War List." The entry written by Donaciano Martinez, December 25, 1943, is in a journal in the possession of the Martinez family. His Bronze Star medal citation is in the possession of the Martinez family. "A Condensed History of the 503d PRCT" is available at http://corregidor.org/heritage_battalion/abbott/ brief_history.htm.

John Riley Brown's story originally came from a Web site prepared by his daughter, Nancy Brown Johnson. Subsequent contact led to further details from Nancy and her mother, Hazel, Brown's widow. The combat narrative of the First Cavalry Division for 1940–1945 is available at http://www.ibiblio.org/hyperwar/USA/OOB/1-Cavalry.html. The best resource for the details of the Luzon campaign, in which Brown participated, is *Luzon 1944–1945,* Center of Military History publication 72–28, part of the U.S. Army Campaigns of World War II series, which is available at http://www.army.mil/cmh/brochures/luzon/72-28.htm. The death of Major General Mudge was reported in "Getting On with It," *Time,* March 26, 1945.

Herman Hansen Jr.'s story was compiled with the help of the U.S. Marine Corps Historical Center. The center provided news releases from later in Hansen's career, which summarized in considerable detail his exploits in World War II. The center also provided certain citations, including one from the August 1944 *Naval Aviators Monthly Achievement Report.* John Condon's *Corsairs and Flattops: Marine Carrier Air Warfare, 1944–1945* (Annapolis, MD: Naval Institute Press, 1998) makes reference to Hansen's accomplishments in several parts of the book.

Kenneth Thompson's story is from Patrick Caruso's *Nightmare on Iwo* (Annapolis, MD: Naval Institute Press, 2001), pages 46–47. Statistics for Iwo are from "Battle for Iwo Jima," *World War II — Statistics and Review,* Marine Corps History, at http://www.usmc.mil/history.nsf/ 54d36a38f1a2851e852564d70059b000?OpenView.

James La Belle's story is from "Who's Who in Marine Corps History," Web site of U.S. Marine Corps History and Museums Division, http://hqineto01.hqmc.usmc.mil/HD/Historical/ Whos_Who/LaBelle_JD.htm. His Medal of Honor citation is in "James La Belle," *World War II Medal of Honor Recipients,* at http://www.army.mil/cmh-pg/mohiia2.htm. Robert Simonsen's "History of the Twenty-seventh Marines," available at http://www.allenaustin.net/history.htm, provided background. Details of all twenty-seven of the Marine and navy Medals of Honor awarded on Iwo are in "Iwo Jima Medal of Honor Winners," at http://www.geocities.com/ rbackstr2000/moh.htm.

Eugene Olson's story began with his State of Minnesota military service record, SAM 232, roll 74, claim 129761. Details later came from his wife, Marion. The medical officer's quote is from "Dr. Robert M. Hall," *The Surgeon's Story,* traveling exhibit presented by the American Academy of Orthopaedic Surgeons, 2004. The column by journalist Ray Coll Jr., "Visiting with Veterans from Iwo," is from an undated newspaper clipping provided to the author by Marion Olson. Olson's Navy Cross citation is from the files of the Department of the Navy, Pentagon, Washington, DC.

Albin Glavan's story is from his son, Tony. The letters and citation are from the Albin Glavan family collection. "The Capture of Ie Shima," chapter 7 of *Okinawa: The Last Battle* (Washington, DC: Center of Military History, 2000, 1948), by Roy Appleman et al., provided background information. This book, one in a long series covering the U.S. Army in World War II, is available at http://www.army.mil/cmh-pg/books/wwii/okinawa/chapter7.htm. The Seventy-seventh Division's combat operations on Guam are covered in *Guam: Operations of the Seventy-seventh Division, 21 July–10 August 1944* (Washington, DC: Center of Military History, 1990, 1946), available at http://www.army.mil/cmh-pg/books/wwii/guam/guam77div-fm.htm.

The Millard Boie story is from the Marine Corps Historical Center. Appleman et al.'s *Okinawa: The Last Battle* provided background.

William Acheson's story originated from the detailed obituary prepared by his wife and son, which appeared in the *Minneapolis Star Tribune,* January 25, 2004. Contact with family led to additional information, including his citation, certain military records, and the letter from William's brother. Center of Military History publication 72–28, *Luzon 1944–1945,* available at http://www.army.mil/cmh/brochures/Luzon/72-28.htm, was a useful resource, as were the "Fact Sheet of the Thirty-eighth Division," available at http://www.battleofthebulge.org/fact/

fact_sheet_of_the_38th_infantry.html; and the combat narrative of the Thirty-eighth Infantry Division at http://www.ibiblio.org/hyperwar/USA/OOB/38-Division.html. The unidentified veteran's comments are from "Zig Zag Pass," by Sergeant Dana Frame, at http://www.subicbaypi .com/sub_stories_battlezigzag.htm.

Lillian Henke's story is from her daughter, Judy Borgeson, who shared a great deal of information, including correspondence, military records, and newspaper articles. For more information about B-29s, see *Boeing B-29 Superfortress* (1998), chapter 10, "B-29 Attacks on Japan from Marianas," available at http://www.csd.uwo.ca/-pettypi/elevon/baugher_us/b029-10.html; and "B-29 Superfortress," at http://www.globalsecurity.org/wmd/systems/b-29.htm.

George Orrben's story is from the "Cantine Family World War II Letters," P863, the Manuscript Collection of the Minnesota Historical Society. The surrender of the Japanese submarine to the USS *Murray* is from "DD-576," at http://www.hazegray.org; and "Naval Warfare, World War Two Forum," at http://www.historic-battles.com/forum/index.php?topic= 2612.msg34454#msg34454.

Robert Stone's story is from National Personnel Records Center in St. Louis. Stone's kills are from the U.S. Air Force Web site, "World War II Victory Credits," at http://www.au.af.mil/ au/afhra/wwwroot/aerial_victory_credits/avc_wwii_sti_str.html. Additional support information came from Major James Tapp's "Seventh Fighter Command," http://www.glorene.com/aviation/ 7th/history.htm.

James Roehl's story originally came to the author's attention from the obituary prepared by his family. His daughters, Diane Blanchard and Debby Rasmussen, provided considerable information, including military records, letters, and photos, from the Roehl family collection.

Catherine Filippi Piccolo's story is from the Catherine Piccolo file, P1220, in the Manuscript Collection of the Minnesota Historical Society. The quote is from an article, "30-Year-Old Story She'll Never Forget," by Gareth Hiebert, which appeared in the *St. Paul Pioneer Press,* August 24, 1975.

George Tani's story originated from Edwin Nakasone's book, *Japanese-American Veterans of Minnesota* (White Bear Lake, MN: J-Press Publishing, 2002). His widow, Yoshi Tani, shared additional information and insight.

Stephen Chicoine lives in Eden Prairie, Minnesota. He is executive director of TURN, Twin Cities Urban Reconciliation Network, a community-based nonprofit organization in north Minneapolis. He is the author of two books on Civil War history, *John Basil Turchin and the Fight to Free the Slaves* and *The Confederates of Chappell Hill, Texas*.